Teaching Speaking:
A Holistic Approach

CAMBRIDGE LANGUAGE EDUCATION
Series Editor: Jack C. Richards

In this series:

Agendas for Second Language Literacy *by Sandra Lee McKay*

Reflective Teaching in Second Language Classrooms *by Jack C. Richards and Charles Lockhart*

Educating Second Language Children: The Whole Child, the Whole Curriculum, the Whole Community *edited by Fred Genesee*

Understanding Communication in Second Language Classrooms *by Karen E. Johnson*

The Self-Directed Teacher: Managing the Learning Process *by David Nunan and Clarice Lamb*

Functional English Grammar: An Introduction for Second Language Teachers *by Graham Lock*

Teachers as Course Developers *edited by Kathleen Graves*

Classroom-Based Evaluation in Second Language Education *by Fred Genesee and John A. Upshur*

From Reader to Reading Teacher: Issues and Strategies for Second Language Classrooms *by Jo Ann Aebersold and Mary Lee Field*

Extensive Reading in the Second Language Classroom *by Richard R. Day and Julian Bamford*

Language Teaching Awareness: A Guide to Exploring Beliefs and Practices *by Jerry G. Gebhard and Robert Oprandy*

Vocabulary in Language Teaching *by Norbert Schmitt*

Curriculum Development in Language Teaching *by Jack C. Richards*

Teachers' Narrative Inquiry as Professional Development *by Karen E. Johnson and Paula R. Golombek*

A Practicum in TESOL *by Graham Crookes*

Second Language Listening: Theory and Practice *by John Flowerdew and Lindsay Miller*

Professional Development for Language Teachers: Strategies for Teacher Learning *by Jack C. Richards and Thomas S. C. Farrell*

Second Language Writing *by Ken Hyland*

Cooperative Learning and Second Language Teaching *edited by Steven G. McCafferty, George M. Jacobs, and Ana Christina DaSilva Iddings*

Using Corpora in the Language Classroom *by Randi Reppen*

English Language Teaching Materials: Theory and Practice *edited by Nigel Harwood*

Teaching Speaking:
A Holistic Approach

Christine C. M. Goh
Anne Burns

CAMBRIDGE
UNIVERSITY PRESS

CAMBRIDGE UNIVERSITY PRESS
Cambridge, New York, Melbourne, Madrid, Cape Town,
Singapore, São Paulo, Delhi, Mexico City

Cambridge University Press
32 Avenue of the Americas, New York, NY 10013-2473, USA

www.cambridge.org
Information on this title: www.cambridge.org/9781107648333

First published 2012
2nd printing 2012

Printed in the United States of America

A catalog record for this publication is available from the British Library.

Library of Congress Cataloging in Publication data

Goh, Christine Chuen Meng.
Teaching speaking / Christine C.M. Goh, Anne Burns.
    p. cm.
Includes bibliographical references and index.
ISBN 978-1-107-64833-3 (pbk.) – ISBN 978-1-107-01123-6 (hardback)
1. English language – Study and teaching – Foreign speakers. 2. English
language – Spoken
English – Study and teaching. I. Burns, Anne, 1945– II. Title.
PE1128.A2G576 2012
428.0071–dc23   2011040647

ISBN 978-1-107-01123-6 Hardback
ISBN 978-1-107-64833-3 Paperback

From Christine: For Paul and Nicole
From Anne: For Ross, Douglas, and Catherine

Contents

Series editor's preface

The mastery of speaking skills in English is a priority for many second language learners. Learners often evaluate their success in language learning, as well as the effectiveness of their English course, on the basis of how well they feel they have improved in their spoken-language proficiency. Oral skills have hardly been neglected in EFL / ESL courses (witness the huge number of conversation and other speaking coursebooks in the market), though how best to approach the teaching of oral skills has long been problematic, partly as a consequence of the complexity of spoken interaction and the difficulty of developing principled pedagogical approaches that reflect this complexity.

Both our understanding of the nature of speaking skills as well as approaches to teaching them have undergone a major shift in thinking in recent years. Traditional approaches to the teaching of speaking often involved the use of dialogues and repetitive drills reflecting the sentence-based view of proficiency prevailing in the methodologies of Audiolingualism and Situational Language Teaching. In the 1980s, the emergence of the constructs of communicative competence and language proficiency led to major shifts in conceptions of syllabuses and methodology, the effects of which continue to be seen today. The theory of communicative competence prompted attempts at developing communicative approaches to the teaching of spoken English. Fluency became a goal of speaking courses, and this was developed through the use of information-gap and other tasks that required learners to attempt real communication, despite limited proficiency in English. In so doing, they would develop communication strategies and engage in negotiation of meaning, both of which were considered essential to the development of oral skills.

More recently, the notion of English as an International Language has introduced the concept of intercultural competence, a goal for both native speakers and second language users, with a focus on learning how to communicate in ways that are appropriate in cross-cultural settings. At the same time, it is now accepted that models for oral interaction cannot be based simply on the intuitions of applied linguists and textbook writers, but should be informed by research on the nature of authentic spoken discourse. Advances in discourse analysis, conversational analysis, and corpus analysis, in recent years, have revealed a great deal about the complexity of spoken interaction and the cognitive processes involved in producing and processing spoken language, as well as the characteristics of spoken discourse itself. Such information can inform the design of classroom instruction and teaching materials.

The brief summary above of approaches to the teaching of spoken English reflects a narrative that is developed with considerable depth and breadth in the present book. Drawing on wide-ranging literature from a variety of relevant disciplines, as well as their own extensive experience in teaching spoken English, the authors give a fascinating, comprehensive, and insightful account of the nature of second language speaking skills. The research and theory they survey then serves as the basis for the principles, strategies, and procedures they propose for the teaching of spoken English. This book will, therefore, provide an invaluable resource for teachers, teachers in training, and researchers, providing both a state-of-the-art survey of the field as well as a source of practical ideas for those involved in planning, teaching, and evaluating courses and materials for the teaching of spoken English.

Jack C. Richards

Acknowledgments

On page 119, extract from de Silva Joyce, H. and Hilton, D. (1999) *We are what we talk: Teaching and Learning Casual Conversation*, Sydney: NSW Adult Migrant English Service, 84; used by permission.

Table 5.1 on page 120, based on Slade, D. (1997) Chunks and chats, stories and gossip in English: The macro-structure of casual talk, *Prospect*, 21(2), 43–71.

Figure 5.2 on page 125, Concordance with search word *worry*, Cambridge English Corpus, Cambridge: Cambridge University Press; extract reproduced with permission.

Figure 8.8 on page 187, adapted from Hammond, J. et al. (1992) *English for Social Purposes: A Handbook for Teachers of Adult Literacy*, Sydney: National Centre for English Language Teaching and Research, 17.

Figure 9.5 on page 217, based on Jacobs and Goh (2007) *Cooperative Learning in the Language Classroom*, Singapore: SEAMEO Regional Language Centre; used by permission.

Figure 10.1 on page 235, adapted from Goh (2007) *Teaching Speaking in the Language Classroom*, Singapore: SEAMEO Regional Language Centre; used by permission.

Figure 11.2 on pages 242–243, adapted from Vandergrift and Goh (2012) *Teaching and Learning Second Language Listening: Metacognition in Action*, New York: Routledge; used by permission.

Figure 12.1 on pages 260–261, Module and learning outcomes for language skills for telephoning in job-seeking contexts in NSW AMES (2008) Certificates in Spoken and Written English, Module IV (E) C, Sydney: NSW Adult Migrant English Service; reproduced with permission.

Every effort has been made to trace the owners of copyright material in this book. We would be grateful to hear from anyone who recognizes their copyright material and who is unacknowledged. We will be pleased to make the necessary corrections in future editions of the book.

Introduction

In our many years as language teachers and teacher educators, we have had many opportunities to observe speaking lessons conducted by teachers in training, beginning teachers, and experienced teachers. We have also had numerous discussions with local and international postgraduate students about how activities for speaking are typically conducted in their countries. It is clear that, in many situations, although a great deal of speaking is done in the language classroom, the activities serve mainly to provide opportunities for talk, and little *teaching* of speaking actually takes place. In some learning environments, the development of speaking is neglected altogether because high-stakes examinations focus more on the written language.

Why teach speaking?

Many teachers we know feel that they should be doing more to help their students develop their speaking abilities and, therefore, are keen to know how they can teach speaking better. When asked why they felt speaking was important, these are some common responses:

- All language learners should be able to converse well with other speakers of the language.
- My students are ESL learners and need the language to do well in their school.
- All my students can read and write well in English, but they are poor at speaking and listening.
- I have seen many learners who memorize words from their dictionaries, but cannot speak or listen in English.
- My students don't like talking to their classmates because they can't correct each other's mistakes; they want me to point out their mistakes to them.
- My students speak a non-standard form of the language and cannot communicate in formal situations.
- Many of my students say they practice a lot on their own (by copying recordings they hear), but when they have to speak to native speakers, they fail terribly.

1

- Some of my students are poor speakers. So I need to help them improve.
- Many of my students are too afraid to talk in class. They are shy and lack confidence.
- Some of my students sound very "bookish" when they speak – it is as if they are reading from a book!
- My students love to speak English, but they make a lot of grammatical mistakes.
- My students speak a colloquial and non-standard type of English. I need to teach them how to speak standard English for formal communication.
- While my students are quite competent in grammar and vocabulary, one glaring gap remains in their general ability to present or communicate well.

Teaching or merely doing?

After considering current practices in conducting speaking lessons, many teachers come to a similar conclusion: although speaking activities occur frequently in their classrooms, learners seldom have the opportunity to learn the skills and strategies and the language to improve their speaking. While learners do a lot of talking in class activities, there is often insufficient teaching of speaking as a language communication skill. We'll illustrate this kind of situation, using the case of Teacher M.

> Teacher M realized from early in her career that it was important to develop her students' speaking abilities. She wanted to make sure that her students had plenty of opportunities to communicate with one another in English, so she set aside two lessons a week for speaking practice. She planned many interesting activities for her students. Her lessons were carefully guided by instructional objectives. These objectives were in the form either of what the students should produce (e.g., presentations, debates, descriptions), or what they had to do (e.g., discuss, narrate, role play). Sometimes, when they had finished the activities, Teacher M would ask them to present the outcomes to the rest of the class. At other times, she would simply move on to another activity, such as reading or writing.

In many ways, Teacher M was successful in carrying out her speaking lessons. Her students used the spoken language in a variety of interesting learning scenarios. They often enjoyed their speaking activities because they could talk with one another and practice the target language. Some also felt that they had a lot of fun. There were, however, limitations in the way she planned her lessons, which resulted in her students missing valuable opportunities to develop their speaking abilities. One of these limitations was a lack of explicit teaching. The students were left almost entirely on their own to carry out each activity. For example, after setting students a discussion task, Teacher M merely observed what went on in each group and made sure that they were on task and finished on time. Sometimes, she prepared her students with some key ideas or vocabulary items before they began their discussion. She did not, however, plan activities for developing their speaking competence further.

Thus, while her students managed to complete each activity by drawing on their existing language and cognitive resources, they did not learn anything new that they would not have done without her help. Teacher M did not teach any skills and strategies or new language items explicitly to help improve their speaking further. There were few activities where she focused the learners' attention on specific speaking skills, and the language and genres related to the speaking activities, after they had completed them. She also did not give much feedback on the one-off oral communication activity that the students participated in. One of the reasons was the large size of the class. Moreover, she was happy just to see that her students participated in the speaking activities and felt that she should not focus too much on the lack of accuracy in their language use.

Another limitation in Teacher M's approach to teaching speaking is the rather passive role that the students played in their own learning and speaking development. Although they participated actively in speaking activities, the students were not encouraged to self-regulate their learning by planning, monitoring, and evaluating their own performances. There were also few opportunities for them to develop greater knowledge about themselves as second language speakers. They were not encouraged to understand the demands of various speaking tasks or to use effective strategies for coping with communication. In short, although Teacher M planned many interesting speaking activities, her students did not progress by way of learning new speaking skills. Speaking occurred frequently in her class, but *teaching* of speaking did not.

There are many things that teachers can do to help their students develop specific speaking skills and strategies, and acquire the language they need for a range of speaking demands. We discuss these ideas in this book by proposing a methodological framework and a pedagogical model that show how speaking can be taught systematically, and in a manner that will engage learners in and outside the classroom. The framework is based on theoretical and pedagogical principles for teaching and learning that we relate specifically to the teaching of speaking. The pedagogical model demonstrates how teachers can apply these principles in what we refer to as *the teaching-speaking cycle*. In addition to explaining the theoretical rationale for the teaching methodology, we also suggest practical ideas for conducting different types of speaking activities, developing learners' metacognition about their learning, and planning classroom-based assessment of speaking.

Approach

In this book, we propose a holistic approach to teaching speaking. The approach addresses language learners' cognitive, affective (or emotional), and social needs, as they work towards acquiring good speaking competence. The approach is grounded in a socio-cognitive perspective on language learning, which takes the view that learning is not just a cognitive, but also a social process. The approach emphasizes four key features of learning:

1. Learning is an active, strategic, and constructive process.
2. It follows developmental trajectories.
3. It is guided by learners' introspective awareness and control of their mental processes.
4. It is facilitated by social, collaborative settings that value self-directed student dialogue.

(Bruer 1998: 681.)

The proposed teaching approach takes into account three key factors in successful language learning: teachers, materials, and learners.

1 Teachers

The role of a teacher is to help learners acquire language and skills that they will not be able to achieve on their own. Teachers need to be aware of their students' learning needs and the demands they face when communicating through the spoken language. Teachers can understand more about language learners' cognitive, affective, and social needs from theoretical ideas, as well as personal observations. The observations can be based on conversations with students, information about their background, and learning goals and assessment results. Teachers also need to intervene actively in students' learning, so as to provide input, scaffolding (or support), and feedback. Planning activities where students can communicate with their classmates is just part of the learning experience teachers can provide for their students. It is not enough simply to get students to talk, because they are unlikely to learn new skills and language if there is little linguistic and background knowledge among them on which to draw. The role of the teacher, therefore, is to structure students' learning experiences so as to support their speaking development, in and outside the classroom. Teachers can do this by designing interesting and appropriate materials.

2 Materials

The materials discussed in this book include activities and resources for facilitating second language speaking development. These materials fall into three categories:

1. Those that provide speaking practice.
2. Those that promote language and skills learning.
3. Those that facilitate metacognitive development.

Materials for speaking practice provide contextualized, varied, and interesting prompts and scenarios for talk to take place. Materials for language and skill learning focus on selected elements of the talk, or model spoken texts to increase learners' relevant linguistic knowledge and control of speaking skills. Metacognitive development materials, on the other hand, aim to raise learners' knowledge and control of learning processes, and train them in using communication and discourse strategies.

Materials can be "instructional, experiential, elicitative, or exploratory" in that they "inform learners about the language," "provide experience of the language in use," "stimulate language use," or "help learners make discoveries about the language for themselves" (Tomlinson, 2003: 2). Learning materials, however, are incomplete if they lack a metacognitive dimension that helps learners understand and manage the learning of skills and language. In a holistic approach to teaching speaking, materials should be varied in form and purpose, in order to engage learners in different dimensions of learning. There should be materials that allow learners the freedom to experiment with their own language use so that they can communicate their meaning as clearly as possible, as well as those where they focus on language-specific speaking skills and strategies. There should also be materials that develop learners' metacognitive knowledge about second language speaking, and encourage them to plan, monitor, and evaluate their own learning.

3 Learners

Successful second language speaking development depends as much on teachers and materials, as it does on the learners themselves. They should be encouraged to take responsibility for managing their learning and improving their speaking. They can do this by developing awareness about themselves as second language speakers, by better understanding the nature and demands of speaking, and by critically considering strategies that can facilitate their oral communication. Although speech production is an individual endeavor, every learner's development of second language speaking can be greatly facilitated through working collaboratively with his or her peers.

Teachers should, therefore, encourage learners to support one another's speaking development, not just as communication partners in a speaking task, but also as learning partners who share their learning plans and goals. Through dialogue, students can co-construct knowledge about what is needed to be proficient speakers, and to apply their knowledge and skills in real-time communication. However, learners should not be left alone to struggle through the learning process. Their efforts must be supported by teachers who can provide the necessary scaffolding, input, and guidance.

The figure below illustrates the interrelationships between the three key factors in successful second language speaking development. Learners are positioned at the apex of the triangle to indicate that their learning needs, goals, and outcomes are the most important considerations. However, they can only achieve their objectives if they are supported by well-informed teachers and effective materials. The roles of teachers, materials, and learners will form the basis for the methodological framework proposed later in the book.

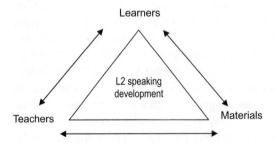

Figure 1: Three key success factors in second language speaking development.

Outline of chapters

This book is organized into four parts. Part 1 introduces theoretical perspectives to help you consider the importance of speaking for second language learners, as well as understand the nature of second language speaking. Part 2 explains key features of spoken discourse and genre, and how these features are relevant to a teacher's understanding of teaching speaking. Part 3 presents principles for designs, and approaches for planning and teaching speaking programs and lessons. In Part 4, tasks and activities for engaging learners in speaking practice and development are presented. These tasks and activities offer many practical ideas for different stages of the teaching-speaking cycle. This part also includes a discussion of classroom-based ways of assessing speaking to promote learning.

Part I: Speaking processes and skills

Chapter 1 discusses the contribution of speaking to second language acquisition and establishes the importance of speaking in academic learning by second language learners. It also highlights affective, or emotional, factors, namely language anxiety and motivation, which influence language learners' involvement in learning to speak. It invites readers to rethink current practices in teaching speaking, and proposes a holistic approach that accounts for speaking outcomes, as well as cognitive, social, and affective (emotional) processes of learning to speak a second language.

Chapter 2 discusses the quality of learners' spoken output in relation to the cognitive demands that they face. The chapter describes psycholinguistic processes involved during speech production, namely, conceptual preparation, formulation, articulation, and self-monitoring. The effects of these processes on language learners' speaking performance in terms of fluency, accuracy, and complexity are discussed. The chapter concludes with some principles for teaching speaking, based on the discussion of the cognitive processes.

Chapter 3 helps teachers understand what constitutes second language speaking competence so that they can teach it systematically and in a principled manner. This chapter first discusses speaking competence in relation to the broader concept of communicative competence. Next, it examines speaking as a combinatorial skill and proposes a model of speaking competence that comprises linguistic knowledge, speaking skills, and communication strategies.

Part II: Spoken discourse

Chapter 4 explains the differences and the relationships between spoken and written language, and the purposes and functions of these two forms of communication. The chapter also examines specific grammatical features of spoken discourse and explains how these features contribute to the maintenance of the flow of spoken interaction. The last section of the chapter considers key aspects of pronunciation, and discusses how the intonation and sound systems of English contribute to the creation of meaning among speakers.

Chapter 5 describes discourse features of spoken language, such as how speakers take turns in extended stretches of speech, how they know when to take a turn, and how they negotiate and manage different conversational topics and provide feedback to other speakers. The chapter then introduces the concepts of interactional (socially motivated) and transactional (pragmatically motivated) interactions. This discussion is followed by an explanation of the concept of genre in speaking, which has to do with the way certain types of interaction have predictable beginning, middle, and end structures. At the end of the chapter, we touch briefly on the contributions made to the study of spoken discourse by corpus linguistics.

Part III: Designs and approaches

Chapter 6 proposes a methodological framework, founded on theoretical and pedagogical principles, to offer a holistic approach to teaching speaking. The framework takes into consideration the respective roles of teachers, materials, and learners, and accounts for the interrelated development of all three components of speaking competence. It also draws on insights from research and theory to present a selection of methods for organizing learning activities for speaking, including part-skill practice, pre-task-planning, and task repetition.

Chapter 7 demonstrates how the proposed methodological framework can be applied in the classroom, in order to approach the teaching of speaking in a holistic manner. It describes a pedagogical cycle that makes the teaching and learning of speaking systematic and explicit. The teaching-speaking cycle consists of seven stages that make use of different types of activities to engage language learners in working collaboratively and individually. The teaching-speaking cycle also demonstrates how different kinds of learning materials can be used to provide learners with opportunities to practice their speaking through fluency-oriented tasks, learn relevant language items and discourse structures, and acquire speaking skills and strategies, as well as develop their metacognitive knowledge for self-regulating their learning.

Chapter 8 guides readers in the steps involved in planning a course to develop the systematic teaching of speaking. It considers the speaking needs of learners, and how teachers can assess and analyze learner needs. It then considers how goals and objectives, based on learner needs, can be developed, after which three possible approaches to planning a unit of work are suggested. The first is a general topic-based approach, where the material is organized around topics that are deemed relevant for particular types of learners. The second is a task-based approach, where the tasks to be completed are linked to the spoken skills to be practiced by the learner. The third is a text-based approach, which draws on the idea of genres of speaking that learners may need to use in various social contexts. This discussion is followed by consideration of the kinds of materials that could be used for these approaches. The chapter ends by discussing how learners' progress and achievements in the course could be assessed, as well as how the teacher can go about evaluating the effectiveness of the course.

Part IV: Classroom practices and processes

Chapter 9 explains how teachers can plan tasks for speaking practice. It describes different types of fluency-oriented tasks: communication-gap tasks, discussion tasks, and monologic tasks. Communicative outcomes for each task type are identified, and explanations for conducting each task are included to guide teachers in using or adapting them for their learners.

Chapter 10 presents activities that help learners focus on language and discourse so as to develop greater accuracy, fluency, and complexity in their speech. It suggests three stages: noticing / sensitizing, analysis, and further practice. It also offers strategies for task repetition so that learners have further opportunities to repeat an earlier task after learning more about the language and strategies needed to enhance their performance.

Chapter 11 discusses metacognition, or thinking about one's thinking, and shows why teachers have an important function in bringing cognitive, social, and affective learning processes into a conscious level. It offers suggestions for metacognitive instruction for L2 speaking development that can help learners plan, monitor, and evaluate their learning.

Chapter 12 highlights the importance of assessment for learning. It focuses mainly on classroom-based assessment, and shows teachers how they can assess learners' speaking performance and development in a principled way, in order to help them further develop as English language speakers. It also discusses ideas for learner self- and peer assessment. The chapter concludes by considering how teachers can rate and score learner speaking performances.

How to read this book

Readers of this book can read each chapter independently of the others if they would like to find out more about a particular topic. To derive maximum benefit from the book, however, we would recommend reading the chapters in sequence. Reading chapters in sequence provides the opportunity to consider the principles embodied in the methodological framework and teaching cycle, and to see how these principles are applied to the practical ideas presented in the three chapters in Part 3. Each chapter in organized in the same way:

- It begins with two or sometimes three questions, and these are answered through a discussion of specific topics.
- There are mini-tasks in each major section that teachers can attempt on their own, or with a colleague or classmates.
- Each chapter concludes with a summary of important principles or practical ideas for teaching speaking, relevant to the topics discussed.
- At the end of each chapter are group learning tasks to help readers deepen their understanding of key concepts and issues presented in the chapter. These tasks are more elaborate and require collaboration with others, and are suitable to be used in courses for teaching speaking. They are also suitable topics for written assignments of various types.

There are various features for enhancing the readability and usability of the material:

- Simple tasks are included at different parts of each chapter to encourage reflection on learning and application of ideas learned.
- Figures are included to present abstract points, tables to summarize key points, bullets to emphasize key points, and numbers to delineate steps or progression.
- Handouts and materials that can be used directly in the classroom are included.
- Relevant articles and books have also been suggested for further reading.

Concluding remarks

This book has been written from our experience and research in teaching speaking to English language learners, but we believe the ideas will be relevant to teachers of other languages. We hope that the book will provide theoretical insights and practical ideas for teachers and teacher educators who choose to use it. On this note, we would like to thank the many English teachers in our teacher education, graduate courses, and other workshops who have implemented the ideas in their classrooms, and who have given us valuable feedback for improvement.

Authors' acknowledgment

It has been a real pleasure for us to work together and to pool our respective theoretical and practical views about the teaching of speaking, an area both of us have worked on for many years. Writing this book has also been an fascinating experience in sharing, refining, and exchanging ideas across two different countries through the occasional meeting, email, and Skype®! In writing the book, we have had wonderful support and feedback from various people. First, and definitely foremost, is Debbie Goldblatt, whose meticulous editorial work has helped us to shape the manuscript's raw edges into this final, more polished version. We cannot thank her enough for ensuring we went the extra distance to attend to details of content and presentation. Karen Brock and, before her, Kathleen Corley, our commissioning editors from Cambridge University Press in New York, were unfailingly supportive, not to mention patient, as we worked towards the final product. We'd also like to thank Kathleen for bringing us together as authors. We do not forget, either, that it was the series editor, Jack C. Richards, who first approached each of us, in one case, many years ago, about a book on teaching speaking. He must have also sensed that we would work well together as a team. Writing a book inevitably takes time away from family life. As always, we thank our families for their continuing support and love and dedicate this book to them.

PART I
SPEAKING PROCESSES AND SKILLS

1 Speaking and the language learner

Speaking is accepted by everyone as an essential language-communication skill, but its importance to language learners goes beyond just day-to-day communication. Speaking can facilitate language acquisition and contribute towards the academic development of many second language learners. It is useful, therefore, to begin our discussion of teaching speaking by examining these benefits and, at the same time, to consider factors that can affect learners' willingness to speak more in the target language. We will do this by answering two questions in this chapter:

1. In what way is speaking important to learners' language acquisition and academic learning?
2. If speaking is important, why do some learners avoid it?

To answer these questions, we will be examining three topics:

- Speaking and language acquisition.
- Speaking and academic learning.
- Speaking and affective factors.

Introduction

All language teachers know that speaking is an important communication skill for their students, but not all are aware of how speaking can directly contribute to other important areas of their students' personal success. In this chapter, we will review some of the research and discussions that highlight the role of speaking in second language acquisition. We will also discuss the importance of speaking for academic learning, in view of the high number of second language learners in different areas of education. Finally, we will address a question that many teachers have: If speaking is important, and my students know it is important, why do some of them avoid speaking in the target language? One of the main reasons, we suggest, is that they are influenced by affective factors, such as anxiety and a lack of motivation. In this chapter, we aim to establish the importance of speaking in the language classroom not just as a communication skill, but also as a means of facilitating the acquisition of the target language and the learning of academic content. We also aim to shed light on the challenges that some second language learners face. Throughout this chapter and the rest of the book, we will use the term "second language" as shorthand to refer to any language that individuals are learning in addition to their first or other dominant languages. While the contexts for learning may be different, we believe many processes and issues pertaining to speaking are common to all language learners.

Speaking and language acquisition

Like many teachers, you may hold the belief that language input is important in acquiring a new language. It may seem clear to you that reading extensively can help learners acquire a second language. You may also believe that listening is equally important in providing learners with the necessary input for learning. However, it is not just input through reading and listening that is important for language acquisition. Research studies have shown that output is also crucial in helping learners become increasingly proficient in the language. Your students' development in the target language can be helped considerably by encouraging them to speak.

To explain the importance of speaking in your students' language development, let's begin by making a comparison between first and second language acquisition. Both processes share a number of common features of acquisition. One of these is the way in which the environment can influence successful language learning. Most people would not hesitate to say that for children to learn their first language, they must be "exposed" to the language. A difference of opinion, however, may arise with respect to the extent and the nature of such "exposure." The view that is the most convincing for us is that the quality of conversations between adults and children play a crucial role in ensuring children's success in learning to use the language effectively. This view, broadly referred to as the interactionist approach in language-acquisition literature, asserts that the language that children hear in the environment serves not just to "trigger" some innate mechanism for language acquisition. Rather, it is through daily interaction with expert speakers (i.e., adults or "caretakers") that children receive valuable input and feedback on their emerging language, thus helping them to acquire the structure and use of the language. Assisted by adults who use conversational techniques when interacting with them, children develop an awareness of language form and its connection with language function (Halliday 1975).

Adults create opportunities for children to use the language to express intentions and interpret the meaning of utterances they hear. More importantly, through conversation strategies such as modeling, reformulation, contingent speech, clarification requests and confirmation checks (see Chapter 3), adults guide and encourage children to use language that is accurate, appropriate, and potentially rich and meaningful. In reformulation, for example, an adult may hear a child say, "I hurted my leg!" To show the child the correct form, the adult rephrases what is said, but, at the same time, makes sure the meaning that the child expresses is retained and the flow of the conversation is not disrupted by overt teaching. So the adult may say something like this, "Oh dear, you hurt your leg! Let me have a look." In reformulations, the child hears a complete and grammatical version of his or her original utterance, which may consist of only a word or two. Contingent speech is used to encourage children to continue talking about a topic that they themselves initiated. Below is an example of how a father creates opportunities for his three-year-old child to use language to express her ideas during pretend play:

CHILD: I going to the shop.
FATHER: You're going to the shops? What are you going to buy?
CHILD: Some more teabags.
FATHER: Who's going to have the teabags?
CHILD: Put in the tea.
FATHER: I think we've got lots of teabags. There are some more teabags in the cupboard.
CHILD: Orange. Some more orange.

(Goh & Silver 2006: 275.)

Besides showing his interest, the father's questions and comments are also an important means of setting up verbal scaffolds for increasing the number of turns the child gets. At the same time, the child knows that what she says has been understood. This type of positive feedback is very satisfying for language learners. When a child's speech is unclear, the adult may also request that he or she clarify the meaning. So, for example, when a child says, "I not got it," the adult may say, "What haven't you got?" thus prompting the child to make his or her meaning more explicit: "I not got the cake." Through a range of conversation strategies, adult speakers help children increase opportunities for using the language they are acquiring and, at the same time, help them notice problems in their speech and express their meaning more clearly.

Input, feedback, and output in second language learning

The types of conversation strategies just mentioned that are used in first language learning play a similarly important role in second language acquisition. When language learners are engaged in using oral language through interaction with expert speakers, they can also be prompted to notice their utterances and produce language that is increasingly more accurate. Early work on oral interaction by Hatch (1978) emphasized the important role that speaking plays in second language acquisition. Hatch, as well as other researchers who followed, argued strongly that by engaging in talk with more competent speakers, language learners will derive two key benefits. Firstly, they will be helped by their interlocutors' input and feedback. Besides hearing input that is modified for their language ability, when they interact with competent speakers, learners also have a chance to hear a more accurate model of language being used. Although comprehensible input is important, it alone is insufficient. Language learners can also develop their language by producing comprehensible output (Swain 1985). Swain's output hypothesis claims that the production of oral language can, under certain circumstances, enable learners to acquire new forms of the language. Language learners can be "pushed" to use language further when what they say is unclear or ungrammatical, and they have to repeat, rephrase, or correct what they have said in order to produce speech that is comprehensible to others. In responding to questions for clarification, learners and expert speakers engage in negotiations for meaning, where constant adjustments are made to the linguistic forms, structure of discourse, and content message so that an acceptable level of understanding is achieved (Long 1991). By engaging in negotiations for meaning with expert speakers, language learners can potentially increase their capacity to use the second language.

Clearly, besides language input, learners also need feedback in the form of questions, comments, repetitions, confirmation checks, requests for clarifications, and reformulations. These types of feedback are also important strategies in the process of negotiation for meaning. Reformulation, for example, has been shown to assist second language development (Mackey 1999), particularly among young second language learners (Mackey & Oliver 2002; Mackey & Silver 2005). An important benefit of negotiation for meaning is that learners have to actively produce spoken output, which is equally if not more important than language input in facilitating learning. Merely speaking the language, however, is inadequate for acquisition to occur. For example, when a group of learners talk among themselves, they may use the language inaccurately or inappropriately. Without appropriate feedback, they may not be aware that they are producing forms that are inaccurate. Thus, even though they may become increasingly fluent, their language does not necessarily increase in accuracy.

According to Swain (1985), who articulated the Comprehensible-Output Hypothesis, language learners must notice language forms in their speech that are causing problems for the listeners, such as pronunciation or grammar, and try to modify their spoken language for greater accuracy. Swain argued that, "Negotiating meaning needs to incorporate the notion of being pushed towards the delivery of a message that is not only conveyed, but that is conveyed precisely, coherently, and appropriately" (Swain 1985: 248–249). When this process of negotiating meaning occurs regularly, it can lead learners to improve their control of language form, as well as meaning. When learners use language that is inaccurate and their meaning is imprecise, they should be asked to correct or rephrase what is said to make their meaning clearer. This will help them pay attention to the formal qualities of the language and lead them to use forms that are accurate in future communication. Swain (1995) summarizes three important benefits that negotiating meaning can have for second language learners. It:

- Helps learners become aware of target language forms that they have not acquired.
- Encourages learners to test their own knowledge of the language when modifying their original output.
- Provides learners with opportunities for developing their metalinguistic knowledge.

The importance of input–feedback–modified output in oral interaction with competent speakers has led to the articulation of various hypotheses about the role of such feedback in second language acquisition (Gass 1997; Long 1999). This research has important implications for the way speaking activities are planned in the classroom. Ideally, the activities should allow teachers to provide input and feedback to every language learner and to "push" each one to produce well-formed utterances. In reality, however, it is not possible for most teachers to do so because of physical constraints such as large class size. Even in small classes, as Lynch (1998) observes, some teachers may not be aware of the importance of modified output and, therefore, neglect opportunities for "nudging" learners to use language this way. This makes it all the more crucial for speaking lessons to include stages where learners can focus on the use of accurate language to accomplish speaking goals. Teachers could plan activities that draw their students' attention to linguistic forms, discourse structure, and vocabulary that can further develop the learners' ability to speak accurately. Explicit instruction on language forms has been shown to contribute to learners' oral language development (Gor & Chernigovskaya 2005; Sheen 2005).

Discuss it

Think about two or three speaking activities that you have carried out or have observed in class. Briefly describe the activities to a colleague. To what extent were the students "pushed" to use accurate and appropriate language? What factors seem to facilitate this type of language production, and what factors work against it?

Speaking and academic learning

Traditionally, English-as-a-Second-Language (ESL) learners consisted largely of university and college students, or adult immigrants learning in English-speaking countries. The age range of second language learners, however, has lowered over the years to include a sizeable number of young and adolescent non-native speakers studying in English-medium schools. In the U.S., for example, there is a high proportion of students in main-stream education who are learning English as a second language. Similar situations are found in the U.K., Canada, Australia, and New Zealand. In England, for example, provisional school census data in 2008 showed that an estimated 14 percent of primary pupils and 10 percent of secondary pupils in government-funded schools did not have English as their first language (Graf 2011). The situation of learners of English as a second or additional language participating in mainstream English-medium education has given rise to scholarly discussions about the role that teachers can play in supporting such learners (see, for example, Gibbons 2002; Graf 2011).

This ESL situation, however, is no longer limited to traditionally Anglo-phone countries. The pattern and contexts for learning and using English have been changing in other parts of the world. Asia is one such example. In Singapore, for example, where the medium of instruction in all schools is English, a large number of the children entering school have Chinese, Malay, or Tamil as their first language. To all intents and purposes, these children are ESL learners, and many teachers would readily endorse this view. Increasingly, the country has also become a favorite choice for all levels of education with students from neighboring Indonesia, the People's Republic of China, Vietnam, and Myanmar. The situation In Malaysia is somewhat different, but no less significant. There are now a large number of private colleges offering exchange programs (known in some countries as twinning programs) with western universities, and at least one British and one Australian university have set up local campuses there. Students in these tertiary programs study in environments where English is the language of the curriculum and general academic discourse. In Hong Kong, as well, English is the medium of instruction in selected schools, and there is an increasing demand for an English-medium education.

While such large numbers of ESL learners in mainstream English classes are not seen in all countries where English is taught, a time may come when more countries opt to have some subjects taught in English as a way of narrowing the knowledge gap between their young citizens and those in English-speaking countries, as well as giving students a head start in the current landscape of globalization. Information available through the Internet would become more accessible to students. More and more teachers in English-as-a-Foreign-Language (EFL) countries are being encouraged to teach English through English. Many learners themselves are also keen to develop their speaking abilities, so as to secure better jobs and places in overseas universities. In sum, the development of good speaking (and listening) skills is no longer a bonus for language learners, but an essential aspect of their language-proficiency development because it can have a direct impact on the personal and professional success of many of them.

Using the spoken language for learning and thinking

What is the connection between language learners' speaking abilities and their academic learning? One obvious answer is that since much formal learning takes place through the spoken language (Wolvin and Coakely 1996), and, increasingly, through the medium of English, being able to speak (and listen) in the language of instruction will greatly facilitate students' participation in class and the learning of the subject matter. To speak in English, second language learners have to develop various pragmatic competencies. Learners need to learn how to initiate and maintain conversations, to sustain group discussions, describe feelings and give reasons in an acceptable manner, and ask for more information or assistance (Brice 1992). In other words, one of the fundamental reasons why second language learners need to develop good speaking and listening skills is to engage in effective day-to-day classroom communication.

While the role of speaking for communication is generally recognised in ESL classrooms, the contribution it makes to academic learning is less frequently highlighted. In situations where the target language is also a language of instruction across the curriculum, speaking is an indispensable tool for thinking and achieving academic success. For second language speakers enrolled in academic or professional programs, training in communication skills is often available to learners through English-for-Academic-Purposes (EAP) courses or English-for-Specific-Purposes (ESP) programs. These courses typically focus on presentation and seminar skills, profession-specific speaking skills, and lecture note-taking skills. ESL learners in primary, middle, and secondary school contexts, however, need to develop some other kinds of oracy skills. The term *oracy*, which was first coined by Wilkinson, refers to the general ability to speak and listen as a sign of being educated (Wilkinson 1965). The concept was extended to include the ability to engage with learning through the spoken language (Barnes 1988). Barnes argued that all school learners need to be able to use speech to develop thinking skills that are specific to different subjects in the school curriculum, and the ability to do this empowers the learners to engage critically with their social and physical world.

Teachers use talk in academic settings as an important tool for helping learners explore, develop, consolidate, and investigate ideas, as well as evaluate propositions; all of these are crucial thinking processes in conceptual learning. Recent research with young children has also demonstrated the power of talk in developing early writing proficiency (Fisher et al. 2010). Due to large class sizes in many situations, however, students are often asked to work in groups. Some classes also adopt group work as a way of promoting cooperative learning. Group activities are, therefore, another academic learning context in which language learners need to use spoken language for thinking and learning. Mercer (2000) uses the term "interthinking" to refer to the process of learners working collaboratively through speech to construct a body of shared knowledge and understanding. Successful group talk that promotes thinking and learning is often said to be characterized by acknowledgement and exploration of the contributions by group members. Although these discussions about oracy are in the context of classroom learning where the learners are first language speakers, the ideas and principles are just as relevant to second language learners participating in mainstream English-medium classrooms (Mercer 2001).

The crucial difference for second language learners, however, lies in their ability or inability to use oral language to engage with other students in the type of thinking and learning processes mentioned above. In English-speaking countries where there are many ESL learners in classes, students who do not have English as their dominant language tend to initiate fewer conversations, make fewer requests, and listen less actively, thus causing them to be less effective at cooperative learning tasks (Brice & Montgomery 1996). It is important, therefore, that second language learners develop speaking skills that enable them to use spoken English effectively in various contexts of learning. It is not uncommon to find second language learners being perceived as less able or intelligent, simply because they cannot use the language to express their understanding, doubts, and opinions clearly. Inability to speak and listen effectively in their second language can cause some learners to abstain from participating in class. When even daily communication becomes a problem, it is not surprising that many second language learners cannot participate in the discourse of academic learning. As a result, they are further disadvantaged in schools because they cannot demonstrate ways of using the "mainstream" language valued in formal education (Corson 2001; Cummins 2000).

Decontextualized oral-language use and academic registers

One set of oral skills, which some scholars refer to as decontextualized oral-language skills, is particularly important for helping students engage with learning (Snow 1991). Decontextualized oral-language skill is the ability to talk about things that are beyond the immediate context of interaction and make information explicit and coherent for listeners who share limited background information with the speakers[1]. Such an oral-language skill is similar to the idea of an elaborated code that is independent of the immediate context and contains linguistic features that are more sophisticated for expressing meaning precisely (Bernstein 1975). In contrast, a restricted code is used when much of the information is retrievable from the context of interaction, and, thus, speakers are not required to make their meaning explicit for their listeners. To use an everyday example, we engage in contextualized talk when we talk about details from a film with a friend who watched it with us. On the other hand, if our friend has not seen the film, our speech will have to be a great deal more explicit so that we can fill in the gaps in our listener's knowledge. We look at these issues again in Chapters 4 and 5, which focus on the features of speech and genres of speaking.

In the school curriculum, activities such as presentations, storytelling, describing procedures, and even show-and-tell are just a few of the many examples that require school children to use decontextualized oral language. To do these tasks effectively, learners have to make their information linguistically explicit through various grammatical and lexical resources. They need to use appropriate vocabulary to convey literal meaning and, sometimes, even need to use metaphors in order to make comparisons that are meaningful to their listeners. In addition, decontextualized language use requires pragmatic competence such as understanding listeners'

---

[1] Some experts find the term "decontextualized" ambiguous and prefer to think of this type of spoken language as more abstracted forms of oral language where speakers need to communicate meaning of a specialized or technical nature.

perspectives so that one knows how much information is common ground and how much needs to be explained.

In schools and other academic settings, decontextualized language use is the dominant form of discourse, so the ability to communicate meaning explicitly in context-independent situations is a highly valued skill. Studies have shown that young school learners' ability to use decontextualized oral language has an impact on the development of literacy skills and their academic success (Snow, Tabors, Nicolson & Kurland 1995). There is evidence to suggest that children who have been socialized into decontexualized language use in speech have a distinct advantage in school learning, while those who have not are often severely disadvantaged by the system (Heath 1983; Dickinson & Tabors 2001). When children have not had the benefit of such language experience at home, they will have to depend on the school to develop this ability. If decontextualized language use is a challenge when there is inadequate exposure at home, even for learners who have English as their first language, we can expect the use of decontextualized oral language to be an even greater challenge for second language learners. The ability to use decontextualized oral language effectively is clearly an asset to all school-age children and is particularly important for ESL / EFL learners who may not have had a chance to develop this skill before they begin their formal education in English.

As Mercer (2001) noted, ESL learners in English-medium classrooms face two big challenges. One is inadequate language proficiency, and the other is a lack of familiarity with the social conventions for using language in the classroom. Teachers, too, may find it difficult to pin down the exact cause of the students' difficulties, experienced when learning a subject. With an understanding of language as a pedagogic tool, Mercer argues, teachers can help students improve their use of language for processing and constructing subject-specific knowledge. Gibbons (2001) also called for academic subject teachers to help develop the language and the thinking of ESL learners in mainstream education through scaffolded interactions or "long conversations" in class. As she points out, subject teachers can be a key mediator of ESL children's experiences and the school discourse (in the target language) that they are learning. Nevertheless, while there are compelling reasons for subject teachers to integrate language with subject teaching, much of the responsibility still falls on the shoulders of the language teachers, who have an important role to play in helping learners develop oral-language skills that can support their academic learning beyond the language classroom.

When we help ESL learners develop their ability to use spoken English for academic learning, this ability is not merely limited to expressing and comprehending basic speech functions in the classroom. Learners have to develop abilities for using speech as a way of both engaging with ideas and subject-specific thinking, and communicating facts and opinions clearly through increasingly abstract use of oral language. They also need to develop effective skills that will help them participate successfully in "inter-thinking" when working with others in groups. The ability to use oral language to convey abstract concepts during group work will also contribute to their ability to understand and express abstract ideas in the written language (Grainger 2004). Being able to use oral language well to engage with their learning of the various academic subjects can help language learners succeed academically and reap the benefits of an education delivered through the second language.

It is important, therefore, for language teachers to bear in mind the demands of oral-language use when planning speaking activities for learners who use their second language in various academic contexts. Although language-learning activities in the language classroom are not perfect substitutes for engaging in talk in "real world" classroom communication, thoughtfully planned oral activities can still help language learners learn important skills and strategies for speaking effectively in their content-area classes. Selected oral-language tasks can be based on the types of genres and topics commonly found in academic subjects (see Chapter 5 for an explanation of spoken genres). Such tasks will further facilitate the application and transfer of oracy skills to learning situations across the curriculum and further develop learners' English in various contexts.

In many EFL situations, as opposed to ESL situations, learners may not necessarily need to develop their speaking for immediate academic learning needs. Nevertheless, it is still important to plan learning tasks that offer speaking practice that can contribute to overall language development. The tasks should have the right level of complexity to engage language learners of different age groups and learning needs while, at the same time, help them improve not only fluency, but also grammatical and phonological accuracy. We will explore these ideas later in the book.

Think about it

Do you know of any language learners who have to join mainstream education conducted in the target language? If you do, or are presently teaching such students, list some speaking problems these learners have in their classes. To what extent could these problems affect the success of their academic learning?

Speaking and affective factors

Although second language learners may understand the importance of speaking, it can be stressful for some, if not most of them. In this section, we will discuss the problem of anxiety among learners and how this anxiety affects their willingness to speak the target language. To understand some language-learning problems and processes more deeply, we need to consider both affective and cognitive variables because emotional reactions can have a significant influence on the effectiveness of language learning and processing (Arnold 1999). We could say that affective factors, such as anxiety, are most strongly linked to speaking and listening, where learners often have to process and produce language spontaneously without any planning or rehearsals.

All of us experience anxiety at different times of our lives. Its manifestations include feelings of tension, states of apprehension, nervousness, and worry, as well as physical signs such as "breaking out in cold sweat" and nausea. According to Arnold, "anxiety is possibly the affective factor that most pervasively obstructs the learning process" (1999: 8). Anxiety may be defined as subjective feelings of tension, states of apprehension, nervousness, and worry. As we know, anxiety is often unavoidable, and it can have an effect on the way one behaves. It is an important affective variable in second language acquisition and is intricately intertwined with other affects such as self-esteem, inhibition, and risk taking (Brown 1993). Psychologists say that some individuals may be more prone to anxiety in a wide range of situations than other people, a phenomenon referred to as trait anxiety. Trait anxiety is a stable personality characteristic of some individuals, and if it occurs in language learners, it may impair cognitive functioning and disrupt memory in language use and learning (MacIntyre & Gardner 1991b).

Another kind of anxiety that individuals experience is less pervasive and more situation-specific; that is to say, the anxiety is triggered by being in a particular situation. This is the type of anxiety that many language learners experience when exposed to situations in which they have to use the target language. This psychological state is commonly referred to as language anxiety, and it is something you have probably observed among some learners. What exactly is language anxiety? It has been described as "a composite of self-perceptions, beliefs, feelings, and behaviors related to the learning process and arising from the unique situation in the language classroom" (Horwitz, Horwitz & Cope 1986: 31). Although language anxiety can be distinguished from trait anxiety, it can still have a negative effect on the learning process. You may notice that some learners focus very narrowly on their performance during a speaking task and tend to evaluate themselves too excessively. They may focus on what they are unable to do and overlook what they can actually do. They also worry about potential failure and other people's opinions and are, therefore, not willing to put themselves in situations that they are unsure about.

Learners who suffer from language anxiety perceive speaking in a second language to be an uncomfortable experience and are not prepared to make mistakes because of perceived social pressure. They are also less willing to take risks and experiment with new ways of expressing themselves in the target language (MacIntyre & Gardner 1991a). Such preoccupations make their cognitive performance less efficient, impairing their ability to process information, retrieve, or produce it when required. Language anxiety has been shown to be associated with performance during high-pressure events, such as oral examinations (Phillips 1992). Being aware of language anxiety and its causes can help teachers take a holistic approach to developing learners' speaking. Therefore, it is useful to anticipate some of the situations that can give rise to language anxiety.

Many learners may also be shocked and disappointed when they have to speak in a second or foreign language in real interactions with competent speakers of the language. They may have learned to speak by repeating or constructing complete sentences modeled after the written language, but when they engage in real conversations outside the classroom, they realize that their way of speaking is too "textbook-like" and unnatural (Goh 2009). This, and unrealistic expectations of what speaking in a second language entails, can create a great deal of anxiety for language learners and cause some to avoid oral interactions altogether.

Motivation to speak

A number of studies on language anxiety used or adapted a 33-item questionnaire called the Foreign Language Communication Anxiety Scale (FLCAS), developed by Horwitz et al. (1986). In this scale, the construct of foreign-language anxiety during oral communication is conceptualized as a composite of three other forms of anxiety, namely communication apprehension, test anxiety, and fear of negative evaluation. A study among Taiwanese learners that focused on both spoken and written communication found that students with higher levels of anxiety tended to have low self-concepts as language learners (Cheng, Horwitz & Schallert 1999). These learners had negative self-perceptions about their language competence. An inverse relationship between anxiety and performance has also been found among Chinese tertiary-level ESL learners studying in Singapore (Zhang 2001). Zhang's study also showed a gender difference, with the male students showing a greater tendency to experience anxiety when they had to speak in English, both in and out of class.

Communication apprehension has also been reported among a group of Chinese ESL learners in New Zealand secondary schools (Mak & White 1998). Results indicated that the main reason for apprehension was the linguistic distance between English and Chinese, while other reasons such as an emphasis on voluntary speaking, inadequate preparation, and fear of negative evaluation also contributed. Research among Japanese language learners revealed that learners who reported a high degree of anxiety did less well in their language assessments (Aida 1994; Saito & Samimy 1996). In a recent study that involved about 200 Japanese learners, more than half of the learners said they did not feel sure of themselves when they spoke in English and claimed that they would start to panic if their teachers asked them to speak without having prepared in advance (Burden 2005). The respondents also reported that they were too embarrassed to volunteer to speak and felt self-conscious speaking in front of their classmates. More than half said they felt overwhelmed by the number of rules they believed were necessary to speak English.

Young (1991) identified six sources of anxiety and argued that there were strong connections between them and learners' cultural and social beliefs. Although these sources of anxiety are not exclusively linked to speaking, it is useful to know what they are, as they can help you anticipate or confirm some of the reasons why your students may not be motivated to speak. The six sources of anxiety are as follows:

- Personal and interpersonal beliefs (e.g., fear of failure, competitiveness, communication apprehension, negative social evaluation).
- Learner beliefs about language learning (e.g., perception of mistakes, views of instructional activities, priorities and preferences).
- Instructor beliefs about language learning (e.g., the role of instructors, relationships with learners).
- Instructor–learner interactions (e.g., manner of error correction).
- Classroom procedures (e.g., oral presentations, skits).
- Language testing (e.g., test format, test items, match between practice and testing).

Classroom procedures and learners' beliefs have been reported to be a key source of anxiety for some language learners. Some Japanese learners, for example, reported that their greatest source of anxiety was fear of negative evaluation by others and, hence, losing face in speaking-related activities such as oral presentations (Okata 2005). The learners also reported that of the four language skills, they felt most anxiety when speaking, and especially when it was monitored or evaluated by others. Listening, which also involved the processing of spoken English, also induced a great deal of anxiety among the learners, a result that is reminiscent of another study that documented the anxiety that listening to another language can arouse in learners (Vogely 1998). Oral presentations were also responsible for causing language anxiety among a group of post-graduate ESL students from various Asian countries studying in a university in Singapore (Lun 2001). English language learners in Singapore secondary schools also reported a high degree of anxiety when they had to speak in standard English in class, especially during oral presentations, where they knew it would be unacceptable to their teachers and classmates to use the localized vernacular English dialect known commonly as Singlish (Han 2003).

One direct result of language anxiety is that learners may become reticent and consequently withdraw from active participation in the classroom, as was the case with a group of Hong Kong learners (Tsui 1996). Reticence, therefore, should not be interpreted as a lack of motivation to learn to speak. That learners may not be willing to communicate in the target language because they suffer from language anxiety has also been shown in other studies among Japanese ESL learners (Hashimoto 2002) and EFL learners (Yashima 2002). Researchers have established relationships between language anxiety, self-perceptions of language competence, and willingness to communicate (Macintyre 2007). Whereas learners who are anxious tend to perceive themselves negatively, and, therefore, are less inclined to communicate, those who demonstrated low language anxiety were more willing to communicate, even if they had overestimated their own language competence (Macintyre, Noels & Clément 1997; Baker & Macintyre 2000). ESL learners studying abroad were more willing to communicate in English if they were more satisfied with their interpersonal relationships (Yashima, Zenuk-Nishide & Shimizu 2004). These findings seem to apply to different cultures, although the way anxiety is expressed may vary. Some studies have also shown that teachers were able to help to lower their learners' language anxiety effectively through classroom procedures such as keeping a journal (Farrell 1993; Foss & Reitzel 1991; Lun 2001; Onwuegbuzie et al. 1999).

These discussions about language anxiety can help us as language teachers in several ways. First of all, we are reminded that students who do not speak up in class are not necessarily unmotivated or uninterested. Failure to participate may not even be due to a complete lack of ability. Rather, students' lack of participation in speaking activities may very well be the result of deep-seated beliefs and fears that lead to great anxiety whenever they have to "perform" in class. From our earlier discussions about the role of speaking in academic learning and language acquisition, we can see that not speaking in the target language can have far-reaching consequences in terms of the personal success of many language learners. Nevertheless, we can take steps towards making the environment in our language classrooms one that is non-threatening and, at the same time, supportive of those students who suffer from high language anxiety. For example, we may consider using guided reflections in the form of journals to help them chart and eventually lower their language anxiety. Not only does journal writing help learners objectively examine sources of their anxiety, it also gives teachers a chance to acknowledge their students' feelings of anxiety and provide positive affective feedback and suggestions. Where it is appropriate, students could also be invited to openly discuss their anxiety.

Discuss it

If you have been a second language learner yourself, try and recall if you have ever felt any anxiety in class when you had to speak in the language. Think of two occasions, and describe them. For each, list some reasons for your anxiety. Can you think of ways in which you or your teacher could have lessened your anxiety?

Rethinking current practices in teaching speaking

The acquisition of oral skills is important for language learners to achieve effective communication, as well as for the reasons we have highlighted earlier. Development of these skills, however, is often influenced by a host of factors, and some affective ones may seem beyond the control of the learners themselves. How are current approaches to second language speaking instruction addressing these learner needs? In the past, oral skills were typically taught with a focus on acquiring correct pronunciation and grammar. Drills may have been used, for example, to ensure that only the correct linguistic patterns were learned. Since the advent of communicative language teaching, however, the pendulum has, at times, swung to the other end. Learners are often encouraged to focus on talking. They communicate their meaning using whatever linguistic resources they have because communicative language teaching places a high premium on providing extensive practice in oral communication among language learners. Most language curricula today emphasize the importance of working in pairs or groups to communicate in the target language, through a range of activities. The aim is for learners to become increasingly fluent in speaking the language. Overt correction and attention to language are minimized during these communicative activities. When learners have problems with what they need to say, they are encouraged to use communication strategies. The learning of correct language forms of grammar, pronunciation, and vocabulary are to be done in context. A lack of attention to accuracy may, in some cases, be a weak link in sequences of lessons on speaking.

Thus, while the use of communicative activities seems like a good way for learners to acquire oral skills in a naturalistic environment, the result may be far from ideal. We cannot underestimate the pressure that language learners experience when speaking. The fact that speaking almost always takes place in the presence of others who may be evaluating their performance or expecting an appropriate response also severely constrains learners' ability to monitor their speech for accuracy. In addition, communicative activities are often not designed with academic settings in mind, so second language learners who need to participate in these settings in schools and colleges may not be adequately prepared for the types of communication and genres involved. Speaking lessons also present an intrinsic challenge for teachers and learners alike. Unlike lessons on second language literacy, speaking lessons seldom allow teachers and learners to have a record of their performance because the spoken language is transient, and there is little record of it once the activities have finished. In a writing class, for example, teachers have evidence of learners' work that they can evaluate and offer feedback on. Speaking lessons, on the other hand, do not normally allow for such documentation of learning. Learners' strengths and limitations shown during a speaking activity, particularly in large classes, may go unnoticed and uncorrected. In spite of the learner-centered orientations of many communicative activities, affective factors that influence learner performance may be overlooked in some classes. In view of concerns about learners' anxiety, fear of speaking up, and lack of motivation, speaking lessons could, in general, do more to help learners develop better control over their learning processes and build up greater confidence in tackling speaking tasks. At the same time, lessons should also aim to provide a balance between using the language to speak, which is primarily the emphasis now, and thinking about the language used to speak. Speaking development should also account for metacognitive dimensions of learning (see Chapter 6 and Chapter 11), helping learners to achieve a positive self-concept as second language speakers, understand the demands and the nature of second language speaking, and use effective communication and discourse strategies to enhance their oral skills in different types of interactions. What this means is that teachers need to help second language learners develop their speaking in a more holistic way.

In this book, we introduce an approach that accounts for both tangible speaking outcomes as well as the cognitive and affective processes of learning to speak a second language. In the chapters that follow, we aim to help readers acquire a good theoretical understanding of the processes and skills involved in speaking, and the features of spoken discourse present in the speech and interactions of competent English speakers. These discussions are presented in Chapters 1–5. Building on the theoretical perspectives presented in these chapters, we will present a set of principles in the form of a methodological framework for teaching speaking (Chapter 6). This is followed in Chapters 7 and 8 by the description of a pedagogical model for putting into practice these principles, and by a discussion of how a speaking program built on these principles can be developed. These discussions are relevant to both general English as well as English-for-Academic-Purposes (EAP) programs. The last part of the book, Chapters 10–12, is devoted to a discussion of practical ideas that enable learners to develop their speaking competence through structured and guided experience.

Summary

Second language learners who attend school or tertiary institutions where teaching is conducted in the target language can engage effectively in the discourse of an academic environment if they have good speaking abilities. Inability to do so can cause learners to be disadvantaged in a system where not only proficiency in the target language is desirable, but also the ability to control the academic register in the spoken mode is highly valued. Speaking also directly benefits learners because it can facilitate second language acquisition. This can occur if learners get a chance to receive feedback on their spoken performance and are pushed to pay attention to linguistic forms that are causing their communication problems. Appropriate feedback can cause students to modify their spoken output to produce utterances that are grammatically accurate. Some language learners, however, avoid speaking up in class because they suffer from language anxiety. There are many sources of this anxiety, including personal beliefs about learning, fear of negative assessment by peers, and "threatening" classroom procedures and instructors' beliefs. Students who can participate effectively in oral interaction, in spite of a lack of language proficiency, are those who have developed useful coping strategies.

Based on what has been presented in this chapter, we can draw out some of our initial principles for teaching speaking:

1. Include activities that can potentially develop learners' speaking skills for engaging critically with their academic learning and social environment.

2. Plan activities that draw learners' attention to linguistic forms, discourse structure, and vocabulary so as to develop the learners' ability to speak accurately.
3. Consider the teacher's role in scaffolding classroom interaction so that learners are guided progressively towards effective speaking skills.
4. Make the classroom environment non-threatening, and encourage guided reflection or discussion to help learners monitor and eventually lower their language anxiety.
5. Teach learners to use strategies for dealing with anxiety and improve their speaking performance.

Group-learning tasks

1. Conduct a simple structured interview or questionnaire survey among your classmates or fellow teachers to find out what they know about the concepts introduced in this chapter.

	A	B	C	D
	I haven't heard of it.	I've heard of it, but don't know much about it.	I understand what it refers to.	This concept is an important guiding principle I hope to use in my teaching of speaking.
Comprehensible-Output Hypothesis.				
Negotiation for meaning.				
Language anxiety.				

2. Do you know of any second language learners who are also participating in mainstream education conducted in English? Are you currently teaching students who will be embarking on academic learning in a school / college / university when they complete your language course? Reflect on some of the key activities used for teaching spoken English. Describe two of these activities, and evaluate the extent to which the activities prepare the learners to do the following:

   a. Use decontextualized oral language.
   b. Explore, expand, and evaluate ideas in small-group discussions.

3. Consult a book or a chapter on second language acquisition theories (such as the ones referenced in this chapter), and make brief
   notes about the Comprehensible-Output Hypothesis. Do you think
   the language classes you are familiar with should provide learners
   with opportunities to use spoken language that is precise, concise,
   and appropriate? How tolerant do you think teachers should be of
   oral language that is imprecise and inaccurate? Consider the pros and
   cons of these questions in the light of the role that speaking can play
   in second language acquisition.
4. Conduct a simple survey among your classmates to find out whether
   they experience any anxiety when they have to communicate in a language that is not their first language. (Consider both speaking and listening.) Refer to the six sources of language anxiety that Young (1991)
   identified, which were cited in this chapter. Classify your classmates'
   responses according to these six categories, and present your findings
   to other participants in class. Compare similarities and differences
   among the different groups of learners.

Further reading

Gibbons, P. (2002) *Scaffolding Language, Scaffolding Learning: Teaching Second Language Learners in the Mainstream Classroom*, Portsmouth, NH: Heine-mann.

Mackey, A. and Silver, R. (2005) Interactional tasks and English L2 learning by immigrant children in Singapore, *System*, 33, 230–260.

Swain, M. (1995) Three functions of output in second language acquisition, In G. Cook and B. Seidlhofer (eds.) *Principle and Practice in Applied Linguistics*, Oxford: Oxford University Press, 125–144.

Tsui, A. B. M. (1996) Reticence and anxiety in second language learning, In K. M. Bailey and D. Nunan (eds.) *Voices from the Language Classroom*, Cambridge: Cambridge University Press, 145–168.

2 Cognitive processes in speaking

When speaking, language learners often seem to falter and pause and experience other difficulties. Like all speakers, they must engage in various mental processes, but for language learners, these processes do not necessarily work optimally to help them produce speech that is fluent and accurate.

Understanding the key mental processes speakers engage in can help us support learners in their speaking development in a more informed manner. To discuss these processes, this chapter will answer two questions:

1. How is speech produced?
2. What effects do psycholinguistic processes have on learners' speaking performance?

Topics addressed in the chapter include:

- Cognitive demands in speech production.
- The rate of speech production.
- Fluency, accuracy, and complexity.

Introduction

Language learners tend to believe that native speakers speak effortlessly. It appears to them that the words of native speakers flow seamlessly, and ideas are conveyed through utterances with flawless grammar. Unseen to learners, however, are the myriad complex mental processes taking place. These processes work interactively, often automatically, and in harmony, making optimal use of the limited processing capacity of working memory. To conceptualize speaking as a process, several applied linguists have applied a cognitive model of speech processing proposed by Levelt (1989). This model has been used to explain second language speech production (McLaughlin 1987; Johnson 1996; Bygate 1998) and the use of communication strategies to facilitate speaking in interlanguage communication (Poulisse 1993). In this chapter, we will present the components of Levelt's model and explain how cognitive processes interact to enable speech to be produced as speakers respond to various pragmatic demands. We will also discuss the effects these processes have on learners' speech and their overall speaking performance, and suggest some principles for helping language learners improve their speaking ability.

Model for speech production

In fluent conversations, a speaker may generate two or three words per second by retrieving them from a memory store that contains tens of thousands of items (Levelt, Roelofs & Meyer 1999). This seemingly effortless performance actually involves underlying processes that are remarkably complex and that express both form, or structure, and meaning, or content. These interrelated processes are represented in a model of speech production proposed by Levelt (1989) that consists of three interrelated stages that are directly involved in the production of speech: a) conceptual preparation, b) formulation, and c) articulation. An important aspect of this model is self-monitoring, a process that operates at a level different from the other three stages mentioned above. Each stage of the model is described separately below (see Figure 2.1), but it is important to bear in mind that the different stages may recur and overlap throughout the duration of speech production. In fact, it is now widely recognized that the "stages" interact with one

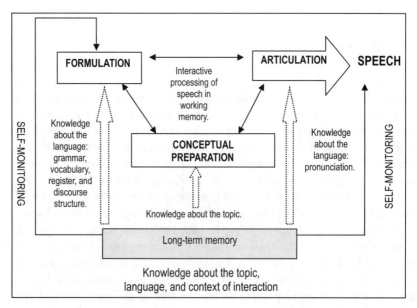

Figure 2.1: Cognitive demands on language learners when producing speech (drawing from Levelt's model of speech processing).

another and occur concurrently when interconnected neural networks in the brain are activated at about the same time (Bechtel & Abrahamsen 1991). This process of how various stages are concurrently activated is key to how individuals access words that are stored mentally when they speak (Bock & Levelt 1994).

Conceptual preparation

Conceptual preparation, also referred to as conceptualization, is where speech production begins. It is the process by which speakers select the topic or information they wish to express. If a topic has already been established, speakers still have to select relevant ideas from their long-term memory to construct their message. These ideas will depend on speakers' background or "encyclopedic" knowledge about the world. The more knowledge they have about the topic, the more choices there are to work from in choosing which message to deliver. Very often, the ideas may exist only vaguely in the speaker's mind, as a mental model or as simple meaning components (a "gist").

In the case of language learners, consider what happens if they are asked to retell a story they have just read or heard. Although the learners might know what the story is about, they will still have to decide which details are important to include in the retelling. Their decision will also depend on how well they have comprehended the story in the first place. One popular speaking activity used in class requires learners to talk informally about a topic they have been given, which may involve producing a narrative, a retelling of a story, or an opinion. Students sit in a group of three or four. One person writes a word on a piece of paper and passes it to the person on his or her left. The person then has to speak in an impromptu manner for one or two minutes. To speak during these activities, learners have to select appropriate content and choose the discourse structure that is appropriate for the genre they are producing. In spontaneous face-to-face interactions, language learners have to construct responses that include relevant information and, at the same time, are socioculturally appropriate (see Chapters 4 and 5). All of these speech events require learners to think about what they have to say before or while they are saying it.

Formulation

Formulation is a process by which the ideas that exist in the speaker's mind during conceptual preparation are mapped on to specific words in the speaker's mental lexicon and strung together (Garman 1990). This process is perhaps the most challenging for language learners of the three stages in Levelt's model. This is because learners have to make a number of lexico-grammatical choices; that is to say, they have to decide which words and grammatical forms are relevant for their intended message. The concepts are "fleshed out" through a stringing together of selected words in the right order (syntax). Tense, mood, number, etc. also have to be indicated by appropriate markers known as bound morphemes (e.g., –ed, –s, –ing). To express these abstract mental concepts clearly, learners have to rely on their knowledge of the grammatical system of the target language.

Some learners may also have to resort to direct translation of key words or entire utterances from their first language. If many utterances need to be produced, learners also have to pay attention to the overall coherence of the discourse as it unfolds. For example, when telling a story, learners have to use words and phrases *(once upon a time, in a land faraway)* to set the context for a narrative. When giving a talk, learners will also need to make use of formulaic, or "fixed," phrases to signpost transitions clearly for their listeners *(moving on to, to sum up)*. Whether learners can do this successfully will also depend on their knowledge of registers, or level of appropriateness, for the social context in which the speech is produced.

Articulation

Articulation is made possible when speakers activate and control specific muscle groups of the articulatory system (consisting of the vocal tract, larynx, and lungs). Through articulation, the message is carried in the form of sound waves to the listener. Although articulation is more of a physiological process, it is closely linked to memory and information processing. When someone who is competent in a language speaks, he or she seldom has to pay close attention to how the words should be pronounced or where the stress for certain words should be. These phonological encodings have largely been automatized and are, therefore, second nature to the speaker. This knowledge also allows competent speakers to draw listeners' attention to specific details, by assigning stress in appropriate places. (See Chapter 4 for a discussion of intonation in context.)

Many language learners, on the other hand, have to recall how some sounds are produced or consciously assign stress to the right syllable in an important key word, as they speak. They may also have to make conscious attempts at adopting intonation patterns that they believe will help them convey their message in a socially acceptable manner. Learners who are very conscious of their pronunciation will give a lot of their attention to the articulation process. This, however, may also be a source of anxiety for some learners because they feel their pronunciation is not good enough or cannot be understood by others, and they avoid speaking up as a result. Sometimes, learners may also find that they have a particular written word in their mind's eye, but they are unable to articulate it because they are unsure of its pronunciation. In all, articulation can be a challenging stage in language learners' speech processing.

Self-monitoring

Conceptual preparation (thinking about what to say), formulation (how to say it), and articulation (actually saying it aloud) are the three processes that directly contribute to speech production. There is, however, a fourth process that is at work at a higher level. This fourth process is the key metacognitive process during speaking and involves self-monitoring, or checking one's speech for accuracy and acceptability. Competent language users normally notice errors in pronunciation and grammar, dysfluencies (e.g., words that are cut off mid-utterance or phrases that are restarted and repeated), and other problems commonly associated with speech production (Levelt et al. 1999). Native-speaker children as young as three-years-of-age have been observed to correct their pronunciation and grammar spontaneously during speech production (Foster-Cohen 1999).

Language learners also monitor their speech, and some may employ oral-communication strategies to help them get their meaning across (Nakatani & Goh 2006). Effective self-monitoring depends on metalinguistic knowledge; that is to say, knowledge of grammar and pronunciation is needed to check the way we speak. Language learners who have limited metalinguistic knowledge will not be able to monitor their speech production well. In addition to monitoring one's speech for structural accuracy, language learners also have to consider pragmatic demands during communication. Basic pragmatic demands include speakers' assessment of the relationship between themselves and their listeners, as well as the interactional and social contexts in which their speech is produced (Burns 1998). Communicatively competent speakers not only produce utterances that their listeners understand, but they also evaluate the appropriateness of what they say in the light of reciprocity conditions; that is, who they are speaking to and under which kinds of circumstances (Bygate 1987). Although self-monitoring is an important strategy for language learners, it may also indirectly put further demands on the other cognitive processes that are already in operation. Language learners may ignore self-monitoring so that they can focus on getting their meaning across as quickly as possible. This factor has implications for teaching speaking, in particular the development of accuracy. We will return to this in some of the later chapters in this book.

Think about it

List three common speaking problems you have observed among second / foreign language speakers. Based on the explanation of speech production given above, suggest the kind of processing demands that might have caused these problems.

Rate of speech production

Language learners do not all produce speech at the same rate, nor do they produce speech at the same rate all the time. On one occasion, a learner may produce speech that is halting and unclear, while on another, he or she may be able to speak fluently and clearly. So what factors influence the rate of speech processing? One important factor is the degree of automatization. Cognitive processes that have been automatized are those that involve skills and knowledge that are well-learned, through constant use and rehearsal (Shiffrin & Schneider 1977; Segalowitz 2003). Automatized processes make little or no demand on processing capacity because they do not require attention or effort to perform.

For example, language learners who are used to narrating stories will automatically begin each story with an orientation or context (e.g., *one day, once upon a time*). The working memory is, therefore, free from one level of processing (how to structure discourse) and is able to attend more closely to other demands (the content of the story). A learner's conceptual preparation and formulation processes in a particular task may become automatized because of his or her prior knowledge of facts, social, or academic conventions; discourse structures; and linguistic knowledge. The articulation process can also be automatized when the learner has developed control over the production of sounds and prosody of the target language.

The rate of speech production also depends on the speed of lexical access; that is to say, how fast or slowly an individual is able to recall and select from words stored in long-term memory (Levelt 1989, Levelt et al. 1999). This access may be instantaneous, or it may require several intermediate steps before the final desired word is recalled. Learners who have a large store of vocabulary will thus potentially have more alternatives to choose from, but this does not necessarily guarantee quicker processing. Some learners lose processing time when deliberating which word to use, and in face-to-face interaction, they may even lose their turn (Hughes 2002).

One way lexical access can be improved among learners is for them to learn to use prefabricated formulaic language (Bygate 1998;

Schmitt 2004). Formulaic phrases may be used for specific occasions (for example, *Congratulations on your promotion, Pardon my ignorance*), or speakers may rely on collocational units – words that usually go together – in normal language use (for example, *a tall order, a terrible mistake, a remarkable achievement*, and so on). (See Chapter 4.) Using prefabricated formulaic language is a facilitation strategy for coping with limited processing capacity and time pressure. To buy processing time, some speakers may even use entire sentences such as, *What you've said is extremely interesting!* (Hughes 2002).

Discuss it

Make a list of formulaic expressions that are commonly used by speakers of English in academic settings or conversations among friends. Have you ever introduced formulaic language in your teaching? If so, what kind of formulaic phrases did you . teach, and who were the learners? Did the learners find the expressions useful?

High-proficiency learners typically produce speech more rapidly than beginning learners because they know more about the language and can apply this knowledge quickly when constructing their utterances. This does not mean, however, that high-proficiency learners can do the same in all situations. The reason is that the degree of automatization varies according to differing demands made on the speaker and the kind of output expected. For example, when talking about a familiar topic with friends, a learner may be able to speak clearly and fluently. The same topic, however, may require greater attention, planning, and monitoring when it has to be communicated to a large audience in a formal situation. On the other hand, in spontaneous interactive talk, learners usually have very little time to plan and prepare what they have to say. Furthermore, they also have to listen to what others are saying and respond appropriately. In contrast, preparation for an oral presentation involves longer planning time, and opportunities for rehearsals are often available. This kind of pre-task planning allows conceptualizing and formulating to take place before articulation, thus creating less pressure and fewer demands on the individual's processing capacity. Planning also enables monitoring to take place before the actual presentation in front of a live audience.

Clearly, learners face many demands when trying to speak in the target language. How can teachers support them in their learning so that they can achieve small successes that can motivate them to further improve their speaking? Teachers can start by planning speaking tasks that provide a realistic level of challenge, in light of the various speech-production processes. If learners have to produce spontaneous speech on an unfamiliar topic, they will experience tremendous cognitive demands on all fronts: conceptual preparation, formulation, and articulation. This may result in cognitive overload, causing some learners to stop talking altogether or to communicate in an unclear manner. If, however, learners have sufficient prior knowledge about the topic, the load may be eased a little, as they need to pay attention only to how to formulate and articulate their ideas.

Another strategy teachers can use is to plan speaking activities that include opportunities for planning and rehearsals. This will help to increase the degree of automatization of one or more of the processes. Finally, it would also be useful to bear in mind that some learners who appear to be quiet or even unmotivated may, in fact, want to participate, but they are unable to cope with the cognitive demands of speaking and, therefore, choose not to participate at all. To understand more about these learners, you can include activities where they are encouraged to describe challenges they face and explore sources of their language anxiety. You can then plan activities that help them alleviate or manage some of these feelings of anxiety.

Think about it

How do you prepare for a talk? Would you take your learners through the same processes? Why or why not?

Fluency, accuracy, and complexity

The interplay of cognitive and affective, or emotional, factors during speech production exerts heavy demands on language learners, and this, in turn, can have a direct impact on the quality of their spoken language. We can talk about the quality of learners' speech according to three characteristics: fluency, accuracy, and complexity (Bygate 1998; Skehan 1996). (See Table 2.1.)

One of the effects of cognitive-processing demands on learners' language use is that they may not have adequate cognitive resources to produce speech that is both fluent and accurate. Under time pressure when speaking, language learners experience limited cognitive capacity for processing meaning and linguistic knowledge at the same time. Thus, even when they know the grammatical "rules" in their heads, some language learners may not always use correct grammar when they speak. Their first priority is to

Table 2.1: *Three key features of learners' speech*

	Definition	Focus
Fluency	Speech where the message is communicated coherently with few pauses and hesitations, thus causing minimal comprehension difficulties for the listeners.	Meaning
Accuracy	Speech where the message is communicated using correct grammar. The notion of accuracy can also be expanded to include correct pronunciation according to target language norms.	Form
Complexity	Speech where the message is communicated precisely. More advanced grammatical forms are used, such as subordination and clausal embeddings, which are appropriate for speech in relation to the social and cultural context, as well as the roles of, and relationships with, interlocutors.	Meaning and form

express meaning (Skehan 1998a). Grappling with limited capacity in their working memory, they will most likely "sacrifice" accuracy when formulating their message. Their immediate aim is to get their meaning across, using the linguistic resources that are available to them at that point in time. There is not always enough time to retrieve rules or access extensively the vocabulary stored in their long-term memory. If you look at Figure 2.1 on page 36 again, you will notice the dotted lines in the arrows linking knowledge and long-term memory. The dotted lines show that the process of retrieval is not always complete.

Beginning learners will not have even developed sufficient grammatical resources to produce utterances that are morphologically or syntactically accurate. Not unlike a child learning a first language, they may initially only try to string content words together (e.g., *Man eat apple*). As their knowledge of grammar develops, words may be supported by greater use of grammatical forms for inflecting verbs (e.g. *Man eating apple* or *The man is eating an apple*). However, when their attention is taxed in face-to-face communication, grammatical accuracy may be compromised, even if they know *about* the type of grammar they are supposed to use. The need to avoid long pauses that might lead to a breakdown in communication or losing their turn often means that learners may not attend to the form of the language adequately.

When some processes, such as lexical retrieval, are partially automatized, language learners may be able to demonstrate language complexity by formulating longer and more precise utterances. They use grammatical resources, such as subordination and clausal embeddings, to increase the preciseness of what they are conveying and to provide additional information. Increase in language complexity within an utterance is an important milestone in children's speech in first language acquisition, and it is also a measurement of second language development. Let's illustrate the relationship between language complexity and preciseness in meaning with the following hypothetical examples of speech, produced during a narrative task based on a picture:

a. The teacher blew the whistle. The children ran as fast as they could.
b. The teacher blew the whistle, and the children ran as fast they could.
c. As soon as they heard the teacher's whistle, the children ran as fast as they could.
d. As soon as they heard the teacher's whistle, the children who were standing at the back ran as fast as they could.

Example a) consists of two independent clauses. The way one idea follows another suggests that the two actions are related to each other, but the relationship is not very clear. In example b), the two clauses are coordinated by the conjunction *and*, thus making the relationship a little more explicit. In example c), we can see the temporal relationship between the two actions even more clearly because of the presence of subordination. This temporal relationship is enhanced through the use of the adverbial phrase *as soon as*. Example d) shows the embedding of a relative clause *(who were standing at the back)* into the main clause, thereby giving more detailed information and making the meaning more explicit.

Research on spoken grammar has suggested that spoken clause structure differs from written clause structure in at least one respect. In spoken grammar, clauses are usually added on to one another through the use of simple coordinating conjunctions, the most common being *and*. What this implies is that language used during speaking may be less grammatically complex than language used in writing. However, this observation is based on spontaneous spoken English where speakers often have to think on their feet. We could argue that in formal discourse, especially where planning and rehearsals are possible, we would expect to see a greater degree of language complexity in our learners' speech. It is also true that in many formal contexts, the spoken language produced contains more features of literate or written English than that produced during spontaneous casual talk. The extent to which complexity is seen in speech will depend on various aspects of the sociocultural context where talk is produced, such as the relationships between speaker and listeners, the extent to which they are familiar with each other, their feelings towards each other, and the distance of the speakers in time and space from the topics being discussed (see Chapter 4).

Language learners' speaking proficiency (and even the proficiency of native speakers) is not a monolithic construct. There are different levels of performance, with some tasks being completed more (or less) fluently and accurately than others. Most of the time, however, language learners' limited processing capacity will force them to attend to meaning before formal accuracy. The implication of this for the classroom, we suggest, is that teachers need to plan different types of activities at different times in order to develop fluency (meaning focused), accuracy (form focused), and complexity (form and meaning focused). However, teachers must judge the abilities of the learners and the extent to which the learners are capable of complexity. When learners, such as beginners, can only focus on either meaning or form at any one time, expecting them to do well in both may frustrate and discourage them.

Try it

Select a topic that you have just read about in the newspaper. Record yourself, giving a spontaneous two-minute talk on the topic in your second language if you have one. Listen to your own speech, and evaluate your production, according to fluency, accuracy, and complexity. If you don't have a second language, ask a friend or colleague who does if he or she will do this exercise and then work with you to evaluate the production.

Summary

The apparent ease with which speech is produced by competent speakers belies the complex cognitive processes involved and masks the many factors which influence the output. These processes are often overlooked in the classroom, where teachers' attention is focused mainly on the product. Teachers tend to focus on how fluent and accurate their students are in communicating their meaning, as well as how well they are able to formulate complex utterances. As a result, learners may be unduly concerned about their performance, when they could be focusing on learning how to develop their speaking abilities.

As we have seen, language learners experience various degrees of anxiety when they have to speak spontaneously. The anxiety is often due to their inability to cope with the cognitive demands of one or all of the core processes described earlier:

a. Conceptual preparation (learners don't know what to say): This could be due to insufficient background or content knowledge, or the inability to select content that is appropriate for the task.

b. Formulation (learners don't know how to express their meaning grammatically): The learner may have a notion of *what* to say, but experiences difficulty in translating that mental model into more precise language, or in selecting the right word.

c. Articulation (learners don't know how to pronounce words in the target language): The learner has formulated a proposition, but may not be able to articulate it clearly. In some cases, learners may be genuinely embarrassed by their poor pronunciation and avoid articulation altogether.

Learners may not, however, experience the same kind of difficulties all the time. These difficulties depend greatly on the nature of the speaking task and the learners' perceptions of the degree of formality, the amount of time pressure, the interest level of the listener, and the background knowledge needed to understand their message. These cognitive and affective factors can affect the quality of learners' performance, giving rise to perceptible variation in their speech, in the areas of fluency, accuracy, and complexity. Based on what has been presented in this chapter, we suggest some principles for teaching speaking:

1. Avoid over-taxing learners' cognitive capacity with activities that concurrently require their conscious attention simultaneously to conceptual preparation, formulation, and articulation.

2. Instead, provide learning experiences that focus separately on different cognitive demands in speaking activities so that learners get a chance to develop their oral language gradually and in a less stressful environment.

3. Vary the level of challenge or difficulty of the speaking activities by providing support during one or more of the cognitive phases involved in speech production.

4. Teach learners to use communication and discourse strategies for buying processing time and negotiating meaning.

5. Recognize that learners' spoken-language performance will vary with the type of demands required by each speaking task. Therefore, be clear about the learning objective for each activity, and assess your learners' performance realistically.

6. Plan activities where learners can focus separately on the expression of meaning and the structuring of the language form, but find a way of weaving these experiences into a coherent whole.

These principles will be demonstrated in chapters where we present a theoretical framework and practical ideas for teaching speaking in a holistic manner.

Group-learning tasks

1. This task requires you to give an informal talk. Organize yourselves into groups of three. Each person writes a topic related to language teaching on a piece of paper. Pass your piece of paper to the person on your left. Nobody should look at what is written on the paper until it is his or her turn to speak. Take turns speaking about the topic you have been given by your group member. Time yourselves so no one speaks longer than 90 seconds. After your group has completed your impromptu speeches, complete the items below individually, before discussing your ideas with one another.

Try to remember as much as you can about what you thought or did when you had to give the informal talk on language teaching.	
Did you think about this?	**Describe briefly what you did.**
a. Conceptual preparation. (Decide what to say.) b. Formulation. (Plan the language to use.) c. Articulation. (Speak clearly so others can hear you.) d. The organization of an informal talk. (Structure your talk.) e. Lexical choices. (Choose the "right" words.) f. Prefabricated chunks. (Include formulaic expressions.) g. Monitoring. (Check what you say while speaking.) h. Evaluation. (Assess the quality of your spoken performance.)	

2. Repeat the task above with the same topic. This time, record yourselves. Listen to the recording in your groups, and evaluate one another in terms of fluency, accuracy, and complexity, using the chart below.

You should also evaluate yourself. Once you've completed the task, compare the results, and explain your opinions to one another.

| Speaker: _____ | | |
| Topic: _____ | | |

	Excellent Good Adequate	Comments on performance
Fluency		
Accuracy		
Complexity		

Do you have consensus on your results? Discuss why your opinions are similar or different.

Further reading

Bygate, M. (1998) Theoretical perspectives on speaking, *Annual Review of Applied Linguistics*, 18, 20–42.

Skehan, P. (1998a) *A Cognitive Approach to Language Learning*, Oxford: Oxford University Press.

Schmitt, N. (ed.) (2004) *Formulaic Sequences: Acquisition, Processing, and Use*, Amsterdam: John Benjamins Publishing Company.

3 *Speaking competence*

The goal of many second language teachers is to help their students become competent speakers of the language. But what does it mean to be a competent second language speaker? This chapter focuses on the notion of second language speaking competence and the implications this has for the way we conceptualize speaking lessons. It will address two questions:

1. What constitutes second language speaking competence?
2. What types of knowledge, skills, and strategies should language learners develop?

To answer the questions, we will discuss the following topics:

- Communicative competence and speaking.
- Knowledge about language and discourse.
- Core speaking skills.
- Communication strategies.

Introduction

To teach speaking effectively, as teachers, you need to understand what speaking competence entails. You also need to know how different aspects of speaking competence relate to one another. This understanding will help you plan and deliver lessons that develop your learners' speaking ability in a balanced and comprehensive way. It will also help you approach teaching materials you work with every day in an informed and critical manner. If your concept of speaking competence is too narrow, the activities you plan will be skewed towards developing only certain features of speaking, and other important features of speaking competence will be neglected. On the other hand, if your concept of speaking competence is too vague, you will not be able to identify specific objectives that your lessons hope to achieve. For example, if you think that good speaking competence simply means speaking fluently, your activities will aim to give learners lots of practice in talking, in the hope that, through cumulative practice, they will become increasingly fluent in expressing their ideas. Practice without a specific focus on relevant speaking skills or linguistic knowledge, however, will not be maximally beneficial to learners in the long run. If you are using prescribed materials in your school or institution, knowledge of what constitutes speaking competence will help you adapt existing activities so as to meet your students' needs more effectively.

Think about it

Take a few minutes to reflect on your own experience as a language learner or as a language teacher, and complete this statement: *"A competent second language speaker is someone who..."*

Here are the combined views of several language teachers. Which of the points below do you agree with?

A competent second language speaker is someone who...
- Has good pronunciation.
- Speaks standard English.
- Can speak fluently and with few or no grammatical mistakes.
- Speaks in a manner indistinguishable from a native speaker.
- Is confident when speaking to a large audience.
- Knows when to say the right things and says them in the most effective way possible.
- Can communicate well with native speakers.
- Can be understood easily by others.
- Can speak effectively and clearly in various situations.
- In bilingual settings, knows how to code-switch from the first to the second language, according to circumstances.
- Can speak fluently and clearly on a wide range of topics.

The statements above show diverse perspectives on speaking a second language. Your view of what a good second language speaker can do will influence the way you conceptualize your teaching objectives. If you think it is important for students to speak with good pronunciation, it is likely that you will spend a great deal of time focusing on their pronunciation. If, on the other hand, your view of what is important is oriented towards grammatical accuracy, you may spend a great deal of time correcting ungrammatical utterances that your learners produce. One consequence of a narrow view of speaking competence is that we lose sight of the larger context where speaking is a social act and the fact that the way we speak will be influenced by many factors related to the social nature of speech.

Communicative competence and speaking

One way in which we can examine the notion of speaking competence is to refer to the concept of communicative competence put forward by Dell Hymes (1979) and expanded on by many researchers who have followed. According to Hymes (1979), an individual's communicative competence is his or her ability to use language effectively in actual communication. This ability consists of both *knowledge* about the language and specific *skills* in using the language. Hymes contrasted an idealized notion of linguistic competence with speakers' actual performance in social situations. Individuals with a high level of communicative competence produce utterances that are grammatically accurate, easy for listeners to process, and contextually appropriate and acceptable. The concept of communicative competence was further developed by Canale and Swain (1980) in order to explain it within second language acquisition contexts (see also Canale 1983). They identified four components that made up communicative competence: grammatical competence, discourse competence, sociolinguistic competence, and strategic competence. Grammatical competence referred to knowledge about grammar, vocabulary, and phonology, while discourse competence was seen as the ability to connect utterances to produce a coherent whole. Sociolinguistic competence consisted of the ability to use language that is accurate and appropriate to sociocultural norms and consistent with the type of discourse produced in specific sociocultural contexts. Finally, strategic competence referred to verbal and non-verbal actions taken to prevent and address breakdowns in communication.

Communicative competence in relation to second language speaking was further highlighted by Johnson (1981) at the beginning of the Communicative Language Teaching era. He summarized what a competent second language speaker was able to do:

> Apart from being grammatical, the utterance must also be appropriate on very many levels at the same time; it must conform to the speaker's aim; the role relationships between the interactants; to the setting, topic, linguistic context, etc. The speaker must also produce his utterance within severe constraints; he does not know in advance what will be said to him (and hence what his utterance will be a response to); yet, if the conversation is not to flag, he must respond quickly. The rapid formulation of utterances which are simultaneously "right" on several levels is central to the communicative skill (Johnson 1981: 11).

From this statement, we see that accuracy ("being grammatical") is clearly an important facet of speaking competence. Accuracy alone, however, is insufficient. Competent second language speakers must also be able to use speech skillfully to achieve their communicative goals. They need to be aware of the socially contextualized nature of speech so that what they say is appropriate and acceptable to their listeners. Thus, they have to consider relationships between themselves and the participants in an interaction, as well as other contextual variables (setting and topic, for example) that might influence the way their message is constructed and conveyed. Such an awareness also helps them decide on the amount and the type of information needed, and the way in which the message is to be conveyed. Johnson's observations allude to the importance of oral communication strategies in second language speaking. For example, language learners often experience problems with vocabulary and this can cause communication to break down. To prevent this breakdown from happening, learners can use strategies such as asking for clarification or repetition that will help in their negotiation of meaning and, at the same time, keep the interaction alive. This ability to employ strategies for facilitating communication is a key component of second language communicative competence (Canale & Swain 1980; Canale 1983).

Another characteristic of second language communicative competence is discourse competence. Discourse competence comprises linguistic knowledge about the structure of spoken genres and the skills needed to organize various genres according to sociocultural context (Burns 1998). Native speakers are familiar with the way different types of spoken genres begin, progress, and end, which greatly helps them to anticipate the overall structure of spoken discourses and to respond appropriately (Burns, Joyce & Gollin (1996); see also Chapter 5. Language learners, however, are not familiar with the way different types of spoken discourse unfold (particularly within the target language culture) and will benefit from learning about spoken genres through explicit teaching. Since second language learners are operating with an incomplete mastery of the language, discourse knowledge can help them predict the type of message they are likely to hear so they can respond appropriately. They can also translate this knowledge into discourse organization skills to enhance the structure, clarity, and appropriateness of their message.

From our discussion so far, we have seen that second language speaking is a "combinatorial skill," like other language communication skills, because it "involves a high element of doing various things at the same time" (Johnson 1996: 155). Our aim in teaching speaking is to help learners become better at combining various skills and processes during language production (Littlewood 1992). Due to the cognitive, affective, and social demands of speech production that we have discussed in the previous two chapters, learner speech may suffer from problems such as dysfluencies and a lack

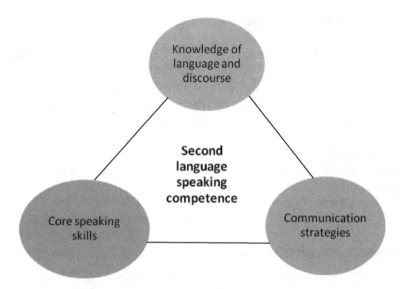

Figure 3.1: Aspects of second language speaking competence.

of grammatical accuracy and complexity. Nevertheless, the speech process can be facilitated by the use of communication and discourse strategies that compensate for gaps in linguistic knowledge, and enhance the overall structure and clarity of the message.

Taking into consideration the various dimensions of second language competence, we propose a model of second language speaking competence that comprises knowledge of language and discourse, core speaking skills, and communication and discourse strategies (see Figure 3.1). The components of this model, and how they relate to one another, are explained in the rest of the chapter. Based on this model, we will define second language speaking development as the increasing ability to use linguistic knowledge, core speaking skills, and communication and discourse strategies in order to produce utterances and discourses that are fluent, accurate, and socially appropriate within the constraints of cognitive processing.

Think about it

Consider the three aspects of second language speaking competence mentioned above. What challenges do you think learners at the beginning level of language learning will face?

Knowledge of language and discourse

To speak well, learners must have sufficient knowledge of the language. But the notion of "language" can be vague and sometimes too narrowly defined. The discussion in this chapter is based on a definition of linguistic knowledge that encompasses knowledge of structure, meaning, and use (Canale & Swain 1980; Canale 1983), and includes the following:

- Grammatical knowledge.
- Phonological knowledge.
- Lexical knowledge.
- Discourse knowledge.

Grammatical knowledge

Grammatical knowledge is fundamental to the development of any language skill. Learners need to know, for example, how verbs in English are inflected to denote tense (e.g., using *–ed* for past tense in regular English verbs). In addition, they need syntactic knowledge; that is, how words are strung together to express specific grammatical structures and meanings. For example, to ask a question in English, learners would normally need to invert the subject and verb positions used in normal declarative utterances or include auxiliary verbs. *(She likes jazz.* → *Does she like jazz?)* Grammatical knowledge is important during the formulation of utterances and self-monitoring in speech processing. In face-to-face interaction, learners also need grammatical knowledge to parse utterances they hear so that they can make further responses (Rost 2001). That is, they need to divide utterances into segments according to syntactic structures or semantic cues, in order to create a mental representation of the combined meaning of the words. In addition to conventional grammatical knowledge, learners also need knowledge about spoken grammar if they are to produce speech that is natural and not entirely modeled on the written language (Carter 1995; McCarthy and Carter 2001).

Phonological knowledge

Another kind of knowledge learners need is knowledge of the phonology (the sound system) of the target language. Phonological knowledge is necessary for three levels of production: word, utterance, and discourse. First of all, language learners need to know how the sounds of the target language are pronounced and how to avoid some common problems associated with transferring sounds from their first language (Kenworthy 1987; Hewings 2004). These aspects of knowledge have to do with the segmental (or micro) features of pronunciation at the word level. Learners also need to be aware of the presence of suprasegmental (or macro) features of speech beyond the word, such as stress, rhythm, and intonation. More importantly, they should know what communicative and discourse functions are served by features such as prominence (placing weak or strong emphasis on certain sounds) and tones (chunking sounds to provide meaning) during speaking and listening.

Lexical knowledge

Language learners' lexical knowledge develops at two levels. The first is the number of words and their meanings that learners know. In other words, this is their individual vocabulary size. It has been estimated that native speakers of English have a vocabulary size of 80,000 words by the time they leave secondary school (Owens 2001). In the case of second language learners, this number is expected to be smaller. Moreover, we need to make a distinction between words that learners know as part of their productive vocabulary; that is, available for use when speaking or writing, and what they know as their receptive vocabulary; that is, available for recognition during listening and reading. An individual's productive vocabulary is generally smaller than his or her receptive vocabulary. Thus, one of the problems that many language learners face is that they do not have sufficient words to express their messages precisely. At a more advanced level, learners' vocabulary knowledge is enhanced by their semantic knowledge of relationships among words. Examples include knowledge of lexical sets such as kinship terms (*mother, father, brother, sister*, etc.) and the relationships of words to abstract concepts such as denotative and connotative meanings (that is, the literal meaning of nouns such as *angel* and *rat* and what idea the words suggest when we call someone an "angel" or a "rat"). Learners' speech will also be enhanced by knowledge about fixed formulaic and idiomatic expressions. Many such expressions are used for signaling discourse organization (e.g., *let me begin by*), to express vagueness (e.g., *this, that, and the other*), and to express modality. Modality in language is an expression of a person's stance, attitudes, and level of certainty. In writing, it is typically signaled by the use of modal verbs, such as *should, must*, and *will*. In speech, however, modality is usually signaled by lexical phrases and simple adverbs such as *I think, I suppose, definitely, apparently*, and *to all intents and purposes*.

Discourse knowledge

Spoken texts are structured in various genres to serve different communicative purposes and social contexts (see Chapter 5). As learners need to use their second language to communicate in target language contexts, it is important that they know how these purposes and contexts influence the structure of the discourse they produce. They need to know what linguistic resources can be used for organizing and structuring stretches of speech to form coherent spoken texts that are appropriate for the setting and the participants. For example, if they want to retell the story of a movie, an awareness of how narratives are structured is useful – that all stories have an orientation, a complication, and a resolution, and that the person who is narrating the story often includes a short personal interpretation or reflection on the story. When language learners want to recount an incident, they need to know that events are typically sequenced in chronological order. In addition to extended monologic discourses, such as those just described, some conversations have predictable structures, too. For example, three-part exchanges are typical in short conversations between British native speakers (Carter 1998: 44):

A: What part of London are you staying in?
B: In Hyde Park.
A: Oh, are you? That's a nice district.

Learners' knowledge of spoken discourse structures also needs to be complemented by pragmatic knowledge about speech acts and sociocultural practices. In other words, not only do they need to know how discourse is typically constructed, but they also need to be aware of the norms in communication in different societies, even when these societies speak the same language. This is part of second language learners' sociolinguistic competence (Canale & Swain 1980). To use the example above of three-part exchanges, we can see that language learners will benefit from knowing about the social function that is served by the last part of the exchange.

Nevertheless, English is increasingly being learned for communication with non-native speakers. In view of the role of English as an international language, knowledge about discourse in English also needs to include intercultural pragmatic knowledge that extends beyond traditional "native and non-native speaker" scenarios to include cultural practices of English speakers from other cultures (McKay 2002). For example, it is common for Chinese speakers of English in many parts of the world to greet one another in English with, "Have you eaten?" or "Have you had your lunch?" if they meet in late morning or early afternoon. Introducing learners to the concept of intercultural and cross-cultural communication is now an important area of teaching practice for language teachers.

The interrelationships of knowledge about language and discourse

The types of linguistic knowledge we have described are closely linked in speech production. In order to communicate clearly, speakers must use appropriate vocabulary and grammar, while structuring the information in a way that is easy for the listeners to understand. For example, to describe an accident, a speaker needs to know words for expressing objects, actions, locations, and people. At the same time, the speaker needs to use grammatical resources such as past-tense verb forms consistently when recounting the incident, but then must switch to present-tense verb forms or the use of modal verbs when he or she wants to give an evaluation of the whole incident (e.g., "People should not drive so fast in the city"). Grammar items such as prepositions and prepositional phrases are also needed to convey the dynamic relationships between the various actors in the event ("The pedestrian was just stepping onto the intersection, and the driver was coming from the opposite direction"). In addition, all of this information has to be structured in a logical order using connectors and discourse markers (e.g., *first, then*). More importantly, learners need to be aware of the differences that exist between spoken language and written language.

Linguistic knowledge is clearly an important component of second language speaking competence. Without it, learners will not be able to formulate and articulate the ideas they want to express. This has important implications for the way we conceptualize speaking activities and lessons. Firstly, we should plan speaking activities that make realistic demands on learners in terms of the type of linguistic knowledge they need to produce spoken language. For example, if the objective of an activity is for learners to develop the ability to describe an event, we need to ensure that this objective is not defeated because learners do not have sufficient linguistic resources to practice the skill. Rather, we can provide learners with some linguistic support so that they can practice the skills without having to worry too much about the language. The second pedagogical implication, we suggest, is that it is useful to think of speaking lessons not merely as opportunities for learners to practice speaking, but rather as structured learning experiences where learners can develop relevant linguistic knowledge. Materials should also account for the interactional contexts of language use and emphasize the role of discourse and register (the topic, the speakers, and their relationships and the type of language required) in fulfilling social functions through speech (Halliday 1985). Speaking lessons should, therefore, include tasks where learners pay attention to language features needed for participating in various types of interactions and producing relevant discourse.

Try it

Refer to a language syllabus or a language textbook, and examine the types of linguistic knowledge that are specified as outcomes. Can you find examples of phonological, lexical, grammatical, and discourse knowledge mentioned in this chapter? How is this knowledge applied to the practice of speaking?

Core speaking skills

It is not enough for learners to just know *about* grammar, vocabulary, pronunciation, and discourse. They must also be able to proceduralize their linguistic knowledge through increasing use of this knowledge in various communicative contexts (Johnson 1996). The term "skills" will be used to refer to learners' knowledge about language and communication that is "put into action" when in speech production. There are four broad categories of speaking skills that learners need to develop, and these are referred to here as core speaking skills (see Table 3.1). Within each core skill are more specific skills (sometimes referred to as sub-skills) that are appropriate for a range of speaking and communication needs.

Focusing on the four broad categories of speaking skills can help teachers in two ways when conceptualizing lessons. Firstly, some teachers may use textbooks or refer to language syllabi that include long lists of specific speaking skills. The categories explained below can serve as a frame of reference to help teachers keep in mind the broad aims of speaking development when planning lessons or sequences of activities. Secondly, some teachers may be working in situations where speaking is rarely taught in an explicit manner. The speaking objectives may be vague, such as "Learners will discuss a problem in a group" or "Learners will practice their story-telling skills." The core speaking skills outlined in this chapter can help teachers identify which set of skills should be focused on so that learners are not just left to their own devices. In other words, the skills that learners need to engage in when carrying out the activities should be made explicit.

Table 3.1: *Four categories of core speaking skills*

Core skill	Specific skills*
a. Pronunciation Produce the sounds of the target language at the segmental and suprasegmental levels.	• Articulate the vowels and consonants and blended sounds of English clearly. • Assign word stress in prominent words to indicate meaning. • Use different intonation patterns to communicate new and old information.
b. Speech function Perform a precise communicative function or speech act.	• Request: permission, help, clarification, assistance, etc. • Express: encouragement, agreement, thanks, regret, good wishes, disagreement, disapproval, complaints, tentativeness, etc. • Explain: reasons, purposes, procedures, processes, cause and effect, etc. • Give: instructions, directions, commands, orders, opinions, etc. • Offer: advice, condolences, suggestions, alternatives, etc. • Describe: events, people, objects, settings, moods, etc. • Others.
c. Interaction management** Regulate conversations and discussions during interactions.	• Initiate, maintain, and end conversations. • Offer turns. • Direct conversations. • Clarify meaning. • Change topics. • Recognize and use verbal and non-verbal cues.
d. Discourse organization Create extended discourse in various spoken genres, according to socioculturally appropriate conventions of language.	• Establish coherence and cohesion in extended discourse through lexical and grammatical choices. • Use discourse markers and intonation to signpost changes in the discourse, such as a change of topic. • Use linguistic conventions to structure spoken texts for various communicative purposes, e.g., recounts and narratives.

* These are important speaking skills within each category of core skills. The lists are not exhaustive.
** Some linguists refer to this as "discourse management."

Pronunciation skills

Pronunciation skills are the ability to produce the segmental and suprasegmental features of the target language. These are important enabling skills for speech production because the ability to pronounce words and phrases clearly can directly influence the articulation process of speaking (see Chapter 2). In addition, the ability to adopt appropriate intonation patterns will help learners enhance the clarity of their meaning when speaking. Learners need to articulate the individual sounds or "segments" (vowels and consonants) clearly, but this alone is inadequate for the production of clear speech. It is even more important that they know how to signal to their listeners the way their discourse is organized. This signaling of discourse organization is achieved through appropriate stress of prominent words and various pitch movements. Studies have indicated that prosodic features such as stress and intonation have a greater impact on the intelligibility of learners' speech production than clear articulation of single sounds or phonemes (Derwing, Munro & Wiebe 1998; Hahn 2004). Thus, learners need to develop their ability to use prosodic or suprasegmental features of English, such as the use of intonation, to organize spoken discourse (Brazil 1985 / 1997). (See Chapter 5.)

It has been argued that English language learners do not need to develop the full range of sounds and prosodic features that native speakers have, and that learners should only learn those features which have been shown to affect intelligibility (Jenkins 2000). While this perspective is a time-efficient approach to preparing learners for communication, it may not necessarily align closely with language learners' own personal goals (Timmis 2002). Some EFL learners aim to develop pronunciation features that are similar to, or approximate, the British or American native-speaker models that they have selected (Goh 2009). This is often considered by many learners to be not only desirable but necessary for their personal, academic, and professional development (Kuo 2006). In the case of young learners, it has been shown that some can eventually acquire the speech patterns of native speakers of the target language (Oyama 1976). Nevertheless, in many situations, native-speaker pronunciation is not a realistic goal, and teachers should encourage students to feel comfortable with their own pronunciation and work towards achieving intelligibility.

Speech-function skills

Knowing how to express and interpret speech functions is an important part of learners' pragmatic competence. Some basic functions in interpersonal communication include expressing thanks or disagreement, explaining, declining, complaining, complimenting, encouraging, or praising. An inventory of such functions can be found in many language syllabuses or coursebooks. Lists of formulaic expressions are also commonly included to help learners with expressing these speech functions. For example, when learners wish to disagree, they may use *I see your point, but . . .* or *I'm afraid I only partially agree with you.*

One important factor to consider is the appropriateness of speech functions in different cultural contexts in which English is used. In many Asian societies, for example, it is considered impolite for younger speakers or those in subordinate positions to disagree openly with those in positions of power and seniority. Even when disagreement occurs, the speakers usually have to include a preamble to the voicing of disagreement. This may include acknowledging explicitly the value and experience of the senior participant in the interaction so that he or she can save face. In other words, the normal politeness markers or language for hedging used in some Western English-speaking societies may be insufficient. While this added attention to seniority may appear to be unnecessary, or even bewildering, to speakers outside of the cultures concerned, it is, nevertheless, an essential aspect of appropriate and successful communication. Thus, in this regard, language learners should develop speech-function skills that are not only appropriate for communicating with native-speakers of English, but also other speakers of English from cultures they are likely to encounter.

Interaction-management skills

As communication is a two-way process, it is not enough for learners merely to know how to express their basic wants and intentions. They also need to develop speech skills that enable them to manage interactions and, in the process, learn to influence the direction these interactions take. For example, when learners are no longer interested in continuing with a particular topic during a conversation, do they know what they can do to steer the conversation away from this topic? In some sense, the skills listed under Interaction management in Table 3.1 can be considered speech-function skills, but they have been categorized separately because they have a specific regulatory purpose. To use interaction-management skills effectively, learners will also need to recognize what the speaker is trying to achieve through his or her words, as well as understand non-verbal cues such as body language. Learners also need to recognize signs that they do not understand each other and that some negotiation of meaning is in order. Bygate (1987) noted that learners need skills to help them initiate and sustain face-to-face interactions and negotiate control of a conversation, and these skills include agenda or topic management and turn-taking skills. Such skills enable language learners to choose topics that they are familiar with, which, in turn, maximizes opportunities for using the target language, as

well as enabling them to handle turn-taking (both theirs and other speakers')
effectively and in culturally appropriate ways.

Discourse-organization skills

Effective speaking is also dependent on the ability of speakers to organize
extended discourse in accordance with accepted linguistic and sociocultural conventions. Learners, therefore, must develop skills for structuring
talk and for responding appropriately as listeners. This requires knowledge of discourse routines, i.e., how a specific speech genre is structured
(Bygate 1998), as well as lexico-grammatical knowledge for establishing
coherence and cohesion (Burns et al. 1996). Linguists use the term "coherence" to refer to a quality in spoken texts that enables listeners to follow the
thread of the message easily. Learners can learn to establish coherence by
using devices such as pronouns for referencing and words for reiterations.
Cohesion in a spoken text means that various parts "hang together" clearly,
giving listeners a sense of its overall structure. This can be achieved by
using words or phrases to highlight different parts in the text. Speakers
can also use expressions to signpost additions or changes as the message
unfolds. Some common discourse markers are *on top of that, on the other
hand, to summarize*, and *to conclude*. To apply discourse-organizing skills,
learners need to draw on their linguistic knowledge about the structure of
spoken discourse.

When planning speaking activities or lessons, teachers need to ask themselves, "What *exactly* are the skills that I want my learners to learn from
participating in this activity?" Let's take the objective, "Learners will practice their story-telling skills" as an example. If our overall aim is to improve
our students' narrative abilities, we should consider which narrative skills
the activities are aiming to develop: a) Do we want the students to learn
to structure a story appropriately? b) Do we want them to develop skill in
describing events and people? c) Do we want them to tell the story using
appropriate stress, rhythm, and intonation so that the meaning is conveyed
appropriately and in an interesting manner? Trying to do all three simultaneously would be unrealistic. Teachers should identify one category of
core-speaking skills, such as pronunciation or interaction management, and
spell out the relevant objectives. So if our aim is a), rather than just asking
learners to work in pairs and practice telling or retelling stories to each
other, we can make sure that our lesson includes activities that will teach
learners how to structure a narrative. We could also include activities that
help learners focus on the language that is needed to signpost transitions
in the narrative. In other words, when we spell out specific speaking skills

as clear learning objectives, we will plan lessons that really *teach* speaking and not just *do* speaking.

Discuss it

Refer to a language syllabus or a language textbook. Which of the four categories of core speaking skills have been identified for teaching and learning? Is there a balanced coverage of all skills? Do some skills appear to be more important than others in the language program? What implications might this have for the students' speaking development?

Communication strategies

Clearly, speaking in a second language is a demanding process for language learners. Learners in face-to-face interactions do not have the benefit of preparing everything they want to say in advance. How do they cope with the cognitive constraints in speech processing and attend to meaning and language form at the same time? How do they respond quickly to prevent the conversation from flagging? What happens when language learners have trouble expressing themselves? Learners who are easily embarrassed and risk-averse might immediately stop communicating, withdraw, or give up. So, for example, in a hypothetical language class, we may have Student A who suffers from language anxiety and avoids participation. In contrast, we may also have Student B who, in spite of limited linguistic abilities, tries to cope with the problem and hold on to his or her turn to speak. We can say that both A and B are using communication strategies to manage their oral interaction with others, but clearly the strategy that B uses is more beneficial to his or her language development. The ability to use strategies appropriately to keep an interaction going is a reflection of language learners' strategic competence.

Broadly speaking, communication strategies are used for two purposes. Firstly, they are used by learners, such as Student A, to avoid having to speak too much. Strategies used for this purpose are referred to as reduction strategies, partly because the scope of communication is reduced. These strategies may be useful as face-saving devices, but they limit the users' opportunities to speak in the target language. The second purpose for using communication strategies is to enable speakers to convey their messages by using whatever resources they have access to. This is the case for Student B. Such strategies are called achievement strategies. They help learners maximize opportunities for speaking in the target language and to achieve their communication goals. Through the use of various achievement strategies, Student B engages in the process of meaning negotiation and receives feedback to help modify what is said. This, as we know, will help Student B not only to participate more effectively during oral communication, but will develop his or her language further.

Cognitive strategies

During oral communication, it is common for language learners to experience problems finding suitable words for expressing their intended meaning. To compensate for this lexical problem, some learners use various psycholinguistic strategies. For example, instead of the word *chipmunk*, they may use a more common word, *squirrel*. In this case, the learner is trying to communicate the concept of the chipmunk holistically by comparing it to a squirrel, which is quite similar in appearance. Sometimes learners are unable to make a holistic comparison when one is not available. If this happens, learners may decide to list different features of the animal in question in the hope that the listeners would identify the animal or object for themselves. Learners may also coin new words, paraphrase, and use circumlocution, like describing something to get to the meaning, or even use words in their first language. All the strategies mentioned above are *cognitive* in nature; that is to say, they are used to mentally manipulate the information being conveyed. They are also commonly referred to in the research literature as psycholinguistic strategies (Kellerman & Bialystok 1997).

Metacognitive strategies

Some learners use a second type of mental strategy that has a metacognitive function; that is to say, the strategies are used to manage thinking and speech production. Learners may decide to plan what they want to say beforehand so that, when they are actually speaking or participating in an interaction, they will not be totally unprepared. For example, before making a telephone conversation, a learner may write down some words or expressions that are needed for the conversation. While speaking on the phone, he or she may notice that some words have not been articulated clearly, and the listener is having problems comprehending what is said. After the telephone conversation, the learner may evaluate his or her own speaking performance during the telephone conversation. Metacognitive strategies are very important for language learning and communication, but learners tend to use them infrequently especially in oral communication (Cohen 1998).

Interaction strategies

Interaction strategies are used by learners to address pragmatic aspects of communication, particularly with regard to negotiating meaning between various participants. Also referred to as "oral communication strategies," these are "strategic behaviors that learners use when facing communication problems during interactional tasks" (Nakatani 2006). For our discussion here, we will focus on strategies by which learners engage the people they are speaking with to help them with expressing and comprehending meaning. These strategies include making comprehension checks, repeating an utterance, giving examples, and using gestures and facial expressions. It is important to note that, in the context of oral interaction, listening is as important as speaking, and problems can arise in either of these processes. When language learners do not understand what is said, they can try to use interactional communication strategies, such as checking comprehension, confirming what is understood, and requesting clarification.

Table 3.2 lists some useful communication strategies that competent language learners use in order to find alternative ways of expressing their meaning, correct their mistakes, buy processing time, elicit help from expert speakers, and keep their turn in an interaction. The use of these strategies, however, may not come naturally to all learners, and such strategies are clearly something that many will need to develop. By learning to use these strategies, learners will get more opportunities to produce modified output, which will in turn facilitate their overall language development. It is important, therefore, that speaking curricula and lessons include activities for strategy training. These activities should raise learners' awareness about communication strategies, as well as provide opportunities for practice in using the strategies. When teaching learners about communication strategies, we should also introduce the language that is needed for using these strategies. For example, learners would do well to learn what to say when they need their interlocutors to clarify or repeat what has been said. (For a review of communication strategies and their effects on speaking performance, see Dörnyei & Scott 1997; Nakatani & Goh 2007). Interactional strategies are similar to what is often referred to as "discourse strategies" for managing spoken discourse. For a detailed discussion of discourse strategies, see Chapter 5, where we illustrate some key strategies for openings and closings, and feedback or backchaneling.

Table 3.2: *Communication strategies for second language speaking*

Communication strategies	Specific strategies
a. Cognitive strategies Techniques to compensate for gaps in lexical knowledge and related linguistic problems.	• Paraphrase: Circumlocuting or describing an object, person, or event to get the meaning of a specific word across. • Approximation: Using an alternative term, e.g., *squirrel* for *chipmunk* • Formulaic expressions: Using language chunks, e.g., *What I'm trying to say is . . .* to buy processing time. • Message frames: Setting the global context for what is being described before attempting to describe it.
b. Metacognitive strategies Mental operations to regulate thinking and language during speaking.	• Planning: Preparing the contents and the form of the message. • Self-monitoring: Noticing one's language and message during message production. • Self-evaluation: Noticing one's language and message after message production.
c. Interactional strategies Social behaviors for negotiating meaning during interaction.	• Exemplification: Offering an example to make one's point clear. • Confirmation checks: Asking listeners whether they have understood the message. • Comprehension checks: Paraphrasing what is heard to confirm one's understanding. • Repetition: Repeating all or part of what is said to check one's own understanding. • Clarification requests: Asking the speaker to explain a point further. • Repetition requests: Asking the speaker to say something again. • Exemplification requests: Asking the speaker to give an example. • Assistance appeal: Asking the listener for help with difficult words.

Discuss it

Think of a group of students whom you teach or will teach in the future. Choose three communication strategies that may help your students in their oral interaction. Explain why these are relevant and important for this group of students.

Summary

This chapter examined second language speaking competence and the implications our understanding of this competence has for teaching speaking. Briefly, here are the answers to the questions posed at the beginning of the chapter:

1. Speaking is a combinatorial language skill. It requires the ability to fulfill various communicative demands through efficient use of the spoken language. When problems occur, speakers should have ways of coping with them. Second language speaking competence, therefore, requires knowledge of the target language as a system for making meaning and an awareness of the contextual demands of speaking. It also calls for the use of various skills for using speech effectively and appropriately, according to different communicative purposes. Last, but not least, speaking competence includes the ability to use a range of strategies to compensate for gaps in knowledge and ineffective speaking skills.

2. The linguistic knowledge needed for second language speaking development includes knowledge about grammar, pronunciation, words and their meanings, and discourse. Language learners' wider linguistic knowledge should also include pragmatic knowledge about speech acts and sociolinguistic knowledge about sociocultural practices of speakers of English. Core speaking skills are skills for pronunciation, expressing speech functions, managing interaction, and organizing discourse. Communication strategies are also crucial, and these include cognitive or psycholinguistic strategies, metacognitive strategies, and interactional strategies. They enable learners to overcome lexical gaps, negotiate meaning, repair communication breakdowns, and enhance the discourse that they and their interlocutors are jointly producing.

In answering the questions presented at the beginning of the chapter, a number of concepts and theoretical perspectives on language learners' speaking competence were explored. Based on the discussion, the following principles for planning speaking activities and lessons have been suggested:

1. Speaking activities should make realistic demands on learners in terms of the type of linguistic knowledge they need for producing spoken

language. Activities that aim to help learners practice using specific speaking skills should not tax learners' linguistic processing at the same time. Teachers should consider different ways of providing the language that learners need.

2. Speaking lessons are not just opportunities for practicing speaking. You should conceptualize them as structured learning experiences for developing relevant linguistic knowledge. It is important that learners be guided to notice features of language needed for various types of interactions and discourse.

3. When planning a speaking lesson, you should identify one category of core speaking skills that learners will focus on through the activities. Specific skills should be clearly identified as lesson objectives. Based on these objectives, you can plan procedures for carrying out the activities that can help learners to develop the skills. You may also need to help learners focus on the language that is needed for using the skills.

4. The speaking curriculum and the lessons developed need to include strategy training. The training should involve activities that raise learners' awareness about important communication strategies, provide practice in using the strategies, and teach relevant phrases and expressions for using some of these interactional strategies.

Group-learning tasks

1. Second language speaking competence is articulated differently in different language syllabi and language teaching frameworks. For example, the Common European Framework (2001: 251) focuses on what learners are able to do with speech at the end of different levels of proficiency and stages of learning:

   Lowest level: Learners are able to participate in simple factual conversations on a predictable topic.
   Highest level: Learners can advise on or talk about complex sensitive issues.

   a. Discuss the benefits of articulating speaking competence in terms of broad communication objectives like those in the Common European Framework. What limitations are there?

b. Identify the types of linguistic knowledge and core speaking skills that are necessary for attaining the competence at the lowest and highest levels mentioned above.

c. Imagine you have to teach a low-proficiency class on how to engage in factual conversations on a predictable topic. How would you translate this broad objective into specific instructional objectives for your speaking lessons?

2. Consider the following learning objectives for spoken English taken from a syllabus for a four-year language program in high schools. What feature of speaking competence does each objective relate to: knowledge of language and discourse, core speaking skills, or communication strategies? Do you think the syllabus has provided a balanced coverage of all important components of speaking competence?

Learning objectives	Speaking competence
By the end of the program, learners will:	
• Use the stress patterns and rhythm of English appropriately.	
• Use an appropriate register.	
• Vary pitch, tone, pace, and volume to suit purpose.	
• Use grammar appropriate to speech, and vocabulary appropriate to the topic and context.	
• Understand and use verbal and non-verbal cues appropriately.	
• Plan and organize a talk with purpose, audience, setting, and media in mind.	
• Select an appropriate focus and format, and develop main ideas.	
• Support ideas with audio / visual and print resources during presentations.	
• Monitor and adjust presentation to sustain audience interest.	
• Emphasize salient points in speech.	
• Use cohesive devices to link ideas within a presentation.	
• Respond appropriately to questions raised during a presentation.	

3. Read the excerpts from transcripts below. Describe what the speakers are doing in each case to improve the way they express meaning. You do not need to give a label to the strategy if you are not sure what label (cognitive, metacognitive, or interactional) is appropriate, but you should try to infer from the excerpt what the learner is trying to do. Do you think the strategies these learners have used are useful for language learners?

Communication strategies

---

a. This is what some ESL learners said when describing things in English[1]:
   - "Like chicken, but bigger."
   - "It's used to cut a carpet."
   - "You can see it in the laboratory."
   - "The Samurai used it for fighting."
   - "It's made of plastic."
   - "It has three lines on it."

---

b. Some EFL learners took the part of the customer at a travel agent in a role play[2]. The following are some of their responses.
   - "My reservation, no? No bargain?"
   - "I have a little money, so change to double room. Do you see?"
   - "Do you available traveler's checks?"
   - "The place for ships . . . like bay."
   - "How can I go . . . (pause) *minato* (harbor) . . . *yotto* (yatch)?"

---

[1] The data are cited from Rossiter (2003).
[2] The data are cited from Nakatani (2004).

4. In this chapter, we considered the importance of different types of linguistic knowledge and skills and how they contribute to learners' development of speaking competence. Many learners are also aware of their importance. Here are some excerpts from journals kept by a group of graduate students who were ESL learners in a university in Singapore[3]. If you were their language teacher, what feedback would you offer to each of the learners? Share your thoughts with your classmates or other teachers you work with.

[3] The data are cited from Lun (2001).

Learner A

"The rhythm and accent in English sentences are very interesting. It can also help us to speak English words clearly. Sometimes I don't know when we speak English which word should be stressed, which word shouldn't. I think I'll practice more often outside the English lessons."

Learner B

"On the oral presentation, I feel a little nervous. . . . It reminds me that a good speaker includes so many meanings, such as proper tone, compatible body gestures, and so on. Many Asian people aren't accustomed to use body language when they speak, maybe the Asian traditional conservative character. I think I'll pay more attention to my gestures when I speak. Proper body language is so important for speaking."

Learner C

"When I talked to my classmates in English, maybe I made wrong pronunciation of several words, but they didn't correct me because they know what I meant – the result is that I am so used to several wrong pronunciation and is not good to improve speaking English level. Today I pronounced 'apes' wrongly. I didn't know when I was speaking – thanks my teacher for correcting it."

Learner D

"Today's English class begins with the discussion about customs of addressing people. The norms are very difficult from one country to the other. In Chinese, people seldom call each other with first names, but it's just contrary here. However, I think we will soon get into the habit of it. Teacher J call me "Xinbo," a name only called by my parents before I came here, and that let me feel we are already friends."

Further reading

Bygate, M. (2005) Oral Second language abilities as expertise, In K. Johnson (ed.) *Expertise in Second Language Learning and Teaching*, Baisingstoke: Palgrave Macmillan.

Canale, M. (1983) On some dimensions of language proficiency, In J. W. Oller Jr. (ed.) *Issues in Language Testing Research*, Rowley, MA: Newbury House, 333–342.

Canale, M. and Swain, M. (1980) Theoretical bases of communicative approaches to second language teaching and testing, *Applied Linguistics*, 1, 1–47.

Nakatani, Y. and Goh, C. (2007) A review of oral communication strategies: focus on interactionist and psycholinguistic perspectives, In E. Macaro and A. Cohen (eds.) *Language Learner Strategies: 30 years of Research and Practice*, Oxford: Oxford University Press, 207–228.

PART II
SPOKEN DISCOURSE

4 Speech: features, grammar, and pronunciation

We have already suggested that it is important that second language teachers and their learners develop knowledge of the nature of spoken language. In order to appreciate distinctive features of spoken language, it is useful to contrast speech and writing. Although spoken and written language are clearly related, they are typically characterized by different kinds of linguistic patterns. Understanding something about the typical patterns of each is very useful knowledge for second language teachers who must help learners improve their speaking skills. This chapter focuses on the relationships between spoken and written language, and some of the typical grammatical features of spoken discourse. This chapter will address two questions:

1. What are the relationships, similarities, and differences between spoken and written language?
2. What grammatical and pronunciation features are common in spoken language?

To answer the questions, we will discuss the following topics:

* Relationships between spoken and written language.
* Grammatical features of spoken language.
* The characteristics and discourse functions of pronunciation.

Introduction

Despite the fact that communicative language teaching has encouraged teachers to prepare learners for realistic and authentic communicative situations, it is ironic that materials and tasks for teaching speaking have traditionally relied largely on grammars of written language (and often still do). Thornbury and Slade (2006: 2) comment that, "For a long time spoken language was taught as if it were simply a less formal version of written language," and there are still vestiges of this way of thinking when it comes to teaching speaking. It is quite typical in many coursebooks to find "scripted" dialogues that rely on the material writers' intuitions, or introspections, about what kinds of spoken exchanges happen in particular contexts. Unfortunately, however, these texts do not usually reflect the kind of language people might actually use in natural situations outside the classroom. Materials may even limit learners' opportunities to extend their repertoires of speaking because they focus on mastering particular language forms (such as using the present perfect) or functions (such as apologizing), rather than on meaningful communication.

There are various problems related to scripted or introspected texts. Generally, they are based on traditional grammars derived from written language. They often represent spoken exchanges as neat, fluid, predictable, and unproblematic for the speakers. Burns, Joyce, and Gollin (1996, drawing on Porter and Roberts 1981) refer to the following characteristics as typical limitations of scripted dialogues:

- Utterances often occur as fully formed and complete sentences.
- Certain structures are repeated rather unnaturally.
- Each speaker takes distinct turns with no overlapping of talk, hesitations, or listener feedback.
- Each speaker says about the same amount.
- The speakers use formal and standardized language forms.
- Vocabulary is usually restricted to one topic or field of discourse.
- Speakers tend to make overly explicit references to people, objects, or experiences.
- Contextual knowledge is very explicitly provided throughout the text, and there is often no reference to shared knowledge.

If the materials are accompanied by recordings, the speakers' pronunciation is usually standard, and utterances are made with greater than usual precision. The pace of speaking may also be slower than what is found in normal speech.

Think about it

Examine a language textbook you are familiar with, or that you use regularly. To what extent does the material presented for speaking practice reflect these characteristics of scripted dialogue? Are there any features included that you would consider to be representative of natural speech?

There may be some good reasons why materials for language learning commonly portray the characteristics of scripted dialogues mentioned above, and why teachers may need to make use of them. At various points, new structures will need to be introduced by the teacher, and opportunities for using them as "pushed output" (see Chapter 3) through controlled practice will be important. By restricting vocabulary, learners' comprehension and use of the language they are required to produce will also be facilitated. Rather than having to deal with the overlaps, hesitations, and competition for turns in natural speech, it is easier for learners to manage quite defined exchanges of information. Beginning learners in particular are unfamiliar with the sounds and pronunciation of the language and may, therefore, benefit from hearing speech at a slower than normal pace. Problems arise, however, if language learners continue to be presented only with a diet of scripted speech as learning progresses (Carter 1997; Gilmore 2004). Since learners need to use the language for more complex exchanges outside the classroom, it is important for teachers to be able to draw their learners' attention to features of natural speech and give them opportunities to practice understanding and using these features in different contexts. As McCarthy and Carter (1997: 338) put it:

> Whatever else may be the result of imaginative methodologies for eliciting spoken language in the L2 classroom, there can be little hope for natural spoken output on the part of language learners if the input is stubbornly rooted in models that owe their origin and shape to the written language.

In this chapter, we explore what kind of knowledge about spoken language is useful for teaching and how it might be applied in the classroom.

Relationships between speaking and writing

In order to follow from the comments made above about typical models for teaching speaking, in this section, we look at the similarities and differences between spoken and written language. We consider the social purposes and broad features of each and suggest that different forms of speaking and writing occur across a continuum, depending on the level of formality and distance in time and location from the concepts discussed.

Social purposes of spoken and written language

Clearly, spoken and written language are related to each other and overlap in various ways as they have obvious similarities of lexis (or vocabulary) grammar, and structure. Even though some kinds of spoken discourse may deal with the same or similar topics to written discourse, they may also serve different social purposes and have different audiences. So, although the spoken and written language draw on the same linguistic resources, they utilize them in different ways. As Halliday (1985: 45) notes, "The kinds of meanings that are transmitted in writing tend to be somewhat different from the kinds of meanings transmitted through speech."

In acquiring the ability to convey meaning, humans develop spoken language before learning to communicate through writing, and speech dominates in daily social interactions. As their language develops, young children learn through spoken communication how language operates to fulfill a wide range of social and personal needs and functions, and their understanding of how these functions are expressed continues to evolve into adulthood:

* Asking for things they want and need.
* Getting other people to respond to requests.
* Expressing who they are as individuals.
* Socializing with those around them.
* Exploring their world and finding out how things work.
* Verbalizing things that go on in their thoughts and imagination.
* Exchanging information with other people.

(Based on Halliday 1975.)

Even though there are still traditional societies that rely more heavily on oral communication, written language plays a crucial role in modern communities and, indeed, written texts are often more highly valued by society. Over time, written language and spoken language have evolved to achieve different communicative functions, and it is valuable for language teachers to have a sense of how the nature and purpose of speech and writing may differ.

Think about it

Consider the disadvantages of being unable to utilize written texts in contemporary daily life. Think about the use of technology, as well as traditional print forms.

The nature of speech and writing

As already noted, spoken interaction involves fulfilling various functions in recognizable cultural ways. In that sense, we can say speech is always socioculturally purposeful. One obvious difference between speech and writing is that speech is produced "online" as a person speaks, and, the ability to now record speech notwithstanding, it is essentially impermanent. We can say that speech is situated in "real time." Because of its fleeting

Table 4.1: *Typical features of spoken and written text production*

Spoken language	Written language
Dialogic / interactional.	Monologic / non-interactional.
Co-constructed spontaneously by more than one speaker.	Constructed over time by individual writers / readers.
Shared knowledge of context.	Assumed knowledge of context.
Unplanned and negotiated.	Planned and redrafted.
Impermanent (produced for "real time").	Permanent (produced for the "long-term").
Close to action in time and space (context-embedded).	Distant from action in time and space (context-removed).
Uses more informal language.	Uses more formal language.

(Based on Eggins 1994: 55.)

nature, typically speakers do not plan what they will say in advance, but (co-)construct their interactions with others, as the talk unfolds. To do this, they must not only give themselves time to think by using various linguistic strategies (hesitations, pause fillers, and so on), but they must also take feedback from their interlocutors (or speaking partners) into account. Spoken interaction is face-to-face (or at least voice-to-voice), and so getting listener feedback is an important part of making sure no misunderstandings are occurring. Table 4.1 summarizes the features involved in producing spoken and written language.

It must be stressed that these features *typify* the production of spoken and written language; there will be great variation in the actual contexts and conditions under which language is produced. For example, it is, of course, possible to produce speech that is planned or rehearsed, as in news broadcasts or political speeches, although in such cases, speakers are usually working from written texts. Similarly, writers may work collaboratively to negotiate pieces of writing, which will, nevertheless, exhibit features of written text when completed. Written texts can be "speech-like" as, for example, in notes left for a family member (e.g., "Gone to movies, back at 6:00"). Therefore, language production can be thought of as a kind of continuum, with "most spoken" texts that relate to immediate action at one end and "most written" texts that are abstract and reflective at the other. Somewhere around the middle of the continuum lie texts that have characteristics of both modes, so they blur the typical distinctions outlined above.

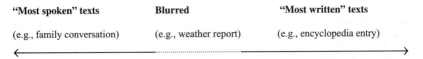

Figure 4.1: Continuum of spoken and written language.

When developing spoken activities with learners, teachers can consider where on the continuum the activities may lie. For example, for learners in "conversation classes," teachers may need to think about the appropriate register, including what level of formality is needed for the kinds of conversations being targeted. Are learners practicing in order to have conversations with host family members, classmates, workmates, regular acquaintances, strangers, and so on? Are they speaking about activities as they are being performed, or retelling previous events? Do they need to use specialized vocabulary or informal vocabulary? As discussed in the next section, the lexical and grammatical features of the language used are affected by who the speakers are, their relationships with each other, the topics being discussed, and the context of language use.

Try it

Listen to a discussion (e.g., on the TV, radio, or online) on a current topic of interest to you. If possible, record a segment of the discussion. Then find a written account on the same topic (e.g., in a newspaper, magazine, or reference book). How does the spoken and written language differ? How does the relationship between the speakers affect what they say? How does the writer seem to position him- or herself in relation to the readers (as an equal, an expert, or an informant)?

Spoken and written language

In the discussion above, we looked at the concept of a spoken-written continuum. In this section, we explore this concept further by examining related examples of spoken and written discourse. We also look at the concepts of lexical density and grammatical intricacy.

Comparing linguistic features of spoken and written language

In order to illustrate further how written and spoken language differ in terms of the patterns of language they draw on and the way they are affected by context, time, space, and speaker relationships, let's consider the following series of texts. They are all concerned with the sport of basketball (adapted from Burns, Joyce & Gollin 1996: 50–51). In the first text, two fans are discussing the game as they actually watch it:

Text 1

A: Oh, man, what a play!
B: He can really get it on from downtown –
A: Go, go, go!

In this text, the speakers express their evaluations of the game and the players. They have no need to make direct reference to the context, as their utterances are produced in relation to the immediate action of the game. Therefore, only a few of the lexical items used (i.e., nouns, verbs, adjectives, adverbs) have to do with expressing content (e.g., *man, downtown*). This is because the speakers can assume understanding from their references outwards (anaphoric reference) into the context of the action *(What a play! he, get it on from downtown, go)*. Their language is interpersonally tuned to their relationships with each other. They use colloquial, informal language appropriate to, and understood by, the group they identify with; that is, basketball fans *(get it on from downtown)*, but which is unlikely to be understood by people not familiar with the game. Just overhearing these speakers would not necessarily lead to comprehensibility, as the language is vague and highly embedded in the actual happenings. Also, there are no specific references to what kind of activity is really taking place. In the second text, the game is being reported on the TV news. The broadcaster is commenting on the footage:

Text 2

And we pick up the game in the third quarter . . . so, score is 13–10, the Jets . . . and Ellis is being guarded by Davis . . . and Johns is trying to get a piece of it . . . but so far we haven't seen any pressure by the Bombers . . . and there we go pass from Johns to Ellis . . . oh, and he nails the three!

In this text, the speaker constructs speech directed at an inclusive and generalized audience of basketball fans. He expresses solidarity with his audience by using the inclusive pronoun form *we*. He does not have to rely on feedback or reactions from another speaker, but in selecting language for the commentary, he uses his knowledge about how his listeners are likely to be engaged by what he says. Even though this is a recording, he selects language that describes the game as if it were actually happening in real time, and, as a result, draws on the present tense to describe the action. He uses more content words than in the first text (e.g., *game, quarter, guarded, pressure*), and specific actors are named *(Jets, Ellis, Davis, Bombers, Johns)*, but the language is still relatively informal. Even thought the audience can see the context of the match, he explains aspects of the physical context, highlights the action of specific players (e.g., *We pick up the game in the third quarter, Ellis is being guarded by Davis)*, and names events as they happen for the audience *(There we go pass from Johns to Ellis)*. The commentator's focus is on describing, commenting on, and evaluating the action *(So far we haven't seen any pressure by the Bombers)*.

For the third example, we turn to an example that sits in the "blurred" area of the continuum in Figure 4.1. Here is a series of texts sent by one of the fans from the first text as SMS messages to a friend unable to attend the match:

Text 3
Smithy did this mad slam dunk.
Just left the ground man, like he was flying.
Ellis did this three-pointer from half way.

Here the language focuses on specific aspects of the action selected by the message sender. The writer uses past tense as he recounts action that has just happened. He selects content words *(ground, flying, half way)* and names the actors *(Johns, Ellis)*, as he needs to recreate the context for his absent reader. Although the text is written, it could equally be spoken. It is colloquial and informal, as appropriate to the relationship with the reader. Because of their group membership and solidarity as baseball fans, the writer can use technical terms related to the game *(slam dunk, three-pointer)*, knowing the reader shares his knowledge. In text four, below, part of a magazine article about basketball, the writer is again recreating the action for his reader, but here the language differs again:

Text 4
When you look into the eyes of guard Bill Elliott, you see a lot of things. Fear, however, isn't one of them. Ellis's no-fear style came of age in Game 3 of the finals. With 12 seconds left, Ellis calmly accepted a pass from Johns and casually sank a three-pointer to put the team ahead 89–88.

Here, the writer reconstructs the action distant in time and space from its immediate context. The writer must attract the reader's attention away from competing articles in the magazine; he does this first by "personalizing" a possible reader relationship with the player *(When **you** look into the eyes . . .)* and presenting the key player as a "basketball hero" who is worth reading about *(Fear isn't one of them; Ellis's no-fear style)*. Because the language selected has to do the work of reconstructing the action for readers who may not have been present at the match or seen the TV footage, the author must increase the number of content words so that context *(Game 3 of the finals, 12 seconds left)* and action *(calmly accepted* a *pass, casually sank* a *three-pointer)* can be spelled out explicitly. The writer makes the assumption that these technical terms, used to describe the goal scoring, will be understood by his "in-the-know" audience of fans. The language used falls into the written, and not spoken, mode. Even if this text were used in a news broadcast, it would clearly have been pre-scripted.

The final text comes from an official guide published by the National Basketball Association (Vancil 1994).

Text 5

The record books are full of names and numbers; superstars and stats. Individuals win scoring titles and block all shots. They pass out assists and lead the league in steals. But all of them operate within the context of a team. The greatest of these teams manage to combine diverse individual talents into a singular battle plan. We can see this in the work of Ellis, Smithy, and Johns, who work together, combining their individual skills to lead their team to victory.

In this text, even though specific players are named, they are referred to in order to generalize about, and exemplify features of, the game of basketball. The text is at a much greater level of abstraction and distance from the context of a specific match than the previous ones; this effect is created by a much higher level of content words *(record books, names, numbers, superstars, stats* − in just the first sentence). The references are to generalized aspects of basketball, with technical terms about the game *(scoring titles, block, assists, steals)* permeating the text, since it is written for a specialist and authoritative volume. Thus, "prestige," formal lexis *(operate, manage, combine, individual talents, victory)* is used in preference to the informal language of the spoken texts.

We can see from these brief descriptions how language is shifted by users along the "abstraction continuum," as it moves in distance (i.e., time and space) away from "happenings" in the world. Language teachers may come across learners who have not grasped the implications of these differences. Their spoken language comes across as too formal; they "speak like a book." Similarly, learner writing for academic purposes may be lacking in depth and sophistication because the learners "write as they speak." They may have been advised to write down what they would say. To help these learners, it is valuable for teachers to be able to explain that "[w]riting and speaking are not just alternative ways of doing the same things: rather, they are ways of doing different things" (Halliday 1989: vii).

Lexical density and grammatical intricacy

A common assumption about speech is that it is less organized, systematic, or structured than writing. Because of its apparent "formlessness," it has tended to be seen as less open to description than written language. This is why, as the McCarthy and Carter quote suggested earlier, grammars of written language have usually taken precedence as the basis for language teaching, even where spoken language teaching is concerned. Halliday argues that both modes of communication are structured and organized, but in different ways. Speech is not formless, but, by its very nature, is "low in content" (1985: 77). In the five text descriptions above, we noted how content words increased as the language becomes more abstract. Written language is high in lexical density; that is, the number of content words compared with function words in a clause, which is the basic grammatical unit of meaning:

> Content words are words that carry a high information load, such as nouns, adjectives, and lexical verbs. Function words are those that serve mainly a grammatical purpose, such as articles, auxiliary verbs . . . of all registers, both spoken and written, conversation has, by far, the lowest lexical density. (Thornbury & Slade 2006: 44.)

We can see these differences more clearly if we compare the content words in two single clauses from the first and last texts above.

He can <u>really get</u> it on from <u>downtown</u> . . . (lexical density 3).

The <u>greatest</u> of these <u>teams manage</u> to <u>combine diverse individual talents</u> into a <u>singular battle plan</u> (lexical density 10).

In the second clause, the lexical density is much higher, reflecting the close "packaging" of information to carry the relevant content.

Try it

Go back to the two texts you collected for the previous task. How do they compare in the way they shift across the spoken to written continuum? Underline the content words in some of the clauses from each text, and compare the lexical density.

Compared with writing, speech also displays less lexical variety, or fewer different words in a text (Ure 1971). Same-word repetition is common in spoken language giving a low type–token ratio (or low number of different words compared with "repeated words").

While written language is complex in terms of lexical density, spoken language displays a different kind of complexity – grammatical intricacy. Speech is intricate in the sense that clauses are generally woven together, often by conjunctions that link one clause to another. The second text of the five above shows how the seven clauses spoken by the commentator are all linked, or conjoined, by common conjunctions *(and, so, but)* that are used to create the grammatical intricacy of the talk:

> <u>And</u> we pick up the game in the third quarter . . . <u>so</u>, score is 13–10, the Jets . . . <u>and</u> Ellis is being guarded by Davis . . . <u>and</u> Johns is trying to get a piece of it . . . <u>but</u> so far we haven't seen any pressure by the Bombers . . . <u>and</u> there we go pass from Johns to Ellis . . . oh, <u>and</u> he nails the three!

In contrast, the written text in the fourth example uses sentences and punctuation to separate clauses. Rather than being conjoined, clauses tend to be embedded, or subordinated, as in:

> When you look into the eyes of guard Bill Elliott *(subordinate clause of time)*, you see a lot of things *(main clause)*.

Halliday (1989: 91) explains that apart from lexical density and variety, grammatical metaphor is also a characteristic of written language. By grammatical metaphor, he means that in the changes of vocabulary and grammar that take place from speech to writing, human experience is represented rather differently. He states that, "The spoken form appears to be nearer the bone" (1989: 94). To be more specific, speech is typically *congruent*; in other words, it draws more on verbs to represent actions (e.g., *complete*), experiences (e.g., *enjoy*) and states of being (e.g., *are*) or mind (e.g, *believe*). In contrast, writing is typically *incongruent*; verbs become transposed into nouns (e.g., *completion. enjoyment, existence, belief*) as writing moves across the continuum towards greater abstraction. Keeping to the baseball theme, we can see how this process works in this example:

Spoken version:
Ellis scored the three-pointer and the fans cheered wildly.

Written version:
Wild cheering followed Ellis's scoring of the three-pointer.

Speech describes things that are going on in the world as they happen *(scored, cheered)* and so relies on words to do with action processes (verbs); writing gives language a "sort of metaphorical quality" (Halliday 1989: 94) by using a process of *nominalization*, or turning verbs into nouns.

These features enable written language, in particular, to be removed from immediate experiences and to report in a more abstract way, from a greater distance in time and place.

Having looked more closely at the linguistic features of speech and writing, it is now possible to summarize some noticeable differences that *typify* each mode of communication.

Spoken language	Written language
Lower number of content words / higher number of function words.	Higher number of content words / lower number of function words.
Clauses linked by conjunctions *(and, but, so,* etc.).	Clauses linked by subordination *(who, which, when,* etc.).
High use of personal pronouns *(I, you, we,* etc.).	Low use of personal pronouns.
Inexplicit references to the surrounding context *(over there, it,* etc.).	Explicit references within the context *(in the corner, the desk,* etc.).
Relationship aspects emphasized (interpersonal foregrounded).	Content aspects emphasized (information foregrounded).
Relies more on verbs to carry meaning.	Relies more on nouns to carry meaning.

So far, we have looked at broader "macro" features and characteristics of spoken and written language. In the next section, we look at some of the "micro" features of grammar that occur in natural speech.

Grammatical features of spoken language

Over the last two decades, considerable advances have been made in indentifying various distinctive grammatical features of spoken language (see for examples, Biber et al.1997; Carter & McCarthy 2006). Here we look at several of these features.

As already mentioned, speakers must produce their utterances under pressure of real time and cognitive processing demands. Speech production can, therefore, be described as dynamic and spontaneous. Biber et al. (1996: 1067) refer to three vital construction principles of "online" speech production that influence spoken grammar:

- "Keep talking" (speakers must avoid communication breakdown). This principle leads to speakers producing hesitations, backtracks, or having to give up a turn.

- "Limited planning time ahead" (speakers have limited working memory). This principle means that speakers must be as concise as possible and avoid over-elaborating the structure of their utterances, especially at the beginning and middle points.
- "Qualification of what has been said" (speakers may need to add or "tag on" to previous utterances). This principle is a consequence of the first two and enables messages to be elaborated or modified.

These fundamental principles of speech production have an impact on how spoken language is realized as continuing discourse. In this section, we look briefly at some of the major effects.

THE "ADD-ON" STRATEGY: GRAMMATICAL COMPLEXITY

"Add-on" is the term used by Biber et al. (1999: 1068) to describe how speakers build up utterances semantically in order to maintain speech fluency. In spontaneous talk, speakers maintain their turns by adding on "clause-like" structures; that is, using coordinating clauses (such as those joined by *and* or *but*) and embedded clauses (such as those beginning with *because*). Clauses are identified as units that can be analyzed as subject + verb, or subject + verb + object. The text below comes from a discussion among colleagues about a book they have all just read. For the sake of simplicity, the structures the speaker uses are shown by dividing them into basic clause-like chunks:

> When I read it for the first time / I found it quite an interesting way of approaching the whole argument / but reading it for the second time / I felt slightly uneasy / because she never really defined the reasons / why the changes were introduced / I mean / she doesn't really go into any depth / and feel that that the idea of a gift is great / and I accept that totally / but it was never used as such previously / because it was kept very much as . . . (interruption by another speaker). (Authors' data.)

This is a relatively long utterance, where clauses follow each other rapidly in sequence. The speaker is able to maintain the turn by adopting the strategy of piling clauses one on top of the other and by using simple conjunctions *(but, and)* and by embedding clauses *(because she never really defined the reasons, why the changes were introduced)*. Compare the way in which the clauses are woven together in the example of talk above and the following written sentence:

> This well-known author adopts, in her usual engaging style, an interesting way of approaching the whole argument through the idea of presenting the concept

of the social and cultural gift, and the application of this concept to a particular societal group.

In contrast to the spoken extract above, there is only one clause in this example and the complexity lies at the level of phrase groups (e.g., *in her usual engaging style*). Biber, et al. point out that not all units in speech contain whole clauses (which are defined as "a structure consisting of an independent clause with any dependent clauses embedded within it" (1999: 1070). Speech is also characterized by segments that are not part of clauses. In the next section, we discuss the idea of clausal and non-clausal units further.

Try it

If possible, make a recording of a discussion on a teaching topic (e.g., your favorite classroom activity) among your colleagues. You should ask their permission first. Then transcribe a short extract where one speaker takes quite a long or sustained turn. Analyze the sample to see how grammatical complexity is built up over several clauses. Mark off the clauses, and look for the conjunctions used to link them.

CLAUSAL AND NON-CLAUSAL UNITS: CLAUSES AND PHRASES

As mentioned, typically speech is interactive, unlike in extended written language where complete clause constructions within sentences can be expected. Speakers, unlike writers, rely instead on complex and fluid grammatical constructions, where clauses are piled on top of each other to keep the speaker's turn going, as we saw in the section above.

It is also difficult to conceive of "sentences" in spoken language, as this way of looking at language reflects the "product-oriented" perspective of written text. Instead, a speaker's "utterance" fits more comfortably as a term to describe the process of unfolding speech. McCarthy (1998:79–80) observes that:

> Anyone who has looked at large amounts of informal spoken data, for example, cannot fail to be struck by the absence of well-formed "sentences" with main and subordinate clauses. Instead, we often find turns that are just phrases, incomplete clauses, clauses that look like subordinate clauses, but which seem not to be attached to any main clause, etc.

In the previous section, we discussed the concept of clause (that is, a unit which consists of subject + verb, or subject + verb + object) and showed how these were built up in speech. In the following short exchange, we can see the use of utterances that are phrases (that is, segments which do not have the full structure of a clause). Pippa (P) and Vic (V) are talking about the Festival of Sydney, which is an annual event in Australia in January.

P: *Well*, I saw in The Herald there . . .
V: *Did you?*
P: *Mm* . . . today's the Festival of Sydney . . . *the big eighty-page cover* . . .
V: *Oh yeah, I didn't* . . . saw something in the Tele I think . . . about the plays that are on . . .
P: *Yes*, worth getting because it covers everything . . . *and a lot is free*.
V: *Oh, yes, OK.*
P: Because I just love Sydney at that time.
V: *You going?*
P: When I get round to booking . . .

(Authors' data.)

The features of speech that McCarthy describes are all illustrated in this interaction. The speakers use some clauses, but there are also segments of speech (in italics) that cannot be categorized as clauses. There are phrases, such as the *big eighty-page cover*, as well as incomplete clauses, like *I saw in the Herald there* and *Oh yeah, I didn't*. Pippa produces *because I just love Sydney at that time*, which seems like a subordinate clause, but does not refer back to any main clause. At one point, Vic uses a series of rather fragmented utterances, including the subordinate clause *the plays that are on*. The speakers are thinking on their feet and building up utterances sequentially, as they process what they want to say interactively.

Biber et al. (1997) note that utterances that are not full clauses are of two types: inserts such as responses *(oh yeah)*, discourse markers *(well)*, and backchannels *(mm)*; and fragments or phrases that are not linked grammatically to other structures *(the big eighty- page cover)*.

Second language learners are often encouraged to "answer in complete sentences" or are corrected when they fail to practice "the full structure" for a new grammatical concept. While teachers often have good reasons for wanting to check that learners have internalized grammatical knowledge, it can also be useful to raise learners awareness that natural speech is characterized by incomplete and fragmented grammatical structures. Otherwise, learners may become inhibited when using English outside the classroom or may run the risk of sounding overly formal and stilted.

ELLIPSIS

The "situated" nature of speech means that speakers employ ellipsis; that is, words, phrases, and even whole clauses that are left out because their meaning is redundant in the immediate linguistic or situational context. Speakers must make judgements about what their interlocutors (speech partners) will be able to retrieve from the context, and what is mutually intelligible because of shared situational knowledge.

If we return to Pippa and Vic's interaction in the last section, we can see several examples of ellipsis. We have inserted the information (in brackets) that the speakers have left out of the conversation, but without affecting the meaning.

P: Well, I saw in The Herald there...

V: Did you [see in The Herald]?

P: Mm... today's the Festival of Sydney... the big eighty page cover...

V: Oh yeah, I didn't [see it in The Herald]... [I] saw something in the Tele [Telegraph] I think... about the plays that are on [in the Sydney Festival]...

P: Yes, [it's] worth getting because it covers everything... and a lot [of it] is free

V: Oh, yes, OK.

P: Because I just love Sydney at that time.

V: [Are] you going?

P: [I'm going to the Sydney Festival] if I get round to booking...

(From the Telegraph, a Sunday newspaper: Authors' data.)

Even though the elements in brackets have been omitted, the speakers negotiate the interaction perfectly well. Items that are left out consist not only of single words (*I*, when it is obvious Vic is referring to himself), phrases (e.g., *in the Sydney Festival*, when it would sound pedantic to mention it again since it is the topic of conversation), but also whole clauses (*I'm going to the Sydney Festival*). Ellipsis has been shown to be common in subjects (*I, they, she*) and in auxiliary verbs (*are, were, did*) (Thornbury & Slade 2006).

It can be very valuable to discuss the concept of ellipsis with language learners and to raise awareness of the kinds of contexts and structures where it occurs. McCarthy (1998) notes that examples of ellipsis barely occur in some popular pedagogical grammars (but see Swan 1995), and that research studies (e.g., Scarcella & Brunak 1981) have shown an absence of these types of ellipsis in non-native speaker interactions.

DEIXIS

Deixis (from the Greek, *finger*) refers to elements that are used to point out outwards into the linguistic and situational context. It is used, particularly, in casual informal conversation where speakers are familiar with each other. In this next extract, two children, Cathy and Doug, are at home doing an activity with their mother. The deictic items are highlighted in italics.

C: Give me *that now* . . . I want *it.*
D: It's my turn . . . *you* get *it* after *me*, Mum said, Mum . . .
M: What's *that* . . . what you using *there*, Cathy?
D: Mum, tell *her* . . . I get *it* first, don't *I?*
C: But want *that* . . .
M: *Here*, Cathy, use *this* instead . . . *you* get a turn *later* . . . *we*'re just getting things ready *now.*

(Authors' data.)

The interaction is full of expressions that respond to the personal, spatial, and temporal "here and now" nature of the talk: personal pronouns (e.g., *I, you, we*), adverbs (e.g., *now, later, there, here*), and demonstratives (e.g., *it, this, that*). It is also noticeable that very little lexis, or content words, are used (e.g., *want, turn, Mum, Cathy*), and several of these are repeated. Ure (1971) described speech such as this as language-in-action. Unless someone was actually present as the action took place, it would be impossible to know that the family's activity involved cooking.

The choice of grammatical elements in the interaction also says something about the relationships between the speakers; the children are siblings between whom there is clearly a feeling of rivalry, reflected in the use of very direct and unsoftened imperative verbs *(give, tell)* and declarative statements *(I want it, I get it)*. There is also an instance of vague language *(things)*, which is a widely used interpersonal feature of speech. Although vague language expressions *(stuff, thingamajig, this and that, whatever)* are sometimes viewed as evidence of woolly thinking, they actually serve to "hedge a speaker's bets" by avoiding his or her commitment to a proposition or making the speaker appear to be too pedantic (Channell 1994; Thornbury & Slade 2006).

HEAD AND TAILS

Heads and tails fall into the third of Biber et al.'s principles: qualification or elaboration of what has been said by tagging on phrases at the beginning or end of utterances. Because spoken language is complex, speakers often adopt the strategy of orienting their listeners to the main part of their message. Both heads and tails perform this function. We will look first at heads.

Heads are nouns or noun phrases that speakers put before the main message, They establish "a shared frame of reference for what is important in a conversational exchange" (Carter & McCarthy 1997: 16), as the following examples illustrate:

And that hotel in Singapore, it was really central . . .
Ugh . . . marking, I really hate it.
Nice day today, was it?
That guy, Ross, he's always messing around with motorbikes.

In the last example we can see that, in spoken language, heads can result in "ungrammatical" structures like clauses with more than one subject *(that guy, Ross, he)*. The kinds of constructions in the examples above would look very odd in written language, but are a common feature of speech.

Tails are expressions that are used to reinforce, extend, elaborate, or clarify the main message. Like heads, they fill a slot, but this time at the end a clause. One type of widely used tail in speech is the "question tag," consisting of auxiliary verbs and pronouns:

You don't like him much, *do you?*
We've just put the kids to bed, *haven't we?*
That shouldn't be any problem, *should it?*

Notice that the tag may reverse either the negative auxiliary verb in the main clause *(don't* becomes *do)* or a positive auxiliary *(have* becomes *haven't)*, or it may reverse the positive auxiliary verb *(do* becomes *don't)* or a negative auxiliary *(haven't* becomes *have)*. However, reversal in the tag does not always take place, especially in British English, as we see here:

He's from the U.K . . . she's from the U.S., *she is.*

Unlike the first type, tags of the type in the last example serve to establish common understanding between speakers; generally no reply is expected (Carter & McCarthy 1997). Apart from question tags, tails may consist of single words or noun phrases that serve different interpersonal or evaluative functions (Thornbury & Slade 2006), as in the following examples:

That's not a good day for me, *Sunday*. (Identification: specific.)
Want a drink, *or something?* (Identification: vague.)
So that was how it ended, *awful*. (Evaluation.)
You're a good customer, *you are*. (Reinforcement.)
Someone's living there already, *yes?* (Question.)
He'll look for another job soon, *I bet*. (Comment.)
How are you, *Christine?* (Vocative.)

Tails play an important role in creating interpersonal relationships between speakers. They are common features of spoken grammar where speakers display their solidarity and express their attitudes and evaluations.

Lexical repetition

Repetition and "relexicalization" of vocabulary (McCarthy 1998) are other distinctive features of speech. To make spoken exchanges hang together, speakers often repeat key content words related to the topic they are talking about. In the following example, Brian (B), Gillian (G), Fiona (F), and Tony (T) are in a regular Monday morning team meeting where they have been discussing what kind of publications they need to advertise the services their organization offers.

G: So, OK, a newsletter's priority and the *glossy* folder—
F: Well, *information* pack . . .
D: Well, some sort of *information*.
F: *Information*, yeah.
D: Getting our *information* . . .
F: *Information*, and the *glossy*, I think that's quite, that's quite adequate.
B: I'd like to get our own . . .
T: A *glossy* would be good for us, too.

(Authors' data.)

The repetition of the two key words, *glossy* and *information*, leave us in no doubt what the topic is about – they capture the essential topic of the conversation. We can also see an example of ellipsis in this text: after the first mentions of glossy folder and information pack, the speakers leave out the words *folder* and *pack* as they can assume their listeners understand. Repetition works also to bind the text together at the discourse level (see Chapter 3). At the same time, it reinforces the interpersonal relationships between the speakers, as repetition of key words suggests solidarity and agreement with each other's ideas.

Similarly, relexicalization has to do with lexical repetition, but, this time, it occurs when a speaker uses a paraphrase or synonym, rather than repeating the same word. In this example, a visitor to Australia, Sarah (S), is talking to her boyfriend's mother (M) about a trip they are planning:

S: Well, actually, I think we'll be going at the end of March.
M: Yes it's *beautiful* then.
S: I heard it's really *spectacular*.

Awareness of lexical repetition, or relexicalization, in spoken text can be very helpful for teachers and learners. Because repetition focuses on key words, teachers can pre-teach important content words from the text that carry meaning related to the main topic. They can also work on vocabulary extension with learners by identifying relexicalized items, getting learners to recognize them or to suggest others that could be used.

Formulaic expressions

Another way speakers facilitate spoken language production is by using formulaic expressions. These are set expressions, idioms, or colloquialisms that are used over and over again in familiar contexts. They are frequently found at the beginnings or endings of interactions, for example:

> Good morning, Dr Wong's surgery. Ros speaking.
> OK, see you soon. Bye.

Formulaic expressions are made up of words that are prefabricated lexical "chunks" (Pawley & Syder 1983) that over time have become widely accepted ways of saying things. Common formulaic expressions are:

> You'll never guess who I just bumped into.
> Don't mention it.
> That's it in a nutshell.
> Hi, how's it going?
> Could I have a word with you?
> Can I help you?
> See you later.

Pauley and Syder note that formulaic expressions are common in speech because they serve to alleviate the pressure to produce oral language in real time. Using these expressions means that speakers can rely on well-worn and fixed utterances to ease the path in routine situations and to smooth social relations.

Try it

Select a social situation you are familiar with (e.g., a school teachers' room). Listen carefully for about five minutes and note down any formulaic expressions you hear. If you are not in an English-speaking environment, notice how formulaic expressions are used in the language spoken.

Speech: Intonation and sound

Pronunciation, the term used to capture the idea of how sounds are used in communication, plays a very important role in getting meaning across.

Pronunciation, however, is not the whole story in spoken interaction, as speaking is a physical act also involving eye movement, facial expressions, and gesture. However, in this section, we focus on the major features of pronunciation that contribute to the message exchange in the context in which the speech is produced.

Certain elements of pronunciation occur at the macro-level and extend over entire spoken interactions. These are referred to as suprasegmental (or prosodic) features (e.g., intonation). Other elements, known as segmental (or phonological) features, occur at the micro-level and involve the production of individual sound segments (e.g., vowel / consonant sounds). Here, we focus mainly on features at the suprasegmental level because recent research (e.g, McCarthy 1998) has revealed how significant intonation, in particular, is in carrying meaning. We follow Brazil's (1997) notion of a discourse approach to intonation, which describes intonation as it is used in continuous interaction:

> Intonation choices carry information about the structure of interaction, the relationship between, and the discourse function of, individual utterances, the interactional "give-ness" and "newness" of information, and the state of convergence and divergence of the participants (Brazil, Coulthard, & Johns 1980: 11).

Central concepts in Brazil's model of intonation are listener-speaker interaction, shared and unshared knowledge, and conversational control (Brazil 1997). A key principle for Brazil is that of "common ground," or "what knowledge speakers [think they] share about the world, [and] about each other's experiences, attitudes, and emotions" (Brazil, Coulthard & Johns 1980: 15). In the sections that follow, we discuss, briefly, four key intonation sub-systems that are central in Brazil's model: tone units, tone, prominence, and key and termination, In order to explain these concepts, we use examples primarily from the text samples in this chapter.

Tone units

Tone units (also known as chunking) refer to blocks or chunks of sound in continuous speech. Speakers use their voices to chunk information into tone or sense groups, which reveal how the message should be "packaged" from the speaker's point of view. These packaged chunks offer listeners important signposts about how they should process what they hear (Burns & Seidlhofer 2010).

Tone units use pitch movements and contain "either one or two syllables that a hearer can recognize as being, in some sense, more emphatic than the others" (Brazil 1997: 7). Pitch movements are where speakers' voices go up and down and may include pauses. More emphatic syllables are known as "prominent" syllables, and we will look at this concept more closely in the next section. In this example, we can see how a long utterance is chunked by the speaker:

> When I read it for the first time // I found it quite an interesting way // of approaching the whole argument // but reading it for the second time // I felt slightly uneasy // because she never really defined // the reasons why the changes were introduced // I mean // she doesn't really go into any depth // and feel that the idea of a gift is great // and I accept that totally // but it was never used as such previously // because it was kept very much as . . . // (interruption by another speaker).

There can be more than one way of chunking utterances in some instances. For example, some speakers might chunk:

> I found it quite an interesting way // of approaching the whole argument

. . . as two tone units. Others might chunk it as three units:

> I found it // quite an interesting way // of approaching the whole argument.

Thus, tone units relate to the patterning of sound across stretches of language that speakers use to signal their meaning.

Prominence

Within tone units, speakers give emphasis to certain syllables in the words. Typically, emphasis is placed on content words. To give words more salience and to signal their importance for creating meaning, speakers mark them out by making them louder and extending the length of vowels. In Brazil's model, prominent syllables are highlighted by using capitals:

> // Well, I SAW in the HERald there //
> // That's it in a NUTshell //

In the examples above, the pitch movements lead to emphasis being placed on *saw*, *Her*ald, and *nut*. The intonation, or "speech melody," used in these utterances selects certain words from a range of possible choices. The syllable that is given greatest prominence in any utterance is called the tonic syllable. In the first utterance above, where two syllables are given prominence, the first, *saw*, is the onset syllable and the last, *her*, is the tonic. In the second utterance, there is only one prominent syllable, *nut*, which is therefore the tonic. Placing emphasis on the syllable that carries meaning is clearly an important skill. Teachers may need to work with learners to help them understand prominence and, therefore, how they can give salience to the syllables that carry the message they want to get across.

> **Discuss it**
>
> How would a speaker's meaning change by giving prominence to different syllables in the utterances above? Discuss with a colleague the possible new meanings created by the changes in prominence shown below:
>
> // WELL // I saw in the Herald THERE //
>
> // THAT's IT // in a nutshell //

Tone

Tone choices refer to the way in which the pitch of speakers' voices rise or fall within the tone unit. The five tone types found in natural discourse in English are: fall (ﬨ), fall–rise (\↗), rise (↗), rise–fall (/ﬨ), level (→). Brazil notes that the most common of these in naturalistic discourse are fall ("proclaiming" tone) for new information (information not known to the listener), and fall–rise ("referring" tone) for given information (information the speaker already knows).

// Give me that NOW // ﬨ I WANT it // \↗

The level tone, which is commonly found in utterances such as train announcements, (Halliday 1970) is not considered to add much to the expression of meaning, as it is not part of "direct" discourse. Brazil notes that it is a tone that is not listener-sensitive; in other words, it does not respond to the relationship between speaker and listener. A level tone is also found when speakers list points that have been previously raised.

// We've got BEEF // → TURkey // → SALmon // → CHICKen // → or SALad // → sandwiches.

A rise tone is commonly used in questions and has implications for the nature of the role relationships between speakers. Used exclusively, the rise tone can imply an attempt to control or dominate the listener, or contest what people say, and can come across as rude. Where the speakers have equal rights as speakers, it is more usual to find a fall–rise tone. Let us look again at the question tones used in the conversation between Pippa and Vic:

P: // Well // I saw in The Herald there . . . //
V: // Did you? // (\↗)

P: Because I just love Sydney at that time.

V: // You going? // (\↗)

P: When I get round to booking . . .

Think about it

How would the meaning be changed if Vic voiced his questions in the following way:

// Did you? // (↗)   // You going? // (↗)

What would he be implying about the role relationship with Pippa, and his rights as a speaker?

In some cultures, the use of these tones may differ from the way they are used in codified native-speaker versions of English, such as British or American. For example, Goh (2000) points out that the use of fall tone for given, rather than new, information and rise tone for questions where the speaker already knows the answer is common in Singaporean English. In contrast, in British English, fall tone implies new information and rise tone in questions implies the speaker does not know the answer. Thus, teachers may need to sensitize learners to how the patterns of tones they use might impede interactions, give wrong impressions, or even cause offense in intercultural situations.

Key and termination

Key and termination are aspects of pronunciation concerned with pitch level. They have to do with the way speakers manage a topic by contrasting the stress in their utterances. According to Brazil (1997), at the onset of a tone unit, speakers select their pitch from a three level system – high, mid, and low. Prominent tones in the tone unit (known as keys) can thus be made more dramatic, emphatic, neutral, and so on. High key gives contrastive value (expressing difference from what was already said); mid key, additive value (adding on to the information); and low key, equal value (giving information that is to be expected). Pitch also affects the way the utterance is terminated, with the speaker again selecting high, mid, or low pitch on the prominent (tonic) syllable. Speakers use termination pitch to constrain a next speaker's response, to give up a turn, or to begin a new topic. Looking again at the basketball commentary, we can see how pitch is used "to indicate relationships between the tone units in terms of the informational value speakers attribute to them" (Burns & Seidlhofer 2010: 205).

> // And we pick up the game in the THIRD quarter // . . . so, score is 13–10 (THIRteen–ten) the JETS // . . . and Ellis is being guarded by Davis // . . . and Johns IS trying to get a piece of it . . . .

By using high key on *thir*teen, the commentator is contrasting the re-introduction of his commentary (maybe after a commercial break) with the previous quarter. He then jumps to high pitch to dramatize or emphasize the fact that the *Jets* (who may in the past have been a low-scoring team) have scored surprisingly highly against the Bombers. The high pitch on *is* also carries contrastive meaning. It suggests that, unexpectedly, Johns may not have made much attempt to get into the action earlier in the game, but is now doing so. Sensitizing learners to how pitch works to signal the importance of information in various places in the message can greatly enhance intelligibility.

Stress

In general, content words (e.g., verbs, nouns, adjectives, adverbs) are where prominence in utterances is placed. Other words (function words, including pronouns, prepositions, articles, and so on) serve to bind the grammatical structure of utterances and are not usually stressed. Where they are stressed, as in *Johns* IS *trying to get a piece of it* . . . above, they are used for a particular contrastive purpose.

This kind of prominence, or stress, however, still operates at the suprasegmental level, or at a higher level than the word. Stress at the word level is also important in carrying meaning and contributing to the intelligibility of a speaker's utterance. Word-level stress is segmental, relating to prominence that is placed on the syllable and on the phoneme (the smallest unit of sound). Pronunciation of phonemes has to do with the way in which speakers use their mouth, lips, and tongues to produce the sounds of a particular language. Here we look only at the way word-level stress is employed.

In the prominent parts of the utterance, syllables within a word are produced in different ways. In multi-syllable words, stress must be placed on the appropriate syllable if meaning is to be clear. Consider the placement of stress in the content words in the following utterance:

> // I found it quite an INTeresting way // of apprOACHing the whole ARGument // but READing it for the SECond time // I felt slightly unEASY //

Knowledge of syllable stress is often a challenge for language learners. For example, Polli, originally from Bangladesh, who was studying in Australia, had this to say about some of her difficulties:

> My problem is I'm not sure with some words how to say them. For example, I'm used to saying com/FORT/able, but I said it the other day and the woman could not understand me. When my teacher asked the class if something was correct or incorrect, I said CO/rrect, and she told me that was not the right way to say it.

In this section, we have described briefly some of the key features of a discourse model of intonation and stress, drawing on the work of Brazil. A discourse model provides a description of the role played by intonation in the contexts where speech is produced. It reveals how changes in discourse intonation allow for the communicative intentions of the speaker to be made clear (Goh 2000). Having an understanding of intonation and stress assists teachers in diagnosing problems that impede learners' intelligibility. In a globalized world, where English is used as a lingua franca for intercultural exchange, intelligibility is now a particularly important aspect of effective communication among all speakers of English.

Summary

In this chapter, we have considered differences in the way spoken and written language are produced, and some of the grammatical features that characterize spoken language. Knowledge about spoken language grammar has grown very rapidly since technological advances made it easier for researchers to collect spoken samples and research, and analysis of speech over the last two decades has become very extensive. Here we have been able to touch briefly only on a limited number of the features of spoken language and to make some initial suggestions about what can be done in the classroom to focus attention on them.

Based on the discussion in this chapter, we can suggest some implications for teaching speaking:

1. Introduce learners to key differences between spoken and written language. It is quite likely that learners' previous experiences of practicing speaking skills have been based on written grammar and dialogues that are "introspected" by textbook writers, as these features are still common in many textbooks. Introducing learners to authentic examples can sensitize them to the differences between speech and writing.

2. Introduce learners to the idea of the spoken-written continuum and help them to see how language use shifts across this continuum. Begin by asking them to express ideas on a topic in speech, and then help them to construct how these ideas might be expressed in different types of writing. This is particularly important for the development of academic writing skills.

3. Sensitize learners to the fact that spoken language, especially in casual social encounters, does not have to make use of a high level of grammatical, lexical, and structural *(syntactical)* competence. Thornbury and Slade (2006) argue that *pragmatic* use, where learners produce what they can to create meaning according to immediate needs, may be more useful. They advocate a "core grammar" that includes some of the features we have discussed in this chapter: conjunctions, deixis, simple past and present verb tense forms, the ability to formulate questions, and heads and tails fillers.

4. Assist learners to understand how intonation and syllable stress contribute in significant ways to meaning. Provide examples of how speakers use tone units and prominence to construct their messages, and to create meaning. Preferably, use examples of natural speech, or find recent materials that have good, recorded authentic interactions. Also provide opportunities to compare L1 and L2 sound systems to identify contrasts that may be particularly problematic. Encourage learners to develop strategies for coping independently when confronted with pronunciation problems, for example, using a pronunciation dictionary, or soliciting repetition, paraphrasing, and feedback.

Group-learning tasks

1. This task asks you to think about context and the continuum between spoken and written language. Work in groups of three. Discuss what the context might be for each text. Then decide, approximately, where the texts below would fit on the spoken to written continuum. What is it about the language features in the texts that prompts your decisions? Give reasons for your responses.

Text 1

Participants reported on the literature they had read in preparation for the workshop, and various aspects of the literature were discussed in relation to the major focus of the project. The group also spent time defining the concept of scaffolding as it relates to the current project. A working definition was developed to underpin the projects that will be conducted between November and March. The participants also spent time developing a research topic that each person will undertake until March. Methods for conducting the individual projects were also clarified. Each participant has been asked to report on his or her research at the workshop to be held on March 5.

Text 2

Diving is amazing, loving the warm weather! No problem 4 Dan to stay, but will be in aber, then stirling 4 wrk, so won't be there. can give him keys. Talk soon. luv

Text 3

This is very kind of her. Let me know what you want to do, happy to fit in.

Text 4

The state government this week announced that train commuters from the AirportLink stations of Green Square and Mascot will have their fares reduced from Monday, March 7. The cost of a weekly ticket will be cut from $42 to $25.

Text 5

A: Do you have medical expenses of $1,500 in the last financial year?

C: Just for myself?

A: Yes.

C: Now last year. I have had . . . I don't know. I couldn't answer that. I'd have to sit down and calculate all the visits. Would that mean all the visits to the doctor and all the . . . ?

A: Yes, all the out of pocket expenses.

C: OK. It's possible, but I couldn't tell you that right now. But I can claim for that, can I?

2. The text below is a continuation of the conversation between Sarah (S) and her boyfriend's mother (M). S, who is from the U.S., is telling M above a recent trip to the outback of Australia. Work with a partner to find examples in the text of the following grammatical features: 1) non-clausal units, 2) ellipsis, 3) formulaic expressions. Note any other features that are outlined in the section on spoken grammar in this chapter.

S: I saw signs with a kangaroo and a koala bear on it . . . and, obviously, I'm not used to that. It was great . . . I went out and took pictures.

M: You didn't see the real kangaroos or the real koalas?

S: We did.

M: Did you?

S: Yeah, up in the trees.

M: You were very lucky.

S: Yeah, that's what I've been told. Yeah, that's very exciting... I still haven't seen a kangaroo yet, but considering I've been around Sydney, I don't really expect to.

M: Yeah, well, I hope you enjoy your stay here.

S: Thank you.

M: Nice talking to you.

S: Thanks. You, too.

Grammatical feature	Examples
1. Non-clausal units	
2. Ellipsis	
3. Formulaic expressions	

3. Collect examples of your learners' pronunciation problems. Look for at least one example of each of the different features of discourse intonation discussed above. In groups of four, discuss the examples and develop some ideas for teaching activities that could be used to assist your learners.

Further reading

Brazil, D. (1997) *The Communicative Value of Intonation*, Cambridge: Cambridge University Press.

Carter, R. et al. (2008) *Working with Texts: A Core Introduction to Language Analysis*, London: Routledge.

Carter, R. and McCarthy, M. (1997) *Exploring Spoken English*, Cambridge: Cambridge University Press.

Thornbury, S. and Slade, D. (2006) *Conversation: From Description to Pedagogy*, Cambridge: Cambridge University Press.

5 *Spoken discourse and genres of speaking*

Apart from understanding typical differences between spoken and written language, and the grammatical features that characterize speech, knowledge of how spoken language is realized in context, and of what kind of linguistic features enable spoken texts to hang together as they unfold, is also important in language teaching.

This chapter focuses on spoken texts as discourse, or, in other words, extended stretches of text in context. It also considers the notion of genre, or text types, found in speech and highlights some of the genres that have been identified by research to be commonly used by speakers. This chapter will address three questions:

1. What features of discourse characterize language as it is used in a social context?
2. What text types or genres are common in spoken interaction?
3. How can the notion of genre be applied in the classroom?

To answer the questions, we will discuss the following topics:

- Features of discourse.
- The concepts of genre and text type.
- Genres of speaking.

Daily life is filled with numerous types of discourse. Learners may need English to engage with family members, work colleagues, classmates, lecturers and teachers, friends, business, public or health organizations, and many other people in the general community. In order to carry out these interactions effectively, it is useful for learners to have a sense of the nature of the discourses they will be involved in. Discourse analysts study how whole extended pieces of authentic language (written and spoken texts) are patterned in particular ways that are sensitive to the contexts in which they are produced. As already mentioned, approaches to teaching speaking have tended to model themselves on written language and the structures of individual, isolated sentences. In a discourse approach, teachers can raise learners' awareness about the patternings in authentic text that operate to maintain extended interaction. In this chapter, we will look first at some of the major features of spoken discourse. The second half of the chapter looks at the related concept of genre. The chapter, therefore, moves from considering micro-features of speech to looking at macro-features of speech.

Discourse features in speech

Ways of analyzing discourse have come from various sociological and (socio)linguistic origins. Major contributions and approaches include conversation analysis (CA), speech act theory, pragmatics, interactional sociolinguistics, systemic functional linguistics, exchange analysis, and critical discourse analysis. They each have their distinctive theoretical perspectives and systems for analyzing discourse. Here, we look at various features of discourse analysis drawn from these theories that are likely to be useful in planning spoken-language instruction.

Adjacency pairs

The concept of adjacency pairs comes from the field of conversation analysis (e.g., Sacks, Sacks, Schegloff & Jefferson 1974). Conversational analysts note that exchanges between speakers are typically composed of two turns, which make up the smallest units of conversation. They are adjacent to each other and produced by different speakers. Examples of adjacency pairs include question / answer; offer / accept; instruct / receipt; greeting / greeting; request / grant. Types of responses that occur are *preferred* responses (where the speaker responds positively to the first utterance) or *dis-preferred* responses (where there is usually some kind of rejection). Dis-preferred responses are typically accompanied by a justification or explanation.

Question / answer:

A: What's the time?	A: What's the time?
B: Six-twenty.	B: Dunno, haven't got my watch on.

Offer / accept:

A: D'you want to come over to my place tonight?	A: D'you want to come over to my place tonight?
B: Yeah, that would be nice.	B: Can't, got to work late.

Try it

Listen for examples of other kinds of adjacency pairs (instruct / receipt; instruct / reject; greeting / greeting; compliment / response; request / grant) in conversations you hear around you. Try to identify examples of preferred and dis-preferred responses. If you do not easily have an opportunity to listen to English speakers, identify how these adjacency pairs occur in a language you have access to. How similar or different from English are the adjacency pairs?

Conversation analysts are interested in micro-features of talk and pose questions such as:

- Why does only one person speak at a time?
- How do speakers know when to take turns?
- How do speakers know when to initiate new topics?
- How do speakers know when it is appropriate to interrupt?
- How can one speaker complete another speaker's utterance?
- How do interactants recognize when a speaker wants to close a conversation?

(Thornbury & Slade 2006: 114.)

Such questions are very useful for the teaching of speaking, as teachers can focus on these different features of speech and develop activities to help learners manage them in interaction, perhaps providing examples they have collected themselves. Teachers can also discuss with learners how these interactional features in English might compare with other languages they are familiar with. For example, how are dis-preferred responses handled in their languages? In the next section, we look at two other micro-features of discourse identified in the questions above.

Turn taking

Speakers use a variety of discourse strategies to manage turns in conversation. Despite hesitations, overlaps, or interruptions, talk flows remarkably smoothly, and often for long periods of time, because speakers are adept at reading signs about how turns are allocated. Essentially, speakers have two choices in turn taking. They can self-select, using strategies such as asking questions, introducing new information, or announcing a different topic; or they can select others, using eye gaze, asking them questions, naming them, or orienting their stance physically towards them.

Self select:
A: Hey, guess who I just saw . . . Don.
B: No!

Select others:
CATHY: What do you think, Mum? Blue earrings or gold?
MUM: Mm . . . gold, I think.

A key aspect of turn taking is that speakers have a finely tuned ability to recognize points where a new speaker can take the next turn. The technical term for these key change points is *turn-constructional unit* or TCU (Sacks 1974), which is the smallest unit of one turn of talk. Let us look again at the examples above:

A: Hey, guess who I just saw (TCU) . . . Don (TCU).
B: No! (TCU).

CATHY: What do you think, Mum? (TCU). Blue earrings or gold? (TCU).
MUM: Mm (TCU) . . . gold, I think (TCU).

Each of the TCUs in these examples is an opportunity for the other speaker to come in and take a turn during the exchange. In the first example, B could have interrupted A by asking, *Who?* before getting the reply, *Don*. Similarly, in the second example, Mum could have used the opportunity to speak after the first question from Cathy. In casual conversation, which is highly interactional and interpersonal (motivated by personal relationships), turns are dynamic and fluid, and speakers show high competition for the opportunity to speak. In interactions that have mainly pragmatic or transactional purposes (to achieve a goal), such as a doctor's consultation or a job interview, the question of who controls the turn taking is determined more by the person who has the power (or is the more dominant) in the interaction, such as the doctor or the interviewer, as can be seen in the following short exchange:

DOCTOR: Morning, come in . . .
PATIENT: Morning, Doctor.
DOCTOR: Mr. Jones, isn't it?
PATIENT: Yes, that's right, Brian Jones.
DOCTOR: Morning . . . and take a seat . . . How're you today?
PATIENT: Well, not too good.
DOCTOR: So, what's the problem?

PATIENT: Well, I've had a sore throat for a while now.
DOCTOR: Right, so tell me more about how it started.

(Author's data.)

In this interaction, it is the doctor who asks the questions and, therefore, nominates the patient for a turn. The patient's opportunities for competing for a turn at a TCU are noticeably more limited.

In language classrooms, teachers can discuss the interactional strategies that enable speakers to take on speaker turns, such as speaker roles and rights to turns, and how these might differ from other languages familiar to learners; how people get turns and keep them; and how overlaps and interruptions are tolerated in various cultures, and in English. Learners can practice recognizing discourse signals that show desire to speak (e.g., discourse markers, like *well*, that indicate one wishes to enter the conversation and non-verbal signals like eye gaze, posture, and body position).

Topic and interaction management

Topic management is closely related to turn taking as speakers must negotiate turns in order to manage a topic effectively, thereby achieving mutual understanding and appropriate levels of explicitness for their listeners. In daily interactions, speakers are constantly starting new topics, developing the topic, and changing (or recycling) topics. The way speakers manage topics will depend on factors like their interest in the topic, their knowledge about it, and their sense of which topics are culturally appropriate and acceptable to the speaker. Topic selection has also been shown to be influenced by gender, class, age, and ethnicity (e.g., Eggins & Slade 1997; Pichler & Eppler 2009).

Often a new topic is introduced by linking it to what has been said previously *(Well, I had a different experience; That reminds me of. . . , I tell you what. . .)* or signaling what is to come *(Guess who I just met?)*. Once a new topic is established, speakers then have to manage the interaction by using discourse strategies such as checking, clarifying, summarizing, and adapting to meanings expressed by other speakers. We will use the extract below, where a client (C) is completing an Australian tax return form with the help of a professional accountant (A), to illustrate some of these strategies.

A: Do you do work-related studies?
C: Yeah.

A: And you pay for yourself?

C: You mean for like attending courses or something like that?

A: Yes.

C: Well, I haven't done that so far . . . but . . . I mean my workplace is quite strict . . . They have quite a strict sort of policy on that because it's partly government funded.

A: Ah, yes.

C: So it must relate to the interests of the organization; otherwise, I can't claim any funding . . . so I'm quite concerned about that 'cause that could involve being quite big expenses.

A: Yes . . . if work-related studies, they are tax deductible.

C: Right, OK.

A: Do you need to wear protective clothes in your work?

C: I was going to ask about clothing . . . not protective clothing . . . no.

A: OK, all right.

C: So I can't claim for normal clothing?

A: No.

C: What a pity (chuckles).

(Author's data.)

> **Try it**
>
> Identify examples of how the speakers in this interaction check understanding, elaborate on the topic, clarify meaning, provide feedback, summarize the point they are making, and provide evaluations on what they say to each other.

A, as the professional in this exchange, moves the conversation along by asking C a series of questions, each of which introduces new "mini-topics" related to the main topic of completing a tax return. A also uses turns for elaboration so that more information can be obtained about the client *(And you pay for yourself?)*. There are points at which C clarifies what she thinks is meant *(You mean for like attending courses or something like that?)* and checks that she has understood *(So I can't claim for normal clothing?)*. Feedback is provided by both speakers through confirming expressions such as *yeah*, *right*, and *OK*. As the professional expert in the exchange, A also summarizes a point about tax regulations *(Yes . . . if work-related studies, they are tax deductible)*, while C introduces an interpersonal note into what is essentially a transactional or pragmatic interaction, by providing an evaluation or judgement of what the rules say *(What a pity!)* and chuckling.

Managing topics and interactions is something that learners usually already know how to do well in their own languages. Teachers can help raise their awareness of what they already know from their own experience and help them to consider the strategies that would be useful in English. Coursebooks containing speaking activities have not typically shown how speakers check, clarify, summarize, elaborate, or give feedback in authentic speaking situations. Developing activities that help learners to use interaction management strategies, and having learners practice them both inside and outside the classroom, where the opportunity exists, is a valuable way of progressing their spoken language development.

Discourse strategies

Before concluding this section on discourse features, we will look at just two types of discourse strategies that are important features for learners: opening and closing interactions, and giving feedback during interactions.

OPENINGS AND CLOSINGS

Openings and closings have to do with the way speakers manage the initiation and conclusion of interactions. In more formal situations, the opening is usually initiated by the speaker who is more in control of the interaction, as in the doctor's consultation above:

DOCTOR: Morning, come in . . .
PATIENT: Morning, Doctor.
DOCTOR: Mr. Jones, isn't it?
PATIENT: Yes, that's right, Brian Jones.
DOCTOR: Morning . . . and take a seat . . . How're you today?

Here we can see a sequence of simple adjacency pairs operating together: *Morning, Morning* (greeting–greeting); *Mr Jones isn't it? Yes, that's right, Brian Jones* (identification check–confirmation). In casual conversations, however, openings and closings tend not to consist of simple adjacency pairs, but extend over three-part exchanges or more:

ROSS: Hi, Lynne! How're you?
LYNNE: Oh, hi, hi . . . fancy seeing you here.
PETER: Hello, Ross, how're you doing? How's things?
ROSS: Hi, Peter . . . not bad, not bad.

Conversational closings are usually characterized by pre-closing turns where the speaker signals that the conversation is winding down *(I can't talk much longer; In a rush, sorry; Well, Mr. Aziz, I think that's all we need to ask you for the moment).* In the following example, Ross signals that the interaction is about to end, and it then takes several turns before the three speakers conclude their interaction:

ROSS: Better go . . . got to meet Mary soon.
LYNNE: OK, say hi to her from us.
PETER: See you later.
ROSS: Yeah, see you later. Bye.
LYNNE: Bye, Ross.
PETER: Bye . . . bye.

Try it

Listen for the way people begin and end interactions. What differences do you notice between formal exchanges and informal exchanges? If possible, note down or record some examples of how speakers begin and end (you will need to get people's permission before recording them).

Language learners often have difficulty knowing how to open and close interactions. In general, expressions used during openings and closings in extended interaction are formulaic, like *See you later* in the example above (see Chapter 4). However, they are also culturally specific and in some languages highly formulized according to age, social status, and kinship. Teachers can help learners with these aspects of speech by comparing and contrasting English and their learners' own languages, and by introducing them to the kind of formulaic expressions commonly used. Teachers can also show which types of expressions are appropriate to use, according to the relationships that exist between the speakers.

FEEDBACK

Listener feedback, or *backchanneling*, is pervasive in dialogic speech. Backchannels serve an important function, as they show that the listener is following what is said and expressing his or her agreement, disagreement, uncertainty, or interest. Speakers rely on backchannels to know whether their listeners are following their message and paying attention to what is being said. Without appropriate backchannels, breakdown in communication can quickly occur. In the following interaction, where four colleagues are discussing their experiences in a distance-learning master's program, notice how interaction is made smooth, cohesive, and cooperative through the speakers' and listeners' use of backchannels.

A: I was working in Turkey at the time . . . I was lucky to have one of my colleagues doing the same program, started at the same time as me, so we used to get together regularly . . . er, sometimes as often as twice a week, and we would get together and compare our findings, and because our learning styles were different, as well, we compensated for one another.

B: Yeah . . .

A: And we learned a lot from one another, so it was very . . . yeah, happy, challenging, but happy experience at the same time.

C: Yeah, I think it's really worthwhile making the effort to find people to study with . . . I mean, I know people might not be physically close, but these days with the . . . with the technology that's available, I think you can . . . you can still have that.

D: That's right.

A: Yeah.

B: And you can with somebody virtually . . .

D: That's right, that's right.

(Authors' data.)

Think about it

What would be the effect on the main speaker in the interaction above if the listeners had provided no backchannels? Have you experienced an interaction where a listener gave little or no feedback? What was your reaction?

The speakers in this interaction strongly affirm each other's messages through the frequent use of common backchannels: *Yeah*, and *That's right*. Other typical affirmations that show listeners are keeping up and agreeing with a speaker are *mm*, *uh-huh* and *mhm*. *Mhm*, uttered with a rising intonation, can also mark disagreement, however, and *uh-uh* (as opposed to *uh-huh*) functions as the negative, *no*:

A: D'you like horror movies?

B: Uh-uh (shakes head).

Biber et al. (1999) point out that while all the backchannels mentioned above give a sense of casual, non-committal feedback, other forms, like *Really? Fine, No way!* and *I see!* show a high degree of interest on the part of the listener, or what McCarthy calls "engaged listenership" (McCarthy 2003: 34).

The way listeners give feedback varies from context to context, according to the relationships and characteristics of the speakers (age, gender, social status, and so on). It is also culturally specific, and language users from some communities may give more or less feedback than is common in English. McCarthy (1999: 58) points out, for example, that Spanish speakers tend to acknowledge talk "with what translates to English as a machine-gun-like 'Yes-yes-yes!' which frequently indicates impatience or irritation with the speaker in British English." Discussing with learners the concept of feedback, and exploring how they use feedback in their own languages, is a useful sensitizing exercise that teachers can introduce when teaching speaking. Learners can then compare how feedback is typically used in English and practice common forms of expressing it. This kind of exercise is particularly useful as forms of feedback are rarely included in current coursebooks.

Having looked briefly at some key discourse features and the management of spoken interaction, we now consider larger, macro-structures of types of spoken language that shape and pattern the talk as it emerges.

Transaction and interaction

Spoken language is always produced for a purpose; in this sense, we can say it is *functional* as it has the function of fulfilling speakers' everyday goals. Various theorists (e.g., Brown & Yule 1983; McCarthy 1991) have suggested that spoken interaction is driven by two major types of functional motivation: *transactional*, or pragmatic, interaction and *interactional*, or interpersonal, interaction.

Transactional interactions involve speakers exchanging goods and services, as, for example, in business meetings, service encounters, or job interviews. Interactional interactions focus on creating and maintaining personal relationships – they "oil the social wheels" of daily life. Skype® calls to family members, gossiping in the workplace, and personal storytelling between friends having a meal together are examples. Although talk tends to fall broadly into one of these two major types of motivation, any spoken interaction could, in fact, be a mixture of both types: it would be unusual, for example, for business meetings (primarily transactional) not to contain some elements of interpersonal talk. Similarly, a casual conversation between friends (mainly interactional) might contain segments where speakers turn to transactional matters, such as asking for advice about a problem or discussing a situation involving purchasing goods.

On page 115 we present a useful model drawing on Eggins (1990) (in Burns, Joyce & Gollin 1996) that shows these different functions for transactional and interactional spoken language. The model also shows how the relationships between speakers in interpersonal interactions might influence the specific language that is produced. The model is useful for teaching, as it provides a planning base for teachers to make decisions about which type of spoken interactions they want to introduce to their learners. Depending on their choice, teachers are then in a good position to identify the kinds of discourse features they might need to focus on, such as those already described in this and the previous chapter.

The top of the model shows how spoken interactions can be categorized as broadly interactional or broadly transactional. Conversations in this model consist first of *casual* conversations where the participants have more or less equal interpersonal power; that is, no speaker is more dominant in terms of social status, expertise, or other kinds of power. For example, two friends gossiping over coffee is an example of speakers with equal power. *Formal* conversations, on the other hand, are where power is likely to be unequal, as one of the speakers has more status or knowledge, such as a teacher chatting to a student after class, for example. In each case, the speakers select from the repertoire of their linguistic knowledge, and the choices available to them according to their "reading" of these relationships and how they wish to go on maintaining them. Speakers evaluate in finely tuned ways what kind of language is appropriate and acceptable to the other speakers.

Casual conversations are further classified as *polite* or *confirming*. Polite conversations are those where no, or limited, previous or future contacts exist (−contact). In these conversations, participants are unlikely to have developed strong psychological or emotional feelings towards one another (−affect). An example would be meeting someone incidentally at a language teaching conference, or on a train, and chatting politely on that one occasion. Confirming conversations are where speakers have close and continuing contacts (+ contact) and have strong emotional feelings towards each other (+ affect), such as among family members, work colleagues, or members of a sports team.

Encounters, which do not include casual conversations, are categorized as *factual* or *transactional*. Factual interactions are concerned with giving or seeking information. They involve interactions related to inquiries made in a whole range of daily social situations – in educational, vocational, and in community settings – such as asking someone for directions, or getting advice on enrollment from a course administrator. Transactional

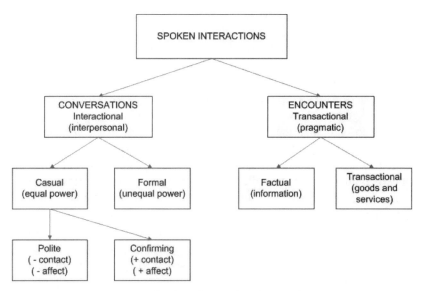

Figure 5.1: Functional motivation for spoken interactions (Burns, Joyce & Gollin 1996:11).

interactions involve the negotiation of goods and services, such as making medical appointments, engaging in transactions at a bank or government office, or purchasing goods in a department store. While Eggins (1990) does not include the dimensions of contact and affect in the categories she gives for transactional encounters (Figure 5.1), again, the language used would be affected by the familiarity of the speakers and their feelings towards each other as people.

In general, transactional talk may be easier to teach in language class-rooms than interactional because it is unfolds in more predictable stages. Transactional interactions are usually easier to identify at the macro-level; for example, a consultation with a doctor is relatively predictable in most cultures and languages. Because of this predictability, at the micro-level, the way the discourse unfolds and the kind of vocabulary and grammar likely to be used (e.g., formulaic greetings, parts of the body, use of imper-ative voice for verbs in a doctor's consultation) are easier to examine with learners. Interactional conversation is more difficult to teach. It is much less predictable, as it is highly spontaneous, jointly constructed turn by turn and very context specific. Because of the nature of the power relations and affective factors discussed above, conversations are interpersonally sensi-tive and more grammatically complex. We will explore these issues further in the next section, where we turn to genres of speaking.

The concept of genre

Genre has been mentioned several times in previous sections of this book and is a useful concept in teaching speaking. The word "genre" means type or kind, and you may be more familiar with its use to describe literature, film, music, or art (e.g., romance genres, thriller genres, folk genres, or landscape genres). However, speakers of any language do not have to be linguists to recognize that certain "types" of talk, or *text types*, recur in speech, or that they emerge in ways that are recognizable and predictable to the listeners. The term "genre" captures the way that different kinds of spoken language events "bundle" the talk towards its goal by moving from stage to stage in ways that are culturally, socially, and institutionally known. McCarthy (1998: 32) refers to genres as "social compacts" or cooperative sets of behaviors, which people use when they engage in unfolding discourses.

Martin (2010: 25) explains that genres have a "distinctive goal-oriented staging structure." Genre descriptions of language use, particularly of service encounters, go back to early work by Mitchell (1957), who investigated the language of buying and selling at markets and shops in Cyrenaica, the eastern part of modern-day Libya (see also Ventola 1987). For example, in certain cultural contexts a typical service encounter genre might go like this:

> To begin, you exchange greetings with a salesperson, who will offer to serve you. You will then state your needs, perhaps helping yourself, or getting the salesperson to satisfy your requirements. When you get what you need, you will be told how much it costs. You then pay your money, say good-bye, and leave. (Martin 2010: 25.)

Martin illustrates these stages visually, using "^" (meaning "followed by") to indicate the sequence:

Greeting^Service Bid^Statement of Need^Need Compliance^Decision to Buy^Payment ^Leave Taking

---

Think about it

Identify a short typical speaking situation you are familiar with (e.g., making a doctor's appointment, reserving a taxi, or ordering a meal). Think about the stages involved in completing the whole interaction. Compare your version with a colleague's version to see how much similarity there is.

Although it is possible to recognize genre structures, like the one described by Martin above, in both transactional and interactional exchanges, the language used to achieve spoken genres in English is not fixed, but involves a great deal of variability and dynamism. Choices ARE made by speakers that are influenced by the topic, their relationships with each other, and the context (Duranti 1983). Sequences of talk, or extensive spoken language events, can also demonstrate genre-mixing, where different kinds of genres may occur in the same event.

Spoken genres (see, for example, McCarthy 1998) have been less well described than written genres (see, for example, Swales 1990) because it has not been easy to capture speech until recently, and spoken language has tended to be viewed as formless and difficult to analyze. Indeed, as we have already suggested in this chapter and in Chapter 4, spoken exchanges are typically composed of very interactive turns, involving several speakers, and are highly context-dependent, where speakers refer to immediate actions or events. However, it is also easy to recognize that there are extended genres such as sermons, jokes, stories, anecdotes, wedding speeches, and so on. These kinds of discourses are usually signaled to listeners by openings (or initiations) like *Did I tell you about the time I...? Ladies and gentlemen...*, or *I've got a great joke to tell you...*, and move onwards through stages that listeners and speakers can usually anticipate until the speakers reach their conclusion. One useful way of identifying these genres for the purposes of spoken language teaching is to distinguish between talk consisting of "chat" and talk consisting of "chunks."

Chat and chunks

The notion of chat and chunks comes from the work of Eggins & Slade (1997), who analyzed genres in casual conversation (see also Thornbury & Slade 2006). Chat segments are "... highly interactive sequences of spoken language characterized by a rapid transfer of turns from one speaker to the other" (Eggins & Slade 1997: 227).

In the following chat sequence, two Australian couples are upstairs in the house of one of the couples where the Sydney Harbour Bridge can be seen in the far distance. Ian, whose house it is, has asked Lynne, who is visiting, to explain how to use a search engine on a computer [A = Anna, I = Ian, L = Lynne, R = Rod].

L: Can we build on the top somewhere ... another little room?
R: No ...
I: ... Right.

R: ... Gee, that's a very good view of the city ... Could you see ... could you have seen the fireworks from here, Ian?

I: Yeah.

R: Could you ... ?

I: Yeah ... right ... Internet connection. (Pause.)

I: OK.

R: OK ... hop in.

L: ... Uh ... oh, I've got to earn dinner now, have I?

A: ... Right ... so.

I: Have you seen these? ... I've been using this chair now for about three years ... Do you know how to use that?

L: Yes, I do ... I'd love one.

I: You won't fall off it?

L: No, I won't fall off it.

I: Aaaagh.

L: We had one at work, but it disappeared, unfortunately, before I could have it.

I: It's bloody brilliant.

L: ... It's absolutely great.

A: So ...

I: I had back problems before I went on this ...

L: ... That's why I think they're great.

I: ... You kneel on it ...

L: Yeah, I know.

(Authors' data.)

In this sequence, we can see that the conversation is spontaneous and informal, as the speakers know each other well. Speakers exchange turns frequently, there is high competition for turns, and the discourse is managed locally turn by turn. For these reasons, and because the talk is highly context-embedded and very sensitive to the relationships between the speakers, chat sequences are difficult to teach.

Chunk segments, on the other hand, are "those aspects of conversation that have a global or macro-structure where the structure beyond the [turn] is more predictable" (Eggins & Slade 1997: 230). One participant takes the floor for an extended period and becomes the principal speaker, there is a recognizable chunk of interaction interwoven into the overall conversation, the chunk appears to move through predictable stages, and the primary speaker uses his or her turn to tell a story, to joke, to gossip, or to give an opinion. In the example below, Gillian has just arrived late at a friend's apartment in Australia, where people she knows well are having coffee together. She goes into an explanation (in the form of a recounting of events) of what held her up [G = Gillian, V = Valerie, T = Terry].

G: It's unbelievable, you know, I've got three ATMs at my bank, right... I'm down there today; there's one working out of three, so I waited in the queue . . . that was all right, put my card in, keyed in my PIN, the shutters came down and ate my card.

V: Oh no . . .

G: So I had to go inside the bank where the queues are practically to the door, and every other person there is a businessman[1] with you know the thousand cheques.

T: Oh right . . .

G: I know, just trying to stay calm and then, finally, there's just me and the little old lady in front of me, and I thought, well, she won't take long, and then she walks up to the teller and picked up this huge shopping bag full of five-cent pieces.

V: Oh no . . .

G: So I left; I felt I just couldn't wait any longer.

T: You didn't get your card back?

G: I didn't get my card, and I didn't get my money.

V: It's all right, darling. I'll lend you a dollar . . .

G: Oh, great. Just don't make it in five-cent pieces. [Laughter.]

(Adapted from de Silva Joyce, H. & Hilton,
D. 1999: 84; used by permission.)

These kinds of longer stretches of talk, even though they are still interactive in the sense that other speakers also play a role, are more amenable to being analyzed as spoken genres or text types. They are much easier to teach than chat, as they have their own internal structures that show identifiable patterns of language. Recognizing that there are key "storytelling" genres is very valuable for the purposes of planning and teaching casual conversation. Drawing on Slade (1997), the table below identifies key genres typical of spontaneous talk and the main features of their generic structure – that is, the various stages the text goes through as it unfolds so that it can be classified as a particular genre.

[1] The term "businessman," common in Australian English, has been retained, rather than the more neutral "businessperson," now used in American English.

Table 5.1: *Common storytelling genres in casual spoken interaction*

Genre	Generic structure
Narrative (facing and resolving a problematic experience).	(Abstract)^Orientation^Complication^Evaluation^ Resolution^(Coda) Narratives first identify a time, a situation, and the participants, and introduce a problem into the setting of the story. They indicate the point of the story and then tell how the problem was solved. They may finish with an evaluation or rounding up of the events.
Anecdote (experiencing a remarkable event).	(Abstract)^Orientation^Remarkable Event^Reaction^(Coda) Anecdotes are similar to narratives in that they focus on a crisis, but they have no explicit resolution. The crisis is reacted to in some way (e.g., through expressions of amazement, frustration, embarrassment, or humiliation).
Exemplum (highlighting a moral point).	(Abstract)^(Orientation)^Incident^Interpretation^(Coda) Exemplums are told to give an explicit message on how the world should or should not be, and to reaffirm cultural and societal values. Fables with "a moral to the story" fall into this category.
Recount (experiencing a sequence of events).	(Abstract)^Orientation^Record of Events^(Coda) Recounts retell events that are sequenced in time order, and have some kind of evaluation running through them. The point is to retell events and share the speaker's evaluation with the listeners.

[^ = followed by; ( ) = optional stages]
(Based on Slade 1997.)

Gillian's interaction with her friends, in the example above, can be identified as a spoken recount; she tells them about a sequence of events that happened to her earlier that day. Looking again at this example, we can see how the generic structure follows the elements of recount noted in the table above, that is:

Abstract:	Used to signal that a recount is about to begin. It is an optional stage, as not all recounts begin by signaling what is to come.
Orientation:	Orients the listener to the places, events, circumstances and people involved *(who, what, why, where, when)*.
Record of Events:	Outlines events in sequence with ongoing evaluation of the meaning or significance of the events.

Coda, or Evaluation: Comments on the overall story and brings it back to the present. The coda serves to round off and signal the end of the recount, provides an evaluation of the recount as a whole, and offers an opportunity for other speakers to begin a shift of topic.

Turning again to Gillian's recount of the bank events, the generic (or macro) analysis of this interaction breaks down as follows:

(Abstract)
G: It's unbelievable, you know.

Orientation
I've got three ATMs at my bank, right . . . I'm down there today; there's one working out of three.

Record of events
So I waited in the queue . . . that was all right, put my card in, keyed in my PIN, the shutters came down and ate my card.
V: Oh no . . .
G: So I had to go inside the bank where the queues are practically to the door, and every other person there is a businessman with, you know, the thousand cheques.
T: Oh right . . .
G: I know, just trying to stay calm and then, finally, there's just me and the little old lady in front of me, and I thought, well, she won't take long, and then she walks up to the teller and picked up this huge shopping bag full of five-cent pieces.
V: Oh no . . .
G: So I left, I felt I just couldn't wait any longer.
T: You didn't get your card back?

(Coda)
G: I didn't get my card, and I didn't get my money.
V: It's all right, darling. I'll lend you a dollar . . .
G: Oh, great. Just don't make it in five-cent pieces. [Laughter.]

If we take these stages in turn, we can also see that each one is characterized by certain patternings of language and discourse features. So it is possible now to analyze the discourse features at the micro-level, and to look at

Table 5.2: *Lexico-grammatical patterns at the micro-level*

Generic stage	Language features and patterns
(Abstract) Signals the story is about to begin and establishes the point of the story.	Generalized *you* (to show general relevance of story). Attitudinal vocabulary (*unbelievable* – to show point of story).
Orientation Orients listeners to events *(who, what, why, where, when)*.	References to specific people involved (*I*). References to place / time *(at my bank, down there, today)*.
Record of Events Outlines events in sequence with ongoing evaluations.	Use of nouns / pronouns for participants *(businessman, a little old lady, she, I)*. Events sequenced in time *(finally)*. Past tense state-of-being verbs *(was)*. Past tense action verbs *(put, keyed, picked up)*. Past in present and reported speech for dramatic effect *(Every other person there is a businessman; There's just me and the little old lady)*. Listener-engaged feedback *(oh, no)* and non-committal feedback *(oh, right)*.
(Coda) Comments on overall events and brings speakers back to the present.	Evaluation of whole story *(I didn't get my card; I didn't get my money)*. Response expressing speaker's attitude *(Oh, great)*. Return to present *(It's all right, darling; I'll lend you a dollar)*.

patterns of vocabulary and grammar (lexico-grammatical patterns) choices made by the speakers as the text unfolds.

The examples above have focused on interactional (or casual) conversation. Spoken genre analysis has also been applied to transactional talk, as the quote from Martin earlier in this chapter suggests. In the following example, a patient is confirming a doctor's appointment with a receptionist. In this example, the stages of the genre have been inserted to show how the interaction unfolds:

Identification
R: Doctor's rooms, can you hold the line for a minute?
P: Yes.
T: Thanks.
(Pause while patient waits for receptionist.)

R: Hello, Bonita speaking.

P: Hello.

R: Sorry to keep you waiting . . .

P: That's all right. It's Sara Morris here.

Request for information

P: I made an appointment for Dr. Hardy next week, and I just wanted to check the time.

R: Right.

P: I forgot to write it down. You told me to call back to check she was in that day.

Response

R: Right, I see what you mean. We weren't sure . . . er, I've just got to check through . . . er, first October, Margaret, Margaret, er, here she is.

P: Oh, good.

R: Yes, 9:30, Sara.

P: OK, fine, thanks.

Closing

R: Good. See you then, Sara.

P: Thanks.

R: Thanks, bye.

P: Bye. Thanks a lot.

(Author's data.)

Try it

For each of the stages above, identify some of the linguistic patterns. Look for components such as openings, key vocabulary, verb tenses, ellipsis, feedback strategies, and closings.

Having an insight into the generic structure of commonly used spoken genres and the grammatical patterns that characterize them allows teachers to begin to plan activities to strengthen learners' speaking skills. Teachers can sensitize learners to the typical stages of various spoken genres and help them practice the key vocabulary needed. Teachers can also help learners think about appropriate strategies, such as recognizing when to take turns and using feedback expressions that keep the interaction flowing. This approach provides a useful alternative to simply rehearsing the kind of introspected dialogue frequently found in coursebook material, as it begins to introduce learners to features more typical of natural speech (Burns, Joyce & Gollin 1996).

The contribution of corpus linguistics

Before we leave this chapter, we need to discuss briefly the contribution made to spoken (and written) discourse analysis by advances in corpus linguistics. Over the last 50 years or so, developments in technology have made it much easier for linguists to collect and analyze large amounts of spoken, as well as written, text. A corpus (from the Latin term meaning body) is "a principled collection of texts available for *qualitative* and *quantitative* analysis" (O'Keeffe, McCarthy & Carter 2007: 1). Using computer software tools, analysts have been able to look at such features as word frequency and how language chunks or collocates to express various meanings (concordances). There are many different types of corpora, which have contributed powerfully to revealing how language is actually used in different contexts. Linguists who build corpora take care to look at how well the contexts they are interested in are represented across the texts included. Traditionally, written corpora have been more common, as written texts were easier to collect. Examples of well-known corpora (the term used for the plural of corpus) that have been developed to analyze large amounts of text include the Cambridge English Corpus (CEC), the Cambridge and Nottingham Corpus of Discourse in English (CANCODE), the Collins Birmingham University International Language Database (COBUILD), and the Brown Corpus and the Michigan Corpus of Academic Spoken English (MICASE).

A core tool in corpus linguistics, and one that has proved to be very useful for language teaching, is concordancing. Concordancing, now performed by high-speed computer analysis "allows for every occurrence of a particular word or phrase" (O'Keeffe et al. 2007: 4) to be identified rapidly through a computer search. The focus word or phrase is the "node" that is presented as a Key-Word-In-Context (KWIC) display, which is accompanied by several words placed on either side of it. Below is an example of a concordance using the search word *worry*.

```
            Opponents of the Bill worry it will mostly benefit affluent pare:
    And of course, the more you worry about it the more it starts er <$E> :
:arry one in the pickup, uh, and I worry about it being stolen.
1 as the business needs it and not worry about the kinds of ups and downs on '
                    The thing I worry about- it isn't that I lose sleep ov
            However, you always worry this, you know, balance, - balance t!
: is also an external agenda and I worry he might concentrate so much on the
        But some africans worry that A shift from aid to trade won't
:er of the United Nations that you worry about it.
                    'They worry about health and safety issues or th
1 member of Parliament people also worry about giving up a good thing.
            and not even worry about it.
        But many historians here worry that in all the excitement, evidence
day you celebrate, and inside you worry because you know the day before it w
and a growing number of Americans worry will be a time of widespread shortag
:he fat cat money managers that we worry about are managing the average perso:
            Still, many worry about long-term consequences should :
: didn't have to <$E>laughter</$E> worry about that before.
1 ex tax inspector you go away and worry about your income tax over the weeke:
            <$3>I really worry?
/ defective, causing confusion and worry for the captains.
            What I worry about is this: the A.n.c.
                    worry cos I 'll look
    so I don't have to, you know, worry about it one way of the other and I
            Some however, worry the longer these unarmed internation:
)rogram which many young Americans worry will be bankrupt by the time they re:
            parents worry it's not enough to stop millions of
            "Then you worry about spontaneous detonation," Smith
```

Figure 5.2: Concordance with search word *worry* (Cambridge English Corpus © Cambridge University Press, extract reproduced with permission).

Try it

Examine the concordance above. What patterns of use can you identify for the word *worry* (e.g., What is the most common grammatical use of this word)? What stands out as the most common word that accompanies *worry*?

The value of a concordance such as this one is that it can create a "lexico-grammatical profile" (O'Keeffe, et al. 2007: 14) of the node, which can tell teachers a great deal about how a word or phrase is typically used in its natural context. By examining a node, one can analyze:

- Collocations: words or chunks that go together or collocate (e.g., *made an appointment*, in the doctor's example earlier in the chapter).
- Idioms / chunks: formulas where words occur as pre-formed chunks (e.g., *this, that, and the other*).

- Grammatical restrictions: restrictions on what words can go together grammatically (e.g., *worry **about*** in the example above, rather than *worry **to*** or *worry **of***).
- Meaning restrictions: restrictions on what words go together (e.g., *excellent* is not generally used with *hair* or with *very*).

Corpus linguists have analyzed corpora in two main ways. One important approach has been quantitative analyses that allow for counts of word frequency. In this way, it is possible to see the most frequently used words across a large corpus of spoken texts. For example, in the Limerick Corpus of Irish English (LCIE), a database of 40,000 words of female friends chatting showed that the ten most common words in order of frequency were *I, and, the, to, was, you, it, like, that*, and *he* (O'Keeffe, McCarthy & Carter 2007: 11). Interestingly, this list reflects what we noted in Chapter 4 – that pronoun references *(I, he, you*, and so on), additive conjunctions *(and)*, and deictic references *(that, it)* are common in spoken language because, in casual conversations, speakers frequently make reference to people and things in the immediate context without specifically naming them, and the number of content words tends to be low.

More qualitatively, another way in which a corpus can be used is to find key words (Scott 1999) in one or more texts on a similar topic. This means that the words that are "key" – that is, the most frequent or salient in those particular texts, can be identified, For example, in spoken language in a particular discipline area, say law or medicine, it is possible to find the words that have the most "keyness" in relation to particular topics. There are important implications here for language teaching, especially in the areas of English for Academic or Specific Purposes (e.g., business English, English for accountants, engineers, airline pilots, and so on), as the lexical items that are the most important for these learners to acquire can then be highlighted in teaching activities, materials development, or the creation of specialized dictionaries. One interesting and practical example of how a corpus can be used for key words is Coxhead (2000). She produced an Academic Word List (AWL) from a 3.5 million-word corpus using written academic texts (journals, textbooks, and coursebooks) in 28 subject areas, grouped into four major disciplines (arts, science, commerce, and law). She then produced 57 word families, which made up around 10 percent of the total corpus, thereby offering academic writers a sense of the main patterning of vocabulary in academic writing.

Corpus analysis can also show what words tend to cluster together into "chunks," such as *a lot of* or *I see what you mean* (as in the doctor appointment example above), and how frequently these chunks occur in certain kinds of interactions. This type of analysis is again extremely useful for language-teaching purposes as it can highlight what chunks, or formulaic expressions, teachers should really spend time focusing on in relation to certain kinds of contexts of spoken language use.

Corpus linguistics has had a huge impact on the analysis of both spoken and written language over the last decade, and its implications for language teaching are slowly beginning to permeate methodologies and materials, although these implications are still by no means widely acknowledged. It would seem clear, however, that work in corpus linguistics will be a very important tool for future pedagogical developments and will be particularly useful for the teaching of speaking. Work in this field means that materials writers and teachers will no longer have to rely on their assumptions and intuitions about what speakers say. Because large amounts of spoken language can be analyzed to show what English speakers, both native and non-native, *actually* say, materials and tasks developed with insights from a corpus will become more authentic and will be able to illustrate, for teachers and learners alike, spoken language as it is really used.

Think about it

How do you see insights from corpus linguistics being relevant for your own teaching context? Discuss your ideas with a colleague.

Summary

This chapter examined some of the discourse features and strategies of spoken language, focusing particularly on adjacency pairs, turn taking, topic management, conversational openings and closings, and listener feedback, or backchanneling. We have also looked at the notion of genres of speaking and considered some of the main types of genres in interactional and transactional interactions. Finally, we discussed briefly the contribution that corpus linguistics is making to our knowledge of the lexico-grammatical features of spoken texts. It is clear that being able to use some of the basic tools offered by these theoretical insights is invaluable for teachers. Teachers who can develop an understanding of spoken genres, and their discourse characteristics and features, are better equipped to meet the challenges of teaching their learners the speaking skills they really need.

Below, we summarize the implications of this chapter for teaching spoken language:

1. Consider how language is structured in different social contexts. Teachers can identify the kinds of social contexts in which learners will need to engage and, therefore, delineate more clearly what kinds of genres should be taught for those contexts.

2. Indentify what genres are implied in the language you are required to cover in the syllabus or coursebook. Are learners required, for example, to tell a story (narrative), to say what they did over the weekend (recount), or to tell about some unusual event that happened (anecdote)? Typically, coursebooks do not provide this kind of information, but simply require students to "speak" about a particular topic or situation. By considering the genre or text type implied in such tasks, teachers can assist students in understanding the stages and the typical discourse and lexico-grammatical patterns of the genre. Scripted coursebook material can be supplemented or extended by more natural examples so that students are exposed to more realistic spoken language.

3. Give students opportunities to practice the key discourse features of natural spoken language. For example, get them to practice recognizing when they can take or give a turn, initiate a new topic, open or close an interaction, and give feedback using appropriate utterances.

4. Introduce students to the idea of concordances. There are several websites that provide data from corpora and also show activities that can be used with students. Have students look for patterns of language use for different vocabulary items, collocations, or spoken expressions they have just heard or find puzzling. Get them to deduce the rule for using such items, and discuss with them how they could use these items in developing their own speaking skills.

Group-learning tasks

1. Consider the genre stages and the language patterns shown below for the recount told by Gillian in this chapter. With your colleagues, brainstorm some activities that you could develop with your students to draw their attention to these stages and patterns. Add ideas for activities to the table below. An example is given for the first stage.

Generic stage	Language features and patterns	Activities
(Abstract) Signals the story is about to begin and establishes the point of the story.	Generalized *you* (to show general relevance of story). Attitudinal vocabulary *(unbelievable* – to show point of story).	1. Have students brainstorm ways of introducing story topics, either individually, if they are in classes where they do not share a common L1, or in small groups, if they do share a common L1. 2. Get them to explain these expressions to the class in English. 3. Introduce students to similar and / or other introductions used to initiate stories in English.
Orientation Orients listeners to events *(who, what, why, where, when).*	References to specific people involved *(I).* References to place / time *(at my bank, down there, today).*	
Record of events Outlines events in sequence with ongoing evaluations.	Use of nouns / pronouns for participants *(businessman, a little old lady, she, I).* Events sequenced in time *(finally).* Past tense state-of-being verbs *(was).* Past tense action verbs *(put, keyed, picked up).* Past in present and reported speech for dramatic effect *(Every other person there **is** a businessman; There**'s** just me and the little old lady).* Listener-engaged feedback *(Oh, no)* and non-committal feedback *(Oh, right).*	
(Coda) Comments on overall events and brings speakers back to the present.	Evaluation of whole story *(I didn't get my card . . . I didn't get my money).* Response expressing speaker's attitude *(Oh, great).* Return to present *(It's all right, darling; I'll lend you a dollar).*	

2. Try out some of your activities in your classroom. If possible, ask one of your colleagues to observe what happens when you try the activities. In return, observe your colleague trying out similar activities in his or her classroom. When both lessons are completed, get together and discuss your respective observations. You could use the questions below to start off your discussions.   ·

   a. How did the students react to the activities? How well were they able to complete them? Did they have difficulties with any parts of the activities?

   b. What changes would you make to a) the activities themselves; b) the steps in the activities; c) the language features you asked the students to practice?

3. Work with your colleagues to collect short samples of natural conversation. Bring your samples to a group meeting, and work to identify a) what genre the samples reflect; b) the stages that unfold in the interaction; c) the key vocabulary used; d) the types of turns the speakers take; e) who gets to speak; f) what kind of feedback the listeners give.

4. If you are unable to record actual samples outside the classroom, note down expressions or brief interactions you hear around you (e.g., openings and closings, what people say to give feedback, or how they take turns). Use these illustrations to demonstrate different features of spoken interaction to your students. Get the students to listen for these features themselves, and bring examples of what they hear to class to discuss with you and the other students.

Further reading

Burns, A. (2001) Analysing spoken discourse: implications for TESOL, In A. Burns and C. Coffin (eds.), *Analysing English in its Social Context*, London: Routledge, 123–148.

McCarthy, M., Matthiessen, C., and Slade, D., Discourse analysis, In N. Schmitt (ed.) *An Introduction to Applied Linguistics*, London: Hodder, 53–69.

Reppen, R. (2010) *Using Corpora in the Language Classroom*, Cambridge: Cambridge University Press.

Wong, J. and Waring, H.Z. (2010) *Conversational Analysis and Second Language Pedagogy*, New York: Routledge.

PART III
DESIGNS AND APPROACHES

6 *A methodological framework*

As many language teachers know, setting up contexts for learners to speak in class is not the same as *teaching* them to speak in a second language. Teaching is a principled and systematic activity. To teach speaking effectively, teachers require a set of theoretical and pedagogical principles that can be applied to the planning and delivery of lessons on speaking. Drawing on insights from theoretical principles about speaking and spoken discourse discussed earlier, this chapter presents a set of principles in the form of a methodological framework for teaching speaking. The chapter seeks to address two questions:

1. What are some of the common approaches to teaching speaking? What are some limitations of these approaches?
2. What theoretical and pedagogical principles are needed to adopt a holistic approach to teaching speaking?

In answering the questions, the following topics are addressed:

- A review of approaches to teaching speaking.
- Presentation of a methodological framework.

Introduction

To speak effectively in a second language, learners have to combine relevant knowledge about language and discourse with speaking skills (see Chapter 3) to produce fluent and accurate output in a variety of communicative situations. This is a challenge for most language learners because they will not have achieved sufficient automatization of knowledge and skills. More critically, working under the constraints of limited time and cognitive capacities, learners encounter numerous obstacles as they attempt to bring their linguistic knowledge and speaking skills to a task. As a result, their language may be inaccurate and their message incomplete. Fortunately, there is much that teachers can do to help language learners improve their speaking competence.

In this book, we offer a framework by which teachers can provide a holistic learning environment where learners not only practice speaking through engaging classroom activities, but also learn about the nature of speaking in a second language and ways they can manage their own speaking development. The aim of this chapter, and the next one, is to present principles by which this type of holistic learning experience can be created, as well as ideas for implementing it. Before going further into the framework, it would be useful to review, briefly, various approaches that have been used for teaching speaking to second language learners.

Approaches to teaching speaking: a review

According to Burns (1998), approaches for teaching speaking can be divided into those that focus directly on developing isolated speaking skills and those that focus on the production of speech during communicative activities. Following Richards (1992), she referred to these approaches as direct / controlled and indirect / transfer respectively (see Table 6.1).

A direct or controlled approach is concerned with structural accuracy and emphasizes practice of language forms, such as pronunciation of the sounds in English. Such an approach also aims to raise learners' awareness about the grammar of the target language, as well as discourse structures and routines. An indirect or transfer approach, on the other hand, is concerned with fluency of speech. It engages learners in functional language use by getting them to talk with other students in class. Teachers typically plan activities to fit common situations in which the learners need to use spoken

Table 6.1: *Approaches and activities for teaching speaking*

	Direct (controlled)	**Indirect (transfer)**
Aim	Develop enabling skills.	Develop interaction strategies.
Focus	Accuracy. Language analysis.	Fluency. Language for communication.
Characteristics	Controlled language use. Skill getting. Pedagogic. Pre-communicative. Part-task practice.	"Authentic" / functional language use. Skill using. Real life. Communicative. Whole-task practice.
Activities	Drills. Pattern practice. Structure manipulation. Language awareness. Consciousness raising.	Discussions. Information gaps. Project work. Role plays. Simulations. Talking circles.
Interaction	Teacher led.	Learner centered.

(Based on Burns 1998: 103–105.)

English. The assumption here is that learners will somehow transfer the speaking skills developed through such communicative activities to real-life situations.

There are limitations in both of these approaches. As Burns (1998) points out, neither of them effectively supports all the processes of second language speaking development. For example, although the direct approach focuses on the development of language form, it does not take into consideration the fact that the accurate use of grammatical resources is often developed through face-to-face communication, particularly in situations where negotiation for meaning is necessary. Controlled language use in speaking classes also cannot account for the development of language complexity. Similarly, as Bygate (2001) observes, the indirect approach gives so much currency to the development of "fluency" through spontaneous talk that a focus on language elements and discourse structures is often neglected. He also notes that the existing approaches do not help learners develop the discourse skills they need for participating in real-world interactions. The approaches outlined here show that the teaching of speaking has been mainly dichotomous, separated from authentic interactions by the emphasis on learning of language form or language use.

The influence of different teaching approaches can be seen in the published materials that language teachers use. In fact, for most language teachers, the approach they adopt is often determined by which coursebook their language programs use. But just as there are limitations within the main approaches, published materials have additional limitations. According to Burns (1998) and McCarthy and O'Keefe (2004), the limitations include:

- Problems with teaching certain speech acts (i.e., using language to accomplish specific communicative purposes and functions).
- Insufficient emphasis on teaching communication strategies.
- A lack of authenticity in the models of speech:
  - Scripted dialogues that do not reflect the fluidity of spoken interaction.
  - Inadequate teaching of formulaic expressions or patterns of language common in speech.
  - Neglect of the grammatical and discourse features of spoken language.

Some experts have, in fact, proposed combining direct practice of language items with indirect practice of communication skills. Littlewood's (1992) methodological framework is an example of such an approach, where a balance between language knowledge and language use is recommended. The framework is underpinned by a theory of "language as a structural system, but one whose primary function is to enable communication to take

Table 6.2: *Part-skill and whole-task practice*

	Learning activities	Characteristics
Part-skill practice	Pre-communication task. Language work.	Controlled, predictable.
Part-skill practice / Whole-task practice	Communicative language practice. Structured communication task.	Variation in degree of control and predictability.
Whole-task practice	Authentic communication task.	Flexible, less predictable.

place" (1992: 8). Pre-communicative task language work is used as a basis for subsequent communicative language practice and eventual free and authentic communication. Table 6.2 shows the type of activities that offer part-skill (direct) practice activities and whole-task (indirect) practice or transfer practice activities. Littlewood notes that some language-learning activities do not fall neatly into either "part-skill" or "whole-task" practice. Simple communicative activities, for example, describing a picture for someone to reproduce, may require learners to exchange messages where the language and content are controlled and predictable. Other activities that require greater interaction may mean that learners produce less predictable language and content, but still within the context of structured communication for classroom learning.

Another approach that combined controlled and transfer activities was proposed by Bygate (1987). He adopted a mainly direct (transfer) approach, but enhanced it by integrating language accuracy, discourse skills, and small group interaction in the teaching of speaking. In particular, he stressed the importance of interaction management and meaning negotiation skills taught in tandem with communicative oral-language practice. A great deal of attention was given to the uses of different types of group work. In connection with interaction skills, Bygate also highlighted the role of communication strategies. He did not, however, present ways of conducting strategy training in the context of teaching speaking.

There is another limitation associated with direct and indirect approaches. They do not directly enable learners to produce spoken discourse that is socially and interpersonally appropriate, and grammatically accurate. Research on spoken English and discourse that emerged in the 1990s provided empirical evidence for differences between spoken and written language (Carter 1995; Carter & McCarthy 1997) and showed that oral communication was a socioculturally situated activity, where each event or genre has predictable discourse patterns and structures (Martin 1992). (See Chapters 4 and 5.) Although findings about lexico-grammatical and discourse features of speech had clear implications for teaching speaking, these findings have not been reflected in teaching approaches until recently.

The relevance of a discourse perspective was highlighted through the work of Burns and her colleagues (Burns 1998; Burns, Joyce & Gollin 1996; Burns & Joyce 1997). Teaching speaking shifted "from regarding the constituent forms of language as primary, to thinking about language from the perspective of larger textual units" (Burns 1998: 107). In this new approach, teachers involve learners in exploring naturalistic data from native speakers' spoken discourse, in order to raise their awareness about register, or the way language is used in an interaction according to the situation, the participants, the topic, and the location. The learning of grammar is also assumed to be closely connected with its function in constructing the various types of discourse. For example, the teaching of imperative forms takes place in texts on procedures (or instructions, such as recipes), while modality (expression of attitude, intention, and possibility) is explored in the context of presenting an argument or opinion. Through language-analysis tasks, learners can develop their metalinguistic knowledge about form-function relationships at the textual level, and improve their knowledge of the social process of oral communication (see also Riggenbach 1999).

More recently, Thornbury (2005) advocated a general approach to skill development for the teaching of second language speaking. The approach consists of three stages: awareness raising, appropriation, and autonomy. Awareness-raising activities aim at helping learners uncover gaps in their own knowledge about speaking. Appropriation activities, Thornbury argues, go beyond controlled practice or restructuring of knowledge for speaking. These activities aim to develop "practiced control," where learners demonstrate "progressive control" or "self-regulation" of a skill (Thornbury 2005: 63). The activities recommended for the appropriation stage consist of a mixture of activities listed within the direct and indirect approaches that Burns (1998) presented above. The third stage of the general approach requires learners to engage in activities that demonstrate a degree of autonomy in and outside the classroom.

As shown in the works of the above authors, there is merit in integrating features of direct and indirect approaches. In reality, however, the approaches remain mainly isolated from each other in most classrooms. A survey of some current coursebooks will show that one of these perspectives tends to dominate the materials. Furthermore, while there is a great deal of emphasis on the doing and the outcome of an activity, insufficient attention is paid to learners' cognitive and affective processes in learning to speak a second language. In addition to these limitations, the pedagogical procedures in some coursebooks do not seem to be supported by any recognizable theoretical principles. Each unit or chapter is typically a series of activities linked together by a common theme. In some general English coursebooks, speaking activities receive even less attention. When they are included, the speaking activities are often meant to prepare learners for a main language-learning activity. For example, learners may be asked to discuss ideas related to a theme as a pre-writing activity, after which the ideas are used to produce a piece of writing. What is needed, therefore, is a holistic and comprehensive approach that reflects a more inclusive understanding about language, language learners, language learning, and speaking. Such an approach should be one that teachers can easily understand and translate into a systematic procedure for teaching speaking. In the next section, we present a methodological framework for implementing such an approach.

Think about it

Examine a coursebook on teaching speaking skills or the speaking practice / activities sections in a general language coursebook. Does the book reflect predominantly a direct (controlled) or indirect (transfer) approach to teaching speaking? What evidence is there to support your observations? If your materials do not fall neatly into one of these categories, comment on the way speaking is approached.

Establishing a methodological framework

In Chapter 3, we discussed the knowledge and skills that language learners need to develop to achieve speaking competence. They must use appropriate speech-enabling skills while, at the same time, produce language that is intelligible and fluent. In order to communicate their meaning more precisely, learners must also master more complex structures of the target language that are important for speaking. For example, simple utterances can be strung together through coordination (use of *and* and *but*), subordination (e.g., "*When you see her*, you'll know what I mean") and embedding (e.g., "The guy *who's wearing dark sunglasses* is his bodyguard"). They also have to use appropriate communication strategies to ensure that they can continue participating in an interaction, even when there are problems. To speak effectively in a second language, learners have to do several, or all, of these things concurrently. This is not something that can be achieved over a short period of time. Nevertheless, teachers can provide the opportunities and support in the classroom and outside it to facilitate development of

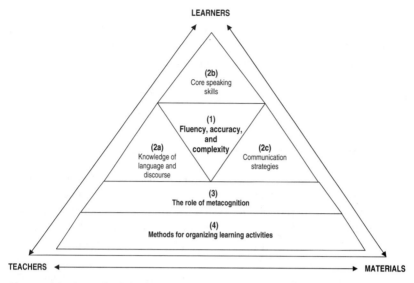

Figure 6.1: A methodological framework for a holistic approach to teaching speaking.

these concurrent skills. The methodological framework proposed for doing this is presented in Figure 6.1.

Based on the concept of "design" in teaching methodology (Richards & Rogers 1986), the methodological framework for teaching speaking shown in Figure 6.1 above identifies key considerations for determining aims and objectives, organizing course or lesson components, and clarifying four important dimensions related to language teaching as follows:

1. Quality of speech: fluency, accuracy, and complexity (see Chapter 2).
2. Components of speaking competence: knowledge of language and discourse, core speaking skills, and communication strategies (see Chapters 3, 4, and 5).
3. The role of metacognition.
4. Methods for organizing learning activities.

Dimension 1, quality of speech: fluency, accuracy, and complexity, is the desired outcome of teaching and learning and holds a central position in the methodological framework. Dimension 2 refers to three aspects of speaking competence presented as three interconnected triangles. These are a) knowledge about language and discourse, b) speech enabling skills, and c) communication strategies. Dimension 3 concerns the role of metacognition, or thinking about thinking / learning in a learner's speaking development.

These three dimensions focus on language learners and underscore the important place learners occupy in the conceptualization of any teaching activities or curricula for speaking. The three dimensions are, in turn, supported by the fourth and last dimension, which pertains to the role of the teacher and materials. The four dimensions, and the interaction between teachers, learners, and materials, provide the conceptual foundation for all teaching and learning activities in the speaking classroom.

Dimension 1: Fluency, accuracy, and complexity

Fluency, accuracy, and complexity – features of learner speech production – are the outcomes of learning (see Chapter 2). These outcomes occupy a central position in the methodological framework. Fluency should be the target for beginning learners and should continue to be the target as learners move towards more advanced stages in their language acquisition. Fluency is sometimes mistakenly thought to be the least challenging aspect of speaking development. If learners can express meaning with few pauses and hesitations, they are often considered to be fluent, even when they make many grammatical mistakes. In this sense of the word, fluency should be an attainable target in early stages of learning. While expressing meaning is one measurement of fluency, it is different from the type of fluency that native speakers or competent L2 speakers demonstrate. At these higher levels of proficiency, fluent speech demonstrates mastery of form-function relationships and is manifested in the accuracy and complexity of the language produced.

Speaking is a combinatorial skill; that is, an ability to do various things at the same time – attend to content, language and rules of use – all under the constraint of limited cognitive processing capacity (Johnson 1996). Greater fluency is achieved when learners process pronunciation and grammar automatically, thus allowing more attentional resources to be used for processing higher levels of communication, such as meaning, appropriateness, and other sociolinguistic concerns (Segalowitz 2003). Achieving the fluency of a competent speaker is the ultimate goal for many second language learners.

Dimension 2: Components of speaking competence

Second language speaking competence comprises knowledge of language and discourse, core speaking skills and communication strategies (see Chapters 3, 4, and 5 again). These are presented in Figure 6.1 as three interconnected triangles that form the main speaking-competence triangle.

The three small triangles (labeled 2a, 2b, and 2c) surround the fluency, accuracy, and complexity triangle (Triangle 1) and are in touch with one another, indicating that the features are all interrelated. The main speaking-competence triangle rests on top of two other dimensions for teaching speaking (labeled 3 and 4).

Learning tasks should provide opportunities for learners to develop the different features of speaking competence, which will, in turn, support their overall speaking performance. Each type of speaking task demands a specific kind of linguistic knowledge about form, meaning, and use. For example, to tell a story, learners need to use verbs for describing events, action, people, and time. They must also know the typical structure of a narrative text (see Chapter 5) and learn how to adopt appropriate stress and intonation to communicate details in the story (see Chapter 4). Speaking tasks also require learners to use specific kinds of speaking skills (see Chapter 3). Teachers should identify the skills as learning objectives and select suitable techniques for developing the skills in the learners. In addition, learners should learn to use communication and discourse strategies where appropriate, for example, when they experience a gap in their vocabulary knowledge, or when they do not understand what they hear and cannot continue the conversation.

Dimension 3: The role of metacognition

The methodological framework acknowledges the importance of metacognition in learning to speak in a second language. Metacognition, or thinking about one's thinking, is an important cognitive process that can be developed through instruction. It foregrounds the role of learners in developing introspective awareness and control of their learning processes and plays a key role in the success of language learning (Wenden 1998; Chamot 2005). Metacognition enables learners to reflect on the process of their learning to speak a second language, as well as enabling them to manage their own performance, emotions, and language development. It comprises three types of knowledge: person, task, and strategy (Flavell 1976; Wenden 2001).

Besides manifesting itself as self-knowledge about learning, metacognition also has an executive function. It enables learners to control and manipulate the way they think and act through three cognitive self-management processes. These are planning, monitoring, and evaluating. Language learners who are metacognitively aware are self-directed and can better take charge their own learning processes (Wenden 1991, 2001). An important part of speaking instruction should, therefore, be in the form of raising learners' metacognitive awareness through introspection and guided self-directed learning. Learners should be encouraged to plan, monitor, and evaluate their speaking development. They should also develop greater knowledge about themselves as second language speakers, and greater understanding of the demands of various speaking tasks and effective strategy use, as identified in the table above. Learners who are aware of useful strategies for developing their speaking abilities are also more likely to use these strategies.

In the speaking classroom, teachers can help learners become aware of their own learning and communication processes by engaging them in dialogues about their experiences, knowledge, and strategies. Together, learners can co-construct further understanding of how to become better L2 speakers. In addition, learners also need to develop effective communication strategies to overcome gaps in their language and to enhance the way they convey their message. We should, therefore, set aside specific time to help learners reflect on their learning, as well as help them learn to use strategies relevant to various speaking tasks. These ideas are elaborated upon in Chapter 11.

Dimension 4: Methods for organizing classroom-learning activities

The fourth and last dimension of the methodological framework shows how learning activities can be organized and forms the base of the large triangle. It draws on principles of task-based learning, part / whole practice, and planning and repetition, and applies these principles to language learning activities for speaking.

TASK-BASED LEARNING

The communicative methodology has been widely adopted in language teaching, and one interpretation of it is found in task-based learning. Skehan (1998b: 268) describes task-based learning as "the way meaning is brought into prominence by emphasis on goals and activities"). Willis (1996, 2005) has characterized task-based learning as follows:

- A task is an activity in which the target language is used for a communicative purpose, in order to achieve an outcome.
- The principal focus of tasks is on exchanging and understanding meaning.
- The outcome of the task can be shared with other learners.
- A focus on grammatical forms comes after the task has been completed.

What are the benefits of task-based learning? According to Candlin (1987), tasks engage learners on both cognitive and affective levels because they:

- Encourage learners to attend to meaning and to purposeful language use.
- Give learners flexibility in resolving problems their own way, calling on their own choice of strategies and skills.
- Involve learners whose personalities and attitudes become central.
- Make learning challenging, yet not excessively demanding.
- Raise learners' awareness of the processes of language use, by encouraging them to reflect on their own language use.

The framework proposed in this book reflects the following principles with respect to using tasks for speaking:

- Increase the frequency of whole-task practice.
- Complement whole-task practice with learning activities that focus on linguistic knowledge and core speaking skills.
- Conduct language-focused and skill-focused activities at appropriate stages of a teaching and learning sequence; hence, not limiting them to the post-task stage, as suggested by Willis (1996).

In Willis's task framework, there is a language-focus activity after the communicative task. In doing the communicative task first, Willis argues, learners would have noticed the gap in their knowledge and would, therefore, realize the need to learn the related forms. In our framework for teaching speaking, the flexible positioning of the language- and skill-focused activities maximizes opportunities for learners to attend to, or notice, important components of language and skills (Schmidt 1990). This flexibility also helps to minimize the cognitive demands learners face during speech processing, thus lowering their stress and anxiety. Moreover, through various metacognitive activities, teachers can help learners become aware of their need for language and skills before a task.

Think about it

Examine the speaking activities used in three consecutive chapters or units in a language course book. How are the activities organized? You can draw a diagram to illustrate the organization if that helps.

PART-SKILL / LANGUAGE LEARNING AND WHOLE-TASK PRACTICE

Language use is a complex cognitive skill. It consists of smaller parts of knowledge, sub-skills, and strategies, all operating simultaneously and interdependently to achieve communicative goals (Johnson 2005). Like all complex skills, the ability to use oral language for communication improves when more of the cognitive processes underlying the use and the combination of various sub-skills are automatized. There are benefits, therefore, in teaching some skills and language items separately, rather than altogether, as a whole, in the hope that learners will "pick up" some of these skills or language. Johnson (2005) noted that it is necessary and feasible to divide complex skills into smaller parts, and this is true of speaking, which comprises many different enabling skills.

Clearly, part-skill practice has a role, and it can be used before or after whole-task or free practice. The "parts" in speaking, however, are not limited to just core speaking skills, but include grammar, vocabulary items, and discourse knowledge. "Part" practice refers to activities where learners' attention is focused on one or more of these areas. We do not recommend, however, including too many areas in one lesson. "Whole-task" practice refers to activities that encourage learners to express meaning in communicative contexts. These are typically speaking tasks we conduct to help learners develop their fluency early on. We will discuss these points further in Chapter 9.

The methodological framework that Littlewood (1992) proposed is a good example of the usefulness of a part / whole approach to teaching and learning speaking. With regard to sequencing of learning activities, he appeared to value putting part-skill (controlled) practice before whole-task (free) practice. Nevertheless, he suggested that it might also be necessary to have whole-task practice preceding part practice. The framework proposed in this book advocates that learners complete whole-task practice at least once before they engage in part-skill practice. This is a feasible approach for communicative tasks involving pairs or small-group work. Nevertheless, in more complex types of tasks, such as oral presentations, narrative productions, and talks, an additional part-practice may be necessary before whole-task practice. There are at least five ways in which part /whole practice can be sequenced in speaking lessons. See Figure 6.2.

In language- and skill-focused activities, we should draw learners' attention to "parts" of oral language that are necessary for fluent and accurate execution of the speaking tasks. In addition, we need to help learners focus on selected speaking skills and help them analyze how these skills are used by competent speakers. This is a vital aspect of teaching speaking.

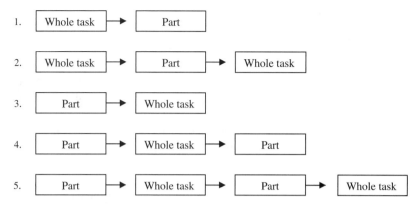

Figure 6.2: Possible sequences of part-skill / language and whole-task practice for teaching speaking.

Many language learners do not have the benefit of sustained periods of communicating with expert speakers, where they can notice language, receive input and feedback, negotiate meaning, and produce modified output. This focus on directed-attention is based on the theory of language learning as a cognitive skill (Johnson 1996; Skehan 1998a), where noticing language is an important part of that process.

PLANNING AND REPETITION

Speaking processes can create a tremendous amount of cognitive load, not to mention stress and anxiety, for language learners. Some learners may experience these negative and often debilitating emotions even when engaged in routine classroom tasks. It has been reported that by modifying the way tasks were normally conducted in a speaking class, teachers were able to indirectly help learners increase the complexity in their oral language, and improve fluency and the quality of content (Bygate 2001; Foster & Skehan 1996). In this section, we will discuss the role of pre-task planning and task repetition for developing speaking.

Pre-task planning

The quality of the language and skills that learners demonstrate during speaking activities is heavily influenced by the cognitive constraints that the learners face. Low-proficiency learners may speak haltingly, producing short utterances with little content. When they attempt to include richer ideas in their speech, their utterances may be grammatically inaccurate. If we compare this type of production with producing writing, it is often the case that in writing, learners first have the benefit of discussing their ideas with classmates or a teacher. They can also try out different ways of writing down their meaning. In speaking, however, pressure or lack of time and the transient nature of speech is invariably a challenge for most learners.

It seems reasonable to infer from this comparison between writing and speaking that when learners have more planning time, they should be able to perform better in a speaking task. Not only would they speak with fewer hesitations, but given time to conceptualize and formulate their messages, they would also incorporate more accurate language forms of the target language. Studies have shown that pre-task time for strategic planning has an effect on all three dimensions of fluency, accuracy, and complexity in learners' speech production, but the results for accuracy have been mixed (Ellis 2005). On the whole, pre-task planning gives learners the "mental space" to pay attention to language form when expressing their meaning, and has clear, positive effects on fluency and complexity (Foster & Skehan 1996; Ortega 1999, 2005). According to Skehan (1998), pre-task strategic planning can have the following effects on some learners' oral language performance:

- Improved complexity in selected tasks.
- More complex content as a result of deeper interpretation of task demands.
- More experimentation with complex or new forms to express complex ideas.
- Better monitoring during task performance.
- Greater fluency.

For teachers, it is important to recognize that pre-task planning is aimed at decreasing the cognitive load that language learners face when they need to attend concurrently to form and meaning, thereby freeing their attentional resources for improving their overall performance. This improvement is more readily seen in the fluency and complexity of learners' speech, and less so in accuracy. Teachers may, therefore, find that it is necessary to include language-focused activities in speaking lessons, so as to encourage learners to notice the language that is needed for performing certain speaking tasks.

Discuss it

Do you usually plan what you will say when you have to speak in a second language? Describe occasions when planning was necessary. How did you use the planning time? Was it useful? Share your experiences with other colleagues. (If you do not speak a second language, interview colleagues who do.)

Task repetition

Task repetition is the repeated use of the same or a similar communication task with the same or different people (Bygate 2001). As a teaching procedure, task repetition exploits the benefits that are afforded by rehearsals of skills and presentation of knowledge. When learners are frequently exposed to similar tasks and contexts for carrying out a task, they become familiar with the demands and may perform better in each subsequent task. The improvement comes from the fact that they no longer need to pay attention to every detail of the task, and this can help prevent their cognitive resources from being overstretched.

As we have already mentioned elsewhere in this book, one problem with learning a second language is that the spoken language lacks permanence and is unpredictable. To provide some stability to the learning and use of oral language, teachers need to provide opportunities for learners to consolidate the linguistic knowledge and speaking skills they have been exposed to in each task. When they do the task the first time and repeat it a second time, the first performance acts as a rehearsal for the second. Rehearsal is related to the now widely accepted concept of schemata, or prior knowledge, which facilitates learning and memory (Rummelhart 1980). When learners repeat a task, they have, by then, developed some knowledge of the relevant language, content, and task routines for accomplishing it. By increasing the frequency of whole-task practice, we ensure that learners' skills at combining different components of their speaking competence can become increasingly automatized through each rehearsal.

When a task is repeated frequently, language learners' limited cognitive capacities are freed up for other more demanding aspects of the task. When learners find themselves repeatedly in similar communication situations, they will develop more and more prior knowledge about the structure of certain discourse types, or genres, as well as the vocabulary and grammar needed for accomplishing the tasks. Learners who repeated tasks, according to Bygate (2001), were also able to produce improved narrative structures. An interesting experiment by Lynch and McLean (2000) made use of a "poster carousel" task. Students stood by their posters and explained them to each "visitor" and, at the same time, answered questions. The recycling of language and content had a positive effect on the accuracy and fluency in their spoken performance. Repetitions of task have been shown to help learners develop:

• Greater fluency.
• More idiomatic and accurate speech.

- Better framing of narratives.
- Greater grammatical and lexical accuracy.
- Greater language complexity.

Discuss it

Have you ever asked your students, or witnessed a teacher asking students, to repeat a speaking activity that they have completed? If you have, what was the result? Were the students interested in repeating the task? Did they seem to improve in terms of language produced?

Summary

In this chapter we have proposed a methodological framework to offer a principled approach for developing language learners' speaking abilities in a holistic manner. The framework accounts for the overall desired outcome of speaking instruction, which is to help learners achieve fluency, accuracy, and complexity in their speaking performance. It foregrounds the components of speaking competence that must be developed to achieve this goal: linguistic knowledge, core speaking skills, and communication strategies. In addition, the framework highlights the important role that metacognition plays in language learning and points ahead to ways in which we can help learners develop metacognitive knowledge and skill in effective speaking. Finally, three principles for organizing learning activities are presented: part / whole practice, planning and rehearsal, and task-based learning. The framework also accounts for the roles played by the teacher, the learner, and the materials in ensuring the successful teaching of speaking. Based on this framework, we suggest the following pedagogical considerations, which will be discussed in detail in the next chapter:

a. Learners' speaking performance can be enhanced through pre-task planning and task repetition, which reduce cognitive load during speech processing. Activities that help learners develop metacognitive knowledge and self-management of their speaking and learning processes, as well as helping them know how to use communication strategies effectively, should also feature in the lessons.

b. Both part-practice activities and whole tasks are necessary to facilitate the automatization of various components of the complex skill of speaking. Speaking lessons should include opportunities to focus on grammar, vocabulary, and pronunciation at appropriate stages of a learning sequence.

Group-learning tasks

1. Select three different coursebooks published in the last 10–20 years for teaching second language speaking. Using Burns' (1998) categorization of teaching approaches, identify and comment on the dominant approach adopted by each book.

2. Select a speaking activity from the materials you have used, or from any published coursebooks.

   a. In a small group, explain to one another what theoretical and pedagogical principles might have influenced the way your selected activity was planned. Refer to specific aspects of the activity to substantiate your observations.

   b. Metacognition plays an important role in learning. Do the activities you have selected develop learners' metacognitive knowledge about learning to speak a second language? If you think they do, which dimensions of metacognitive knowledge does each activity focus on? Make relevant notes for each activity by referring specifically to the appropriate column(s) below:

	Person knowledge	Task knowledge	Strategy knowledge
Activity 1			
Activity 2			
Activity 3			

   c. When everyone has completed the grid above, compare the activities, and identify the activity that may be most or least effective for helping your learners develop their speaking abilities.

3. Observe a lesson on speaking, and examine the implicit assumptions that the teacher makes about teaching speaking and learning to speak. Evaluate the lesson and the tasks and materials used, based on your understanding about teaching speaking obtained from the chapters you have read in this book so far, including this one.

Further reading

Edwards, C. and Willis, J. (eds.) (2005) *Teachers Exploring Tasks in English Language Teaching*, Hampshire: Palgrave Macmillan.

Foster, P. and Skehan, P. (1996) The influence of planning on performance in task-based learning, *Studies in Second Language Acquisition*, 18, 299–324.

Johnson, K. (1996) *Language Teaching and Skill Learning*, Oxford: Blackwell.

7 A model for teaching speaking

Teaching speaking is a principled and systematic endeavor. This chapter shows how the principles embodied in the methodological framework are translated into a pedagogical model for classroom implementation. It will answer the following questions:

1. What kinds of activities provide learners with a holistic experience for developing their speaking?
2. How should these activities be sequenced, and what kinds of materials are needed?
3. How can teachers develop a series of lessons that focus on speaking?

The following topics are addressed:

- A teaching cycle for developing students' speaking.
- Steps for planning with the cycle.

Introduction

Many language teachers recognize the importance of speaking and take great pains in organizing activities for learners to practice their speaking. Many of these activities, however, do little more than set up contexts and opportunities for oral interaction. While learners spend more time talking with one another in the target language, they do not necessarily learn how to speak more effectively. One of the reasons is that, unlike the teaching of writing and reading skills, teachers are often not guided by any particular model for teaching speaking. As a result, learners develop their abilities in a random or incidental manner.

Based on what we have discussed in the earlier chapters, we propose that teachers should aim to help learners develop their speaking competence by encouraging them to do the following:

- Use a wide range of core speaking skills.
- Develop fluency in expression of meaning.
- Use grammar flexibly to produce a wide range of utterances that can express meaning precisely.

- Use appropriate vocabulary and accurate language forms relevant to their speaking needs.
- Understand and use social and linguistic conventions of speech for various contexts.
- Employ appropriate oral communication and discourse strategies.
- Increase their awareness of genre and genre structures.
- Increase their metacognitive awareness about L2 speaking.
- Manage and self-regulate their own speaking development.

In this chapter, we present a teaching cycle that can guide the planning and sequencing of learning activities to develop your students' speaking competence. We will also show how the cycle can be used for planning a series of speaking lessons or a unit of work that focuses on speaking. The principles specified in the methodological framework in the previous chapter are applied through the cycle so that the teaching and learning of speaking is made explicit to both teachers and learners.

Think about it

Select a chapter or a unit of work from a coursebook where speaking activities are used. Consider how these activities may or may not help learners develop their speaking in the ways highlighted in the bulleted points above.

A teaching cycle for developing students' speaking

Many speaking activities in the classroom are transient and occur as standalone or one-off activities. There is little overt attention paid to the process of learning about speaking, and the outcomes of the activities are not always documented. As a result, learners often may not understand or recall the purpose of a speaking activity, and are not able to say what it is that they have learned. Figure 7.1 shows how a series of learning activities are sequenced in the cycle. At each stage of the cycle, the teacher's role is crucial in facilitating practice and learning, and providing input and feedback. Collaboration and dialogue among peers are incorporated into various stages of the cycle so that learners not only benefit from working together, but also get many opportunities to speak.

Every stage in the teaching cycle supports the broad developmental objectives for speaking outlined in Table 7.1 on page 154. Some stages can support more than one objective, and the teacher can decide which objective

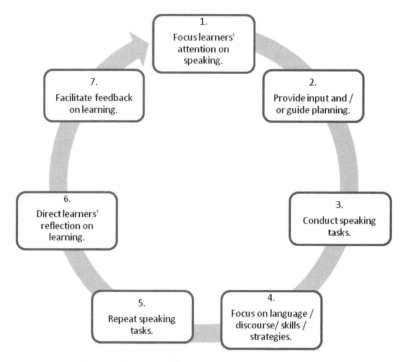

Figure 7.1: The teaching-speaking cycle.

is emphasized in a particular cycle by selecting or planning different learning activities. For example, Stage 4, which focuses learners' attention on features of the speaking task in Stage 3, can potentially help learners develop better control over language, skills, or strategies. It would not be practical or realistic, however, to address all of the objectives in one cycle, and so teachers should focus on just one of them. If the aim is to help learners acquire a particular communication strategy, for example, the use of feedback (see Chapter 5), learning activities that can contribute towards this objective can be planned for Stage 4.

Stage 1: Focus learners' attention on speaking

In this stage, the teacher raises learners' metacognitive awareness about learning to speak in a second language. The focus of these awareness-raising activities is one or more of three recognized types of metacognitive knowledge: namely, person knowledge, task knowledge, and strategic knowledge. Metacognitive activities at this stage can serve one of the two following purposes.

Table 7.1: *How the teaching-speaking cycle supports L2 speaking development*

Stages in the instructional cycle for L2 speaking development	Developmental objectives for speaking
1. Focus learners' attention on speaking.	• Develop metacognitive awareness about L2 speaking. • Self-regulate performance and overall development.
2. Provide input and / or guide planning.	• Acquire appropriate vocabulary and accurate language form relevant to speaking needs. • Understand social and linguistic conventions of speech and speakers' roles and relationships for particular contexts. • Produce a wide range of utterances to express meaning more exactly.
3. Conduct speaking tasks.	• Learn a range of core speaking skills. • Develop fluency in expression of meaning.
4. Focus on language / discourse / skills / strategies.	• Acquire appropriate vocabulary and accurate language form relevant to speaking needs. • Understand social and linguistic conventions of speech for particular contexts. • Learn a range of core speaking skills. • Employ appropriate oral-communication strategies.
5. Repeat speaking tasks.	• Learn a wide range of core speaking skills. • Produce a wide range of utterances to express meaning more precisely. • Develop fluency in expression of meaning. • Employ appropriate oral communication strategies.
6. Direct learners' reflection on learning.	• Self-regulate performance and overall development.
7. Facilitate feedback on learning.	• Develop metacognitive awareness about L2 speaking.

Thinking about your experiences in learning to speak a second language

It is important that you spend some time thinking about your own learning processes. It will help you to have better control over how you learn to speak in another language. You will also gradually become less dependent on your teacher. To help you get started, here are some simple questions. Write short responses to each one.

1. When and how did you learn to speak English?
2. What is your main reason for learning to speak English?
3. What did you like most about learning to speak English? Was there anything you did not like?
4. Do you feel nervous or anxious when you speak English?
5. What kind of learning activities do you like for your speaking lessons?
6. What would you like your teachers to do to help you speak better English?
7. What do you think you can do by yourself to improve your speaking ability?
8. If you are usually quiet in class, what can you do to participate more actively?
9. How would you describe your speaking ability right now?
10. Can you list three things about your speaking that you would like to improve?

Figure 7.2: A learner's self-observation sheet on speaking development.

ENCOURAGING LEARNERS TO PLAN FOR OVERALL SPEAKING DEVELOPMENT

The learners are given different types of prompts to encourage them to think about the demands of learning to speak in a second language and how they can prepare themselves for it. This is best done at the beginning of a course or a unit of learning. Figure 7.2 is an example of a practical task that can be used to encourage learners to plan for overall speaking development at the start of a course or program. Very low-level students could be allowed to answer these questions in their native language.

The questions in Figure 7.2 can also be modified to help learners manage any negative emotions before they prepare to approach a specific speaking task.

PREPARING LEARNERS TO APPROACH A SPECIFIC SPEAKING TASK

The prompts used for this purpose focus on the speaking task that has been planned for the teaching cycle. Through responding to the prompts, learners prepare themselves by familiarizing themselves with the outcomes of the task and by considering strategies they need to complete it. The prompts can also be used to activate learners' knowledge about the demands of the task. Figure 7.3 is an example of how teachers can activate learners' prior knowledge for a speaking task in order to facilitate conceptualization and formulation in speech production (see Chapter 3 again).

Thinking about the overall structure of a spoken text of genre

In the speaking task that you will be doing, you have to speak for about two minutes to your group members on one of the topics listed below. What would you say for each topic, and how would you organize your information differently for each one? Write out your points or ideas for each one clearly.

1. Explain the process of applying for a passport in your country.
2. Compare a place you like with another that you dislike.
3. Narrate your favorite childhood story.

Figure 7.3: Activating prior knowledge of genre for a speaking task.

Stage 1 may take anywhere from 10 minutes if completed individually, to 20–30 minutes if learners are asked to share their thoughts and observations with others. This stage could also be done before class as preparation for Stage 2 below, and other stages that will be conducted in class. For further discussions of activities for Stage 1, please refer to Chapter 11.

Stage 2: Provide input and / or guide planning

Speaking in a second language can create a great deal of anxiety for language learners. Some learners also experience cognitive overload as they try to attend to content and language demands when they speak. For these reasons, it is useful to include a stage where the learners can receive some support for the speaking task that they are about to do, or where they can be given time to plan what they are going to say and how they are going to say it. The purposes of this preparation stage include:

1. Introducing or teaching new language.
2. Increasing the chances for restructuring, or reorganizing, learners' developing linguistic knowledge.
3. Mobilizing, or activating, learners' relatively new linguistic knowledge.
4. Recycling, or reactivating, learners' specific language items for the task.
5. Easing learners' processing load by allowing them to clarify ideas and content for the task.
6. Pushing learners to interpret tasks in more demanding ways and use language to express more complex meanings.

(Skehan 1998a: 137–139.)

By including this stage before the actual speaking task, teachers can scaffold learners as they prepare to meet the demands of the speaking task. Maybin, Mercer, and Steirer (1992: 188) explain the concept of scaffolding as:

> Not just any assistance which helps [learners] accomplish a task. It is help which will enable [learners] to accomplish a task which they would not have been quite able to manage on their own, and it is help which is intended to bring [learners] closer to a state of competence which will enable them eventually to complete such a task on their own.

One type of scaffolding that can be used in speaking tasks is vocabulary support, which can reduce learners' cognitive load so that they can direct more attention to using their available grammatical resources for completing the task (Willis 1994). Other forms of support include content, or information, that learners need to complete a task effectively. For example, if a speaking task requires learners to talk about their favorite authors, teachers can give the learners some time to find out more about the authors by reading up about them in the library or by consulting Internet sources. Learning more about factual details needed to accomplish a task is also a way in which learners can learn new vocabulary in a contextualized manner, and use it in their speech. Teachers can also scaffold learning by talking about their own favorite authors before the students do their task. In addition, teachers can explain how they themselves have prepared for this task. By modeling how a competent speaker accomplishes the task, teachers will show, in tangible ways, how the learners can work towards accomplishing their tasks.

Another type of activity in Stage 2 involves the learners in doing some planning for themselves. Teachers can guide them by identifying features of the speaking-practice task that may be challenging for them. If learners are going to participate in a dialogue or a discussion task, they can consider communication strategies that they can use if they meet with problems during the interaction. Planning is usually needed for complex, rather than simple, tasks. For example, if learners are to carry out a simple information-gap activity, such as completing a text by filling in the blanks with words, they may need nothing more than to review the key phrases to use when asking for clarification and repetition. If, on the other hand, they have to plan a short formal talk to explain a procedure (a genre that has the purpose of giving instructions), or a discussion (a genre that has the purpose of giving both sides of an argument), they will need time to plan the contents and the language (see Figures 7.4 and 7.5 as examples). Depending on the particular group of students, the teacher may need to circulate and help them come up with specific language they may wish to jot down.

Explaining a procedure or process: planning and rehearsing

Part 1: Guidelines to help you prepare for the task

1. Identify a topic you are interested in or know quite a lot about (e.g., how to make your favorite fruit salad).
2. Write the main points you want to cover in the space provided below:

    a. _____

    b. _____

    c. _____

3. Write down a phrase or an expression you would use to show that you will be moving from Point A to Point B, and then on to Point C.

    a. ⎫
    _____
    b. ⎬
    _____
    c. ⎭

Part 2: Rehearsal *(optional)*

Practice giving the explanation. Use the points you have made, and link your ideas by using the signposting words you have just identified. Don't write down everything you want to say, so that you can practice bringing in different points!

Figure 7.4: A pre-task planning guide for giving a talk

Planning for discussion: content and participation

In this lesson, you will be discussing *The best city in the world to live in*. The following guiding questions are meant to help you plan what you can say during the discussion. Write down your answers after each question.

1. Which country will you choose? Jot down three reasons for your choice.

    _____

    _____

    _____

2. When you are giving your reasons, what phrases or expressions will be useful to help you present your views?

    _____

    _____

    _____

3. What would you say to members in your group if they . . . ?
    a. Disagree with you
    b. Support your views
    c. Do not explain themselves clearly
    d. Make a good point

Figure 7.5: A pre-task planning guide for participating in a discussion.

Chapter 11 gives further suggestions on how teachers can help students prepare for a task.

Discuss it

How useful is planning time? What benefits do teachers and learners experience? What challenges and problems should teachers watch out for? Can anything be done to address these problems in advance?

Stage 3: Conduct speaking tasks

The purpose of this stage is to provide learners with context where they can practice speaking through a communication task. The task should encourage the learners to express their meaning with whatever linguistic knowledge, skills, and strategies they have. In other words, this stage of the cycle encourages learners to develop fluency of expression without having to pay too much attention to accuracy of form. Their efforts are also made less demanding by the teacher-guided or individual pre-task planning that has taken place in Stage 2.

Speaking tasks typically involve learners in some pair or group interaction. One of the basic principles for planning these kinds of activity is that, in order to encourage learners to use the target language, we must create situations in which they experience a communicative need and personal motivation to talk to one another. These situations are often in the form of pair or group tasks where information or opinion gaps exist among the various participants in the interaction (see Chapter 9 for examples of such tasks). This sets the stage for oral communication to take place. Equally useful speaking tasks include discussions and problem-solving tasks, as well as talks or other kinds of extended discourse where one person does most of the talking (see also Chapter 5 and Chapter 9).

Stage 4: Focus on language / skills / strategies

A limitation of many lessons on speaking is the lack of attention given to the explicit teaching of relevant language, skills, and strategies that contribute to effective speaking. In fact, it is not unusual to find speaking lessons that consist of only two of the seven stages proposed in the teaching-speaking cycle covered in Figure 7.1. For example, teachers may provide some input (Stage 2), which is followed by students working on a fluency-oriented task (Stage 3), but that is where the activity stops. In some coursebooks, these are sometimes referred to as the pre-speaking activity and the speaking activity respectively. Alternatively, we may find only the speaking activity (Stage 3), which may or may not be related to other parts of the chapter or unit of work. For example, in a unit that has recycling as a theme, students may be given a situation as follows: "You are members of the 'Go Green Society' in your college. Discuss, in your group, how you can encourage the students in your college to recycle and reuse their stationery and clothing." Thus, while language learners may be given an opportunity to practice speaking, there is no scaffolding to help them complete the activity. The "learning" often ends when the task is completed, and the outcomes are simply shared with the rest of the class. More importantly, there is no follow-up or feedback that helps learners develop explicitly their knowledge of the language, skills, and strategies implied in the task.

Stage 4 of the cycle is aimed at addressing this limitation by creating opportunities for learners to improve language accuracy, as well as enhancing their effective use of skills and strategies. In this stage, we draw learners' attention to selected "parts" of the fluency task they have completed. The parts include language features such as pronunciation, grammar, and text structures, as well as vocabulary. Many of the features highlighted in Chapters 4 and 5 can be examined more closely by learners at this stage. For example, they can focus their attention on one of the following: the structure of a genre, discourse markers, or intonation features – thereby allowing them to see how these areas are important for performing the speech functions needed for the task in Stage 3. To focus on these areas, learners can be asked to examine a transcript of the speech of a competent speaker performing the task and to identify language features such as discourse markers used to signal the different "moves" in the text. This activity can help learners see how a particular type of discourse is organized and can help them understand the function of grammar and vocabulary in achieving coherence. More on what can be done at Stage 4 will be discussed in Chapter 10.

Stage 5: Repeat speaking task

At this stage, learners carry out the speaking task of Stage 3 again. The difference between Stage 3 and Stage 5 is that learners have had a chance to analyze and practice selected language items or skills during Stage 4, and, therefore, have been able to apply this knowledge in order to enhance their performance. Repetitions could be carried out in various ways. Bygate (2005) recommends repeating parts of the original task or repeating the entire task, which can be carried out by having students change groups or partners. Alternatively, teachers could introduce a new task that is similar to the one the learners have just done. For example, instead of the topic used in Figure 7.5 above, learners could be asked to give instructions about a topic of their own choice. Thus, they would be rehearsing a procedure genre again, but, this time, with a new focus.

The benefits of task repetition have been highlighted in the previous chapter. Critically, since the task has already been carried out at least once in Stage 3, task repetition, because of reduced cognitive load and the benefit of "rehearsal," can facilitate automaticity in combining various types of linguistic knowledge and skills. Besides the obvious cognitive advantage, task repetition also enhances learner affect. By allowing learners to repeat a task, we offer them an opportunity to build on earlier attempts where communication may not have been completely effective. Being able to revise performance in this way can lead to greater confidence. Because learners have had at least one attempt at a task, they have greater awareness of what to expect and what is expected of them. Getting a second chance to do something right can be immensely motivating for many learners. For further discussions of activities for Stage 5, please refer to Chapter 10.

Try it

Select a speaking activity from a coursebook, and carry it out with another colleague. Record your own speech production. Carry out the same activity again a day later, and record yourself. Do you notice any differences in the way you performed in terms of content, fluency, and accuracy? Explain what the differences are, and why you think they exist.

Stage 6: Direct learners' reflection on learning

The activities in the cycle continue with learners' reflections on their learning experiences. Unlike Stage 1, which directs learners' attention to the task of L2 speaking, Stage 6 encourages learners to self-regulate their learning through monitoring and evaluating what they have learned from the preceding stages. It is also an opportunity for learners to consolidate their new knowledge about language, skills, and strategy use. Reflection need not always be an individual effort. Teachers can encourage learners to think about their learning in pairs, or even in small groups. Individual and group reflection often has a cathartic effect on learners who may be feeling stressed and anxious, and think that they are the only ones feeling that way.

Learners' reflection should be guided by different types of metacognitive knowledge, described in the methodological framework in Chapter 6 and Chapter 11. Reflection can focus on one or more of the following points:

- Demands of the speaking tasks that learners have become aware of.
- The strategies that are useful for meeting the demands of the task.
- Learners' informal assessment of their capabilities and performance.
- Areas of their performance that show improvement.
- Areas to be further improved.
- Plans for improving specific areas.

Learners could also be encouraged to draw on their experiences and to consider how they could prepare themselves for future tasks of a similar nature, whether these tasks are in the classroom or in communicative contexts outside the classroom. Figure 7.6 gives an example of the general prompts that can be used for Stage 6. These prompts can be given to learners as handouts to complete. Alternatively, they can be given to learners as headings to be used in their journals. Teachers can also encourage students

Evaluating my speaking performance	Your teacher's / classmate's response
1. In this week's lessons, I learned to do the following in spoken English: _____ _____ _____	
2. I also learned to use the following useful expressions that can help me speak more effectively: _____ _____ _____	
3. This is how I feel about my learning this week: a. I am confident that I can do this again. ( ) b. I am not very confident that I can do this again. ( ) c. I am still unsure about what I have to say and do in such a situation. ( ) d. I still feel anxious about speaking. ( ) e. I feel less anxious about speaking. ( ) *Put a check (√) next to the sentence that best describes how you feel right now.*	

Figure 7.6: Prompts for learner reflection on learning.

to start a blog to express their thoughts about their experiences in learning to speak a second or foreign language. The use of audio blogs is becoming popular, too, and can be an effective way of combining speech production with reflection (Tan & Tan 2010). This stage of the teaching-speaking cycle is individual work and can be completed at home or in class.

Stage 7: Facilitate feedback on learning

In this final stage of the teaching-speaking cycle, the teacher provides learners with important feedback on their performance in earlier stages of the cycle. In large classes, it is often impossible to monitor student learning and give immediate feedback to every student. However, as students have had to record their thoughts in Stage 6, it is now possible to offer some personal feedback based on what individual learners say or write about their own learning experiences. This feedback can take many forms, and the teacher does not always have to be the one giving it. Learners can also be guided on how to give one another peer feedback. Generally, feedback can take the form of:

- Comments or grades about an individual student's skills and performance from observation sheets used during the speaking task.
- Exchange of written individual learner reflections and comments on each other's progress and achievements.
- Consolidated comments from the teacher, based on written reflections from the class.
- Written comments in students' journal.
- Comments and informal assessment in learner blogs.

The prompts given in Figure 7.6 can be printed and given to learners at the end of every cycle. The column on the right allows you to write comments there. Students can also be asked to comment on one another's reflections. The feedback given can also be based on the students' performance in a spoken task that the teacher has been able to observe. See Chapter 12 for further discussions about feedback in assessment.

Planning with the teaching-speaking cycle

The teaching-speaking cycle is not intended to be conducted and completed in one or even two lessons. It is important, therefore, that teachers pace each stage appropriately and not rush through any one of the stages. For teachers who are familiar with the concept of a unit of work for syllabus

Level:	Pre-intermediate.	
Topic:	Introductions and talking about oneself.	
Speaking skills:	Introduce oneself and others formally and informally.	
	Respond to introductions.	
	Describe personal preferences.	
Language focus:	Formulaic expressions for making and responding to introductions.	
Strategies:	Ask for clarifications and repetitions.	
Duration:	180 minutes (including time for introduction and closure of lessons).	

Stage	Activities	Estimated time	Resources
1. Focus learners' attention on speaking.	Students write short responses to questions about learning to speak in English. (Teacher tells the students that he / she will collect the self-observation notes at the end of the unit of work and will read the notes before returning them.)	10 minutes	Self-observation sheet / prompts; e.g., Figure 7.2.
2. Give input and guide planning.	Students prepare: • A short introduction of themselves. • Some useful phrases for introducing others.	10 minutes	• A pre-task planning guide; e.g., Figure 7.4. • A list of vocabulary items based on the prompts.
3. Conduct speaking task.	a. Students introduce themselves to each other in pairs. b. Next, they ask each other the questions they prepared.	20 minutes	Students own note s based on Stage 2.
4. Focus on language / skills / strategies.	a. Students listen to an audio recording or watch a video recording of different people: • Making self-introductions. • Introducing one person to another. b. They identify and write down expressions that are used for making introductions and responding to introductions, c. Students listen again with the help of the transcript, highlighting the relevant expressions when they hear them. d. Teacher discusses with students the differences between formal and informal registers when making and responding to introductions, and how these are signaled by some formulaic expressions. e. Students listen to / watch the recording again. This time, they are asked to observe any gestures or actions and routines that accompany some of the introductions.	40 minutes	• A recording by the teacher or from another course book. • Transcripts of the recording. Examples of expressions that can be highlighted are: "Hi, my name is Z." "Let me introduce you to Y." "Meet my friend, X." "It's my pleasure to introduce X." "Nice to meet you, X."

Figure 7.7: Planning a unit of work using seven stages of the teaching-speaking cycle.

(continued)

Stage	Activities	Estimated time	Resources
5. Repeat speaking task.	a. Students in their pairs are matched with another pair. One person in the pair introduces himself / herself briefly before introducing his / her partner to the other pair. b. Students do an informal interview activity to meet other members of the class. c. Selected students are asked to use the information they obtained from the activity to introduce a classmate to their teacher formally. (To maximize learner talk-time in a large class, this can be done in groups instead, with selected students taking the role of the teacher.)	50 minutes	An adaptation of the prompts in Stage 2.
6. Direct learners' reflection on learning.	a. Students compare the way introductions are made in English and their first language. b. They compare their observations with a partner's. c. Students refer to their responses to prompts in Stage 1 of this chart. They change and add what they have written. d. Teacher collects the reflection sheets to find out more about the students.	20 minutes	• Reflection sheets • Reflection prompts; e.g. Figure 7.6. Figure 7.2 used in Stage 1 can also be modified for this purpose.
7. Facilitate feedback on learning.	Teacher reads and writes comments on the reflection sheets before returning them to the learners. Students consider how their learning can be transferred to a new task in another unit of work / series of lessons.		Some prompts for Stage 1 that build on the learners' experience in the previous teaching-speaking cycle.

Figure 7.7: Planning a unit of work using seven stages of the teaching-speaking cycle.

planning, it will be useful to think of a cycle as consisting of a series of lessons based on a theme. Depending on the duration of each lesson in the timetable, the various stages of the cycle may spread over an entire week or less. Teachers can use the sequence in the cycle to focus systematically on planning each stage, and on developing tasks and materials. Teachers who teach from prescribed textbooks can also benefit from the principle of organizing learning activities in the cycle by including additional materials on the same topic and purposely repeating some of the activities. Figure 7.7 above shows how teachers can plan a unit of work. This planning can be conducted at the start of a speaking or general language course.

Summary

This chapter presented a model for sequencing and conducting learning activities to develop second language speaking in a holistic manner. The teaching-speaking cycle translates theoretical and pedagogical principles from the methodological framework and can guide teachers in planning activities that engage learners at the cognitive and affective level. The cycle consists of seven stages of classroom procedures. It can be used for planning individual units of work in a speaking course or for adapting materials you are already working with. It demonstrates how various types of metacognitive-awareness, fluency, language, and skills-training activities can be combined to optimize learning opportunities. The cycle emphasizes the following:

1. The teaching of speaking should foreground the respective roles played by the teacher, the learner, and the materials.
2. The main aim of speaking tasks is to help students develop the fluency of expert speakers, where meaning is communicated with few hesitations and in a manner that is appropriate for the social purpose of the message. This is achieved through the use of:
   - Accurate language and discourse routines.
   - Appropriate speech enabling skills.
   - Effective communication strategies.
3. Learners' speaking performance can be enhanced through pre-task planning and task repetition, as these activities can reduce cognitive load during speech processing.
4. Learning involves noticing key information and storing it in long term memory. Activities that focus learners' attention on language, skills, and strategies are, therefore, an important part of teaching speaking.
5. Activities that help learners develop metacognitive knowledge and self-regulation of their speaking and learning processes are also needed to address affective and other cognitive demands of learning to speak a second or foreign language.

By planning lessons according to the stages in the teaching-speaking cycle, teachers can address all these concerns and provide valuable scaffolding for learners as they engage in speaking tasks. Learners will not only practice expressing meaning using their existing language resources, but they will also receive timely input and guidance for improving their performance. In the next chapter, a cycle that takes the *product* – the genre or text – as a starting point will also be presented.

Group-learning tasks

1. Work in pairs to interview some language teachers. Find out from them how they plan and conduct their speaking lessons. In particular, find out how many of these teachers do the following:
   a. Include the explicit teaching of language, skills, and strategies for speaking.
   b. Use activities for raising their students' awareness about learning to speak.
   c. Repeat speaking tasks with the same group of students.
2. Do this task if you have access to a group of language learners. Adapt a speaking activity from a textbook by including some pre-task planning by the students. After you have conducted this activity, reflect on the following points:
   a. How long was the planning time? Why do you think this amount of time is suitable?
   b. What was the purpose of the planning activity?
   c. Did you guide your students in the way they should use their planning time, or did you allow your students to use the time in any way they liked?
   d. Did pre-task planning have any apparent effect on your students' spoken-language performance and overall behavior during the task?
   Interview a small number of students to find out how they used their planning time and whether or not they think pre-task planning is useful.
3. Select one set of activities for speaking from a coursebook. Suggest how you would modify these activities to incorporate the stages in the teaching-speaking cycle. To help you get started, here are some points to consider:
   a. Do the activities support learners' awareness of their speaking development and provide adequate support for the demands of the speaking task? Can you suggest an activity that would offer this support if there is none?
   b. What kinds of preparation, if any, are learners expected to do before carrying out the main speaking task?
   c. Identify one or two language features that can improve your students' spoken performance during this activity. What techniques would you use to teach the language feature(s) you've selected?
   d. How can the students be asked to repeat the main speaking task, either in parts or in its entirety?

Work with a colleague to label the stages in the teaching-speaking cycle below. Then present your ideas to other course participants using the stages in the teaching-speaking cycle as a template.

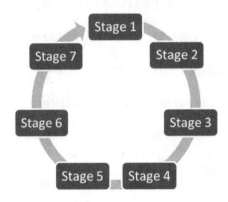

Further reading

Willis, D. (2004) Towards a new methodology, *English Teaching Professional*, 33, 4–6.

Richards, J. C. (2006) Materials development and research – making the connection, *RELC Journal*, 37 (1), 5–26.

Riggenbach, H. (1999) Discourse analysis in the language classroom, Vol. 1: *The Spoken Language*, Ann Arbor: The University of Michigan Press.

Van den Brandon, K. (2012) Task-based language education, In A. Burns and J. C. Richards (eds.) *The Cambridge Guide to Pedagogy and Practice in Second Language Teaching*, New York: Cambridge University Press.

8 Planning a speaking course

In the previous two chapters, we looked at a holistic methodological framework and a teaching speaking model that teachers can use to inform the teaching of speaking. In this chapter, we broaden the discussion to focus on the steps and procedures involved in planning and developing a speaking program. By program, we mean a complete course or syllabus that is developed to assist students in learning more about speaking and to help them practice using their speaking knowledge and skills over an extended period of time. This chapter will address these questions:

1. What features of the learner group need to be taken into account in planning a speaking program?
2. What are the main elements that need to be considered in developing a speaking program based on learner needs?
3. What key aspects must be taken into consideration when considering program outcomes?

To answer the questions, we will highlight the following topics:

- A framework to inform program or course planning.
- The purpose of needs analysis, and how it affects placement decisions and the setting of goals and objectives.
- The main elements involved in creating an appropriate syllabus for the learner group.
- The notion of program outcomes and how they can be evaluated.

These days, English-language teachers work in numerous diverse situations all over the world. Learner groups in English Language Teaching (ELT) are now extremely wide-ranging, covering the whole lifespan from pre-school, elementary, and high school to tertiary and adult classes. In some contexts, English classes are also offered to mature and senior adults who might be learning English for the first time. After their initial training, teachers may find themselves in all kinds of teaching situations for which their pre-service courses did not necessarily directly prepare them. It is very important, therefore, that teachers be equipped to become course developers when necessary, as they may find themselves in new teaching situations that require such skills. Graves (1996: 1) brings this possibility to the fore vividly when she describes a discussion she had with a teacher attending her course:

> One afternoon, a teacher came into my office to discuss an independent study. "I have been asked to design an evening English course for adults in my town in Nicaragua." He paused and then continued, "I've never developed a course before. Are there any guidelines? Is there a procedure to follow? Where do I start?" I realized as I listened to him that I had heard these questions many times before, from many teachers, the difference being the nature of each teacher's situation.

Although in many educational contexts, teachers are required to follow a set syllabus or course book decided by the Ministry of Education, the School Board, or the institution where they work, increasingly English language teachers find themselves having to devise programs from the beginning. They may be given a class and a coursebook and told to teach the students in any way they like. Alternatively, they may be asked to devise a new course for a group of students who hadn't previously been taught English. In this chapter, we respond to some of the questions posed by the teacher in Graves' example. Our focus is, of course, specifically on the teaching of speaking, but the steps and processes we describe could also be applied to other types of course development.

Think about it

What is the nature of your teaching situation? Do you have to work with a required program or syllabus, or are you free to develop your own? How does your course situation affect your teaching? What do you see as the advantages and disadvantages of the syllabus used in your situation with respect to the teaching of speaking?

Program, course, curriculum, and syllabus

A range of terms is used to describe a plan for an extended series of lessons involving teaching and learning. Program, course, curriculum, and syllabus are all terms found in the literature. Often these terms overlap in confusing and ambiguous ways. While the differences between them are often difficult to tease apart, here we make some distinctions for the purpose of clarifying our focus in this chapter.

Curriculum
A broad notion of all the activities involved in teaching and learning. These activities include the content of what students learn, the methods by which

they learn, the roles played by the teachers in their learning, the resources, equipment and facilities used, and the formal and informal requirements and processes used for assessment and evaluation and for further development of the curriculum.

Program
The broad area of study in which students are enrolled, e.g., a business English program, general English program, or certificate program.

Course
The term used for the particular focus of the various components in the program, for example, a conversation course or a speaking-skills course. Within any course, there may be several components, all with separate syllabi, that focus on particular content needed to make up a whole program.

Syllabus
A plan that outlines the areas to be covered in an entire course, typically including rationale, content, topics, tasks, texts, resources, and evaluation.
   The two terms we will mainly use as the focus of this chapter are course and syllabus.

A framework for planning

The framework in Figure 8.1 below outlines the basic phases involved in planning a speaking program. Although it seems to suggest a series of separate steps; in fact, these steps constantly inform and have an impact on each other. For example, assessment, in the sense of continually diagnosing learner needs, is something that the teacher is likely to consider throughout the course. The composition and backgrounds of the learner group will color decisions about goals and objectives, as well as the type of course evaluation that is appropriate for the learner group. The most effective approach is to view the phases and steps in the planning processes as flexible, dynamic, and intertwined. In the discussion below, we will address each of these planning steps, in turn, as a way of responding to the kind of questions asked by the teacher in Graves' illustration referred to earlier.

The learner group

The essential starting point for any planning process is the learners themselves. Without a clear idea of the current knowledge and future aspirations

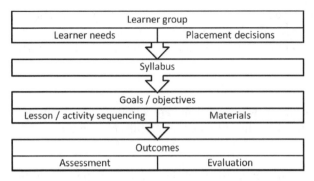

Figure 8.1: Speaking program-planning framework.

of the learners, in terms of speaking in English, effective teaching and learning are unlikely to be achieved. Even when teachers are required to use a pre-set syllabus or coursebook, it is essential that they mediate the teaching requirements from these documents to fit with learners' needs. As most teachers are aware, learner groups vary dramatically in their composition. In some situations, students may be from the same age, gender, language, and national backgrounds, and the teacher can broadly assume a common basis of social and cultural understanding of the classroom situation as it relates to language learning. Elsewhere, classes may be composed of students with diverse cultural and linguistic backgrounds, of varied ages and current language abilities. In these circumstances, the assumptions and expectations between the teacher and learners about what constitutes appropriate learning, and what kinds of content and activities will be taught. may differ dramatically. It is important for the teacher to become as familiar as possible with the nature of the class, the characteristics of the students as a group and as individuals, their previous learning histories, their expectations of the course, and their needs for continued language learning. One of the first steps in planning and designing an effective speaking program will, therefore, be a diagnosis of learner needs.

Learner needs

Needs analysis and needs assessment are terms both associated with the gathering of information about learners at the beginning of a course of study. While these terms are often used interchangeably, they do, in fact, reflect a subtle difference in the ways information on needs is obtained (Graves 1996). Needs *assessment* focuses on collecting information and making formal or informal judgements, for example, on where learners are in their level of speaking ability as rated formally on an assessment scale, informally through an interview, based on their previous experiences of language learning, or the goals and aspirations they have in improving their speaking skills. Needs *analysis* refers to the use that is made of the information collected; that is, how it is analyzed for the purposes of refining the syllabus and its contents, and for making decisions about what activities or resources should be used.

Brindley (1989: 63) distinguishes between a narrow, or "product-oriented," interpretation of needs and a broad, or "process-oriented," view of needs. In the narrow view, the focus is more specifically on linguistic aspects, such as learners' current and future language use. The broad approach goes beyond language use alone to consider how the learner features as an individual in the whole learning situation, which could be described as a more socio-constructivist view of learning. Extending these ideas in order to find "a happy medium," Brindley makes a distinction between *objective needs* and *subjective needs*.

Objective needs are "derivable from factual information about learners, their use of language in real-life communication situations, as well as their current language proficiency and language difficulties" (1989: 70). Subjective needs, on the other hand, are the cognitive and affective needs of the learner in the learning situation, derivable from information about affective and cognitive factors such as personality, confidence, attitudes, learners' wants and expectations, and their given cognitive style and learning strategies" (p. 70). To illustrate Brindley's distinction in more concrete terms, below is an outline of the kind of information that might be collected to evaluate objective and subjective needs in relation to speaking development, with examples to illustrate each point:

OBJECTIVE

- Learner background and experience (nationality, languages spoken, age, gender, years of previous language learning, previous experience speaking English).
- Previous experiences affecting learning (lack of opportunity, short-course duration, life changes, such as attendance at multiple schools or migration).
- Current proficiency in relation to a range of speaking skills and abilities (recent test results / scores, performance on tasks, responses to questions posed by the assessor or teacher, pronunciation skills).
- Broad purposes for developing speaking ability (to pass examinations, for work, for study, for travel, for general communication).

SUBJECTIVE

- Attitudes towards learning English in general (level of enthusiasm, confidence, previous learning experiences).
- Attitudes towards speaking English (perception of future goals or aspirations).
- Motivation / investment in improving speaking skills (willingness to perform in class, out-of-class practice strategies).
- Feelings about speaking in English (anxiety, confidence, shyness).
- Feelings about performing different types of speaking (transactional speaking, class presentations, oral examinations).
- Feelings about speaking with different interactants (with familiar / unfamiliar native speakers, with other competent speakers, with other students / friends or family members, with adults, with children, with teachers or supervisors).
- Preferences about how to learn (learning styles, learning strategies).

Brindley advises that identifying needs should not be a one-off event at the start of a course, but an ongoing process of consultation and negotiation between teacher and learners. A variety of procedures can be used at various points in a course to assess learners' spoken needs including interview, diagnostic assessment, self-rating, observation, informal group discussion, or asking learners to perform particular tasks. In assessing students' current level of spoken competence, teachers may find it useful to make recordings of what speakers can currently demonstrate at various stages. Playing such recordings to demonstrate to learners the progress they have achieved can also be very motivating.

Discuss it

Work with your colleagues to discuss your students' spoken language needs. Consider such areas as the students' age and previous language learning, the reasons they are learning English, the requirements of the syllabus or curriculum, and the outcomes they must achieve. Identify which of the needs you have identified as critical for your students relate to objective needs, and which to subjective needs.

Frameworks for needs analysis

Various instruments can be used for assessing and analyzing information about learner speaking needs. Here we provide some practical suggestions that teachers can use for informal assessment.

The framework below (Figure 8.2) is completed from the point of view of the teacher making the assessment.

Speaking needs analysis checklist

Student name: _____   Date: _____

Teacher name: _____   Class: _____

Learner rating:	Excellent	Very good	Moderate	Poor
1. Answering personal questions.	☐	☐	☐	☐
2. Selecting vocabulary appropriate to the topic.	☐	☐	☐	☐
3. Asking questions appropriate to the topic.	☐	☐	☐	☐
4. Giving feedback.	☐	☐	☐	☐
5. Managing turns in the interaction.	☐	☐	☐	☐
Etc.				

Action plan: _____

_____

_____

_____

_____

Figure 8.2: Framework for teacher speaking-needs analysis.

The next framework (Figure 8.3) is one that provides an opportunity for learners to self-assess their needs. This kind of framework could be used by individuals or by groups, who then reach a consensus on what is most important for them.

The teacher can, of course, modify these types of frameworks by including items on the left that match the teacher's focus for assessment of the

Improving speaking

In this course I / we want to:

	Very important	Quite important	Not important
1. Improve fluency.			
2. Use vocabulary more accurately.			
3. Ask and answer questions appropriately.			
4. Improve pronunciation.			
5. Participate in tutorial discussions.			
6. Other. (Please indicate your ideas.)			

Figure 8.3: Framework for learner speaking-needs analysis.

students' current speaking skills within the aims of the course, and by extending the number of items, as necessary.

The third example can be used by either the teacher or the learner. In the center of the framework, the person completing the assessment writes in the assessment focus. The focus can be on an individual learner or the learner group, but it could also be on a situation in which the learner needs to operate (e.g., a specific workplace, or community context), a particular group the learner needs to communicate with (e.g. patients, in a course for nurses), or a task or text the learner needs to be able to complete. The person completing the framework fills in the components that are the most important for speaking development in the current course. In Figure 8.4, we provide two examples: the learner group, and the patients with whom a nurse needs to communicate.

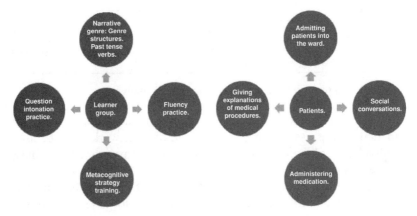

Figure 8.4: Needs analysis frameworks for learner group and communication situations.

A framework can either focus on the most important three or four components (as in Figure 8.4 above) or, alternatively, the number of circles that form the "spokes of the wheel" can be considerably increased to identify other needs (as in Figure 8.5, which shows communication needs for an ESP course and emphasizes, through the thicker, blacker lines, the two situations prioritized by the students).

Try it

Use the ideas above to create your own needs analysis instrument framework. If possible, do this with colleagues with whom you can share the frameworks you develop. Try out the frameworks with your class to see how effectively they work and what kind of information they give you.

Figure 8.5: Analyzing needs through a communication network.

Placement decisions

Placement decisions are related to needs assessment and analysis, as such decisions may be made on the basis of what emerges from these processes. Separate placement tests are sometimes used to provide an initial assessment of learners' speaking skills. Informal placement tests may consist of informal chats or introductions initiated by the interviewer, selection of a topic or visual for the learner to talk about for a few minutes, questions from the interviewer about a topic, questions from the student to the interviewer about the course, or other matters relating to the institution.

In some teaching situations, however, it is the case that learners will be placed automatically, according to their progression in the school system, their age, and the class grades in which they fall. In other circumstances, a placement decision will depend on what has been ascertained about the students' previous achievement, and current skills and competence in speaking, and what kinds of classes are available for the student concerned. Teachers may or may not be involved in these decisions, depending on whether the needs processes occur before, during, or after placement.

Discuss it

In your teaching situation, how are needs assessment and analysis, and placement decisions connected? Who is involved in making decisions about placement? How do these decisions affect the composition of classes and the content that is then selected for teaching and learning? What role do you, as an individual, have in these decisions?

Considering goals and objectives

When the needs processes and decisions about appropriate learner placement are completed, it is then necessary to consider the goals and objectives of the speaking course.

Goals or aims are terms that are used interchangeably in course planning. Here we will use the term *goal*. Developing goals means asking the question: "What is this course for, and what are the learners expected to achieve?" Goal statements are, therefore, broad and highlight the purposes of the course in general terms, in order to indicate what the learners are expected to achieve on the whole. Such statements outline the learning purpose, the general guidelines for teaching and learning, the overall focus of the instruction, and the general skills the learners are expected to acquire. Examples of goal statements for a speaking course are:

- To develop the knowledge and skills for engaging in casual conversations.
- To acquire speaking skills for exchanging personal opinions.
- To develop spoken skills for use in academic study contexts.
- To acquire the ability to deal with inquiries in hospitality contexts.
- To develop speaking skills for seeking and obtaining employment.
- To develop the speaking competencies needed to pass the local authority's oral examination.

The course purpose; that is, the institution or school's reason for offering the course, influences what goals can be set and what specific aspects of speaking skills should be included. In some teaching situations, courses have a pre-determined focus, and the teacher is required to work within that focus, as is frequently the case with English-for-Academic-Purposes (or English-for-Specific-Purposes) courses. This is also the case with many national or regional syllabus documents, where the goals of the program are already specified for the teacher. In other teaching situations, the course purpose is more open-ended, and it is the teacher who must determine the goals and objectives that allow students to reach particular learning outcomes.

Think about it

What is the purpose of a course you teach? Are course goals already specified, or do you need to determine your course goals yourself? If the latter, how do you go about setting goals? Write some goals for your course and discuss them with a colleague.

Objectives extend the overall long-term goals of a course by outlining more specific ways to fulfill the purposes and the learning outcomes. Graves makes a useful distinction between goals and objectives: "The goals of a course represent the destination; the objectives, the various points that chart the course towards the destination. To arrive at the destination, one must pass each of these points" (Graves 1996: 17). One could say that the goals represent the overall map of where the learner must go, and the objectives show the route that should be taken.

There are a number of criteria to consider when creating objectives that can make the task of planning the course easier for teachers. Objectives should be:

- Clear: they set out the key points in the learning process clearly for both teacher and learners.
- Realizable: they should be realistic in relation to the students' speaking competence and short-term needs.
- Achievable: they should be able to be achieved within the timeframe for the course.
- Focused: they should highlight the aspects of speaking that will be of immediate relevance to the students.
- Needs-related: they should be within the current capacity of students to progress in their speaking competence.

These criteria should assist the teacher in setting objectives that are accessible and understandable to their students, and which also take into account where the students currently are in their speaking competence. The duration of the course and frequency of instruction should also underpin the objectives. Attempting to achieve outcomes that are too ambitious within the time available will be demotivating for both teachers and learners.

Goal: To develop the knowledge and skills for engaging in casual conversations.

Objectives related to knowledge

Students will develop their knowledge of:

- Cultural expectations about casual conversations.
- The role of casual conversation in the culture.
- Relevant conversational topics considered appropriate in the culture.
- Speaker and listener roles in casual conversations.
- How casual conversations are structured to achieve a particular social purpose.
- How vocabulary and grammar function in particular kinds of casual spoken interactions.

Students will develop the skills to:

- Initiate a topic in a casual conversation.
- Select vocabulary appropriate to the topic.
- Give appropriate feedback responses.
- Provide relevant evaluative comments.
- Take turns at appropriate points in the conversation.
- Ask for clarification and repetition.
- Use discourse strategies for repairing misunderstandings.
- Use discourse strategies to close a conversation.
- Use appropriate intonation and stress patterns to express meaning intelligibly.

Figure 8.6: Learner knowledge and skills objectives.

Also, objectives should not aim to exceed what is within the students' learning capacity. If objectives and activities are too demanding, given the students' current speaking abilities, the students are not likely to achieve the anticipated outcomes.

The process of arriving at objectives involves asking what specific things learners need to know or do to arrive at the overall goal. If we take one of the broad goals above, we can consider the kinds of objectives that could be developed. In the example above (Figure 8.6), we distinguish between what learners need to know and what learners need to do.

All of the above objectives are stated from the viewpoint of learner achievement. However, it is also possible to express objectives from the teacher's perspective:

The teacher will:

- Assist learners in appreciating the purpose of casual conversation in society.
- Introduce learners to the concept of speaker and listener roles.

- Sensitize learners to the types of topics commonly found in casual spoken interactions.
- Develop learners' fluency when participating in spoken interactions.

This list can be expanded. Again, it is possible to separate teaching objectives in terms of knowledge and skills to be taught.

Discuss it

With your colleagues, discuss the objectives for a course you teach. (If you are not currently teaching, select a course you are familiar with.) How do the objectives aim to meet the knowledge and skills the students need? Are they presented from the point of view of the learner or the teacher? If there are no objectives for the course, develop a set of objectives that highlight the knowledge and skills that will be covered.

While goals and objectives are very useful in determining the direction of the course, they have also been criticized on several grounds. Classroom research has shown that many teachers do not formulate goals and objectives at all, or not until they have taught a course at least once and are more familiar with where their teaching is heading (Graves 1996). Goals and objectives are not always easy to express, and teachers may have difficulty articulating them. Other criticisms relate to the rigidity that might ensue when teaching sticks closely to objectives and does not pursue other learning opportunities that emerge. Some see objectives as trivializing teaching and learning, and turning the learning processes into a rather mechanistic, product-oriented exercise (Richards 2000). The position we take here is that it is very useful for teachers to include goal and objective setting in their course planning, but that both goals and objectives should be used flexibly and, ultimately, with the essential speaking needs of the learners in mind.

The syllabus

The next phase in the planning process involves specifying the various elements in the syllabus for the course. The syllabus consists of components that should arise logically from the learning goals and objectives, and be related back to them.

As we have suggested throughout this book, there is a very wide range of determining factors related to the cognitive, metacognitive, linguistic, and pronunciation components that can potentially be considered in a speaking program. Graves (1996) draws on recent developments in the theory and

Table 8.1: *Elements to consider in developing a speaking syllabus*

Participatory processes Examples: problem posing, experiential techniques.	Learning strategies Examples: self-monitoring, problem identification.	Content Examples: academic subjects, technical subjects.
Culture Examples: cultural awareness, cultural behavior, cultural knowledge.	Tasks and activities Examples: information-gap tasks, projects, skills needed for topic-oriented tasks, such as giving a speech or making a presentation.	Competencies Examples: applying for a job, renting an apartment.
Functions Examples: apologizing, disagreeing, persuading.	Notions and topics Examples: time, quantity, health, personal identification.	Communicative situations Examples: ordering in a restaurant, buying street maps.
Grammar Examples: structures (tense, pronouns), patterns (questions).	Pronunciation Examples: segmental (phonemes, syllables), suprasegmentals (stress, rhythm, intonation).	Vocabulary Examples: word formation (suffixes, prefaces), collocation, lexical sets.

(Adapted from Graves 1996: 25.)

practice of curriculum and syllabus development to suggest that, apart from the specific skills that characterize speaking (turn taking, compensating for misunderstandings, or using cohesive devices), the elements in Table 8.1 are ones that should be considered in developing the content of a syllabus.

The question of which elements to include in the syllabus is a challenging one, and teachers are most likely to select from the components above, making decisions that are based on learner needs, the curriculum they are required to work with, the kinds of materials and resources they have available, and the time allocated to the course. Graves points out also that the elements above overlap; for example, cultural knowledge and awareness would be important in a course on seeking employment, where students need to understand the cultural factors implicit in applying for a job. Teachers will need to make informed decisions about which of these elements to focus on, what is achievable in the time available, and what will assist their learners most.

Lesson / activity sequences

The lessons that make up the syllabus are unlikely to be planned as stand-alone components. In a well-designed speaking program, skills and knowledge are built up from one lesson to the next. One way for teachers to sequence lessons to meet the goals of building learning is to decide on the basis of the unit of work, as we described it in Chapter 7. Here we consider three starting points: a) topic, b) task, and c) text.

STARTING FROM A TOPIC

A unit of work (see Chapter 7) can be developed from topics of interest to students, or from topics that are essential to their immediate goals. For example, if the class is composed of teenage learners (Legutke 2012), the unit of work can be designed around topics that the learners themselves are most interested in, such as fashion, sport, music, film, using technology, adolescent fiction / poetic texts, and drama. One way to involve learners in the topics to be selected is to have them discuss their interests and then list and prioritize in class which ones they wish to see included in the syllabus. Teachers can ask questions such as the following:

1. What topics are students interested in?
2. What authentic, out-of-class contexts do students want to access?
3. Can I (or my students) obtain materials appropriate to this topic?
4. Are the speaking skills students will practice relevant for other topics?
5. Will the tasks selected for this topic allow students to recycle what they have learned?

Topics can also be generated from current local or world events, which are likely to be familiar to the students and for which a substantial amount of material can be found at the time of the event. Figure 8.7 below is an example of a unit of work for intermediate students that a teacher developed on the topic of the soccer World Cup.

STARTING FROM A TASK

The relevance of task-based approaches to designing units of work was discussed extensively in Chapter 6. Designing tasks and activities is for most teachers the most obvious way to think about how they will go about organizing their course content. Teachers inevitably ask questions like, "What tasks and activities will the students do?" and "What materials do I need for these tasks?" As already discussed, tasks focus on the performance of an activity, in contrast to the language focus found in other approaches; for example, PPP (present the structure, practice the structure, produce the structure). In the latter approach, the task is the end point of the process (and may frequently be left out, in some classrooms, because of time pressure),

Learner group	Teenagers
Topic	The World Cup
Objectives.	To discuss personal opinions about teams and players participating in the World Cup. To discuss the teams' chances of winning the Cup. To discuss events reported in the media about the World Cup.
Spoken skills to be developed.	Vocabulary related to sports (soccer). Vocabulary appropriate to interpersonal relations with other speakers. Verbs and verb tenses for different functions: • Giving opinions. • Presenting an argument. • Supporting a point of view. Skills for maintaining a spoken interaction: • Initiating a topic. • Sustaining a turn. • Providing feedback. • Expressing attitudes towards a topic. • Closing a topic.
Classroom tasks.	Class discussion, group discussions, debates, role plays, project work.
Out-of-class tasks.	Internet / media searches for up-to-date reports (L1 / L2).

Figure 8.7: Example of a unit of work on speaking.

rather than the purpose of the learning process. Tasks put the emphasis on fluency in the belief that the communicative nature of the task will promote accuracy, extend learning, and refine speaking skills.

A unit of work based on tasks would allow for the linking and integration of well-connected speaking activities that are related to real-world communicative situations. In the following sequence, all the tasks are related to planning a trip.

Discuss with friends / family where you want to go.	Visit a travel agency to get information.	Plan the trip and the dates with your traveling companions.	Go back to the travel agency to discuss flights, accommodation, and costs.	Decide on places of interest to visit when you get to your destination.	Tell others about your plans for your trip.

In teaching a sequence like the one above, teachers can select from a whole set of different task types, presented below with some examples. For further discussions about speaking tasks, see Chapter 9.

Table 8.2: *Examples of tasks for speaking*

Task types	Examples
Presentations.	Ask learners to prepare a two-minute talk on their favorite celebrity and present it to their group.
Project tasks.	Have learners work in groups to design a poster about a topic they are all interested in. Get them to give a presentation based on the poster to the rest of the class.
Research tasks.	Ask learners to search the Internet for good examples of ESL students talking about how they learn English. Get learners to discuss in groups which suggestions they would use. Ask them to present their conclusions along with their reasons.
Survey tasks.	Ask learners to work in groups to prepare a survey about their favorite films. Get them to interview other learners and present the results to the class.
Creative tasks.	Bring a variety of "dress-up" clothes to class (or ask learners to do so). Help learners prepare for a class "fashion show." Get them to describe to the class what their partner is wearing.
Role-play tasks.	Get students in an ESP class to prepare for future professional roles. In a business class, have students play the roles of professional and client, based on an authentic task performed by the professional (e.g., an accountant advising a client). If possible, record the task using video, and play the video back to the students.

> **Think about it**
>
> What kinds of tasks do you use in your classroom or see used in a class you are familiar with? How do the learners respond to these tasks? To what exent do the tasks link together? How do they serve to build up learners' speaking skills and knowledge?

As students progress through the linked sequences and the particular tasks and activities that accompany them, teachers can monitor their students' spoken production and look for instances where some speaking skills may need to be recycled through extension tasks. Giving students opportunities for further practice of some strategies or structures enables them to improve fluency and accuracy as they go along. See Chapter 10 for activities that help students to do this.

Whereas task-based approaches to planning content tend to focus on the *processes* of speaking, a text-based approach takes the *product*, the genre or text, as a starting point. In Chapter 5 we discussed genres of speaking, and a text-based approach is underpinned by the concept of genre. Text-based approaches first identify the interactional and transactional texts that are important to learners' goals and needs. They then focus the learners' attention on the overall structure of the text, the linguistic patterns that typify the text, the kind of discourse strategies, such as turn taking and feedback, used by the speakers, and other texts that might be related. Instruction using a text-based syllabus is underpinned by a teaching-learning cycle in which teachers structure the students' developing skills and abilities through a series of teaching-learning phases.

In Chapter 7, we presented a teaching-speaking cycle, which is a comprehensive and holistic cycle that guides the teaching and learning of speaking, including the examination of texts for language and discourse knowledge development. While the teaching-learning cycle below also provides a framework for teachers to plan classroom activities, it differs in focus from the cycle in Chapter 7. The aim of the cycle in Figure 8.8 below is to draw attention to the *products* of speaking, in the form of genres or text-types that students will need to manage as interaction. Thus the cycle in Figure 8.8 is associated specifically with a text-based approach and has come mainly from research conducted in Australia (Callaghan & Rothery 1988).

Building the context involves the teacher and learners in whole-class discussions in order to establish the social and cultural purpose of the text, identify the kinds of contexts where the text would occur, identify the topic of the text, and identify students' existing knowledge about the text.

In this phase, the teacher might use images, photos, video or audio material, and objects or illustrations to get students to predict the topic and content of the text. The teacher might then play a video or audio recording and ask students to listen for the key messages being exchanged. Another activity might be to brainstorm vocabulary from the images shown, or to get students to discuss in groups what they know about the text from their own experiences or cultures. The teacher might also ask students to do some research of their own on the topic, using the Internet and other resources. The teacher could also organize class visits or excursions, in order to provide

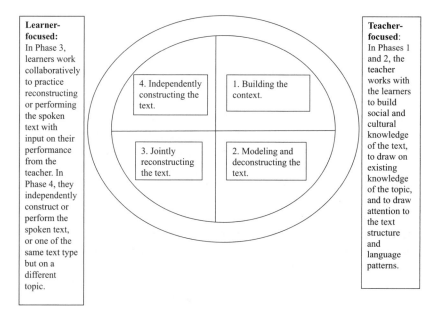

Figure 8.8: The teaching-learning cycle (adapted from Hammond et al. 1992).

learners with experiential opportunities that can then form the basis for extending their knowledge of the topic. The overall purpose of this phase is a preparatory one, to refine the students' cultural and social knowledge about the text and its context, and to prepare them for the linguistic features that they will need to practice in order to perform the text successfully.

Modeling and deconstructing the text is the phase of the cycle where the teacher focuses attention explicitly on the structural aspects of the text. Activities will involve helping students to understand the staging of the text and the way that the linguistic patterns (formulaic expressions, verb tenses, adjacency pairs, and so on) operate at each stage (see Chapter 5). Teachers are likely to consolidate learners' knowledge of text structure by asking them to practice identifying textual stages or focus on the way the relationships between speakers influences vocabulary choices. Learners could be asked to drill certain grammatical patterns, or to complete cloze exercises where they fill in the blanks with appropriate content words.

The *joint reconstruction of the text* is the phase where the teacher begins to hand over responsibility for creating the text to the learners. Learners could be asked to role play the text they have studied, with or without the script, or to do activities where they ask each other questions about various aspects of the text, such as how speakers open and close the text, the kind of language they use at different stages, or the way that they demonstrate their relationships. The teacher could, for example, ask learners to recreate the text to show more formal or informal relationships, making choices of vocabulary and grammar that reflect greater or lesser formality.

The final phase of the cycle concerns the *independent construction of the text*. Here, the learners take full responsibility for creating a text appropriate to an interactional or transactional spoken exchange. Role playing a particular social situation and getting feedback on the performance is likely to be a focus activity at this stage. Students could be asked to choose their own topics so that the kinds of texts they practice are related to real-life needs. For example, a class of mothers with young children might want to be able to handle health appointments more effectively, or participate in teacher-parent consultations. Teenagers might want to speak about their interests to English-speaking family members, or to homestay families. Younger learners might choose to narrate a short account of weekend or holiday activities or memorable events, or to discuss their favorite pets.

The text-based teaching cycle is intended to be used as a flexible framework to guide instruction, so that even though the four phases are labeled sequentially, for various reasons, teachers could begin at different points in the cycle. For example, teachers might begin the teaching unit by asking students to produce a spoken text (Phase 4) that is important for eventual test taking. The purpose here would be to assess current skills, and analyze what might need to be included in the content of a unit of work in order to refine and develop speaking abilities. Alternatively, the teacher might begin by getting students to collaborate in jointly constructing the text. However the teacher decides to use the cycle, it should be borne in mind that the overall aim of this approach is to assist students in understanding and producing whole spoken texts in their contexts.

Try it

Which of the starting points described in the teaching-learning cycle above would work best for your students? Develop a plan for a unit of work, preferably with colleagues who teach a similar type of learner group and class, based on one of these starting points.

Classroom interaction

While the syllabus might highlight the content areas to be covered, it is the nature of the classroom interaction, and its success in bringing the content to life, that can make a difference in what opportunities students are given for learning. The teacher's ultimate role in classroom interaction is rather like that of an orchestra conductor who helps the musicians practice in order to bring all the various parts of the work together, with a result that is not only successful, but also cohesive and harmonious.

Scaffolding or supporting learning across units of work through finely tuned interaction is an important skill for teachers. When tasks and texts are new to learners, providing adequate support as learners' knowledge and skills expand is a necessary foundation for successful learning. The notion of scaffolding is appealing to many teachers who can readily envision how, when a building is constructed, it is supported by scaffolds that are removed as the construction process advances. Here we will discuss the implications of this concept for teachers.

The term scaffolding is associated with Bruner, whose research with his colleagues (Wood, Bruner & Ross 1976) on mother and child interactions led to observations about the role of "more expert others" in supporting and mediating the learning of novice learners. In the study, as children attempted something new, either linguistically or behaviorally, the mothers scaffolded their learning by:

- Providing and naming information or experiences they were not able to express alone.
- Engaging in jointly constructing what they wished to do or say.
- Supplying elaborated forms of expressions or actions.
- Modeling language and behavior so that children could develop their own forms of discourse and action.
- Linking what the children wished to say or do with previous experiences and similar events.

As the child's competence became greater, the mother was able to withdraw support and hand over more responsibility for independent action and expression to the child. The notion of scaffolding has interesting and important implications for classroom interaction. The Russian psychologist, Lev Vygotsky (1978), on whose work Bruner's concept of scaffolding is based, advanced the concept of "the zone of proximal development," or ZPD, which refers to the critical point at which learners, given their current knowledge and competence, require support from other more expert members of their community if they are to develop. In a classroom, scaffolded interaction means that the teacher's role becomes one of providing explicit instruction and guided practice at a key point of need. Scaffolded instruction also involves the teacher in thinking about when it is appropriate to withdraw support, while ensuring that the outcomes of spoken learning tasks and texts will still be successful. We can envision teacher and learner responsibility for learning, as one of "shifting" classroom roles, illustrated in Figure 8.9.

Teacher responsibility	Joint responsibility	Learner responsibility

←——————————————————————————————————→

High teacher support   Low teacher support

Figure 8.9: Shifting teacher and learner roles in classroom interaction.

Whichever syllabus approach a teacher decides to take in a speaking program, it is the nature of the teacher and learner interaction that will create different affordances (van Lier 1996), or significant opportunities for learning. While it may seem to be a truism to say so, in courses on speaking, providing learners with maximum opportunities for speaking in English is a central component of the instructional process.

Discuss it

To what extent does your classroom promote scaffolded learning? How useful do you consider this concept for your teaching situation? To what extent does your classroom interaction shift between teacher responsibility for learning and learner responsibility for learning? What opportunities does your classroom offer for extensive use of English by the learners? Discuss these questions with your colleagues. If you are not currently teaching, discuss a teaching situation you are familiar with.

Selecting materials and resources

Many teachers must work within a mandated syllabus or curriculum where the materials and resources to be used are already selected for them. For many teachers, working in these contexts the textbook may, in fact, become the course that is offered to learners. In these circumstances, rather than following the textbook step-by-step, teachers may be able to pick out particular tasks and activities or modify and extend them, according to their perceptions of their learners' needs. In other situations, teachers are free to select the coursebooks they prefer to work with, or to develop their own materials and select resources. Teacher-made resources and accompanying handouts and task sheets become the medium through which the content is delivered, and, depending on their proficiency level, learners themselves may be able to play a part in developing materials that interest them. Resources that supplement materials could include visuals, radio, television, the Internet, and recordings of spoken interactions collected by the teacher or students (but teachers should be certain to obtain appropriate permission for copyrighted materials). In short, the materials and other resources used in any course will depend on the extent to which a course and its textbooks and resources are mandated, whether by the school, local authority, or Ministry, and on how free teachers are to select their own source materials.

Apart from the degree of freedom accorded to teachers in choosing materials for a speaking course, there are a number of other considerations likely to come into play. These considerations have to do with a) teaching-learning constraints, b) types of materials, and c) teachers' instructional approaches. We outline the factors in each of these three categories below:

Teaching-learning constraints:
• Number of classes taught by the teacher.
• Class length and times per week, and course duration.
• Number of students in the class.
• Age of students.
• Extent of disparity in student levels (mixed-ability classes).
• Resources and time for materials development.
• Level and type of support from supervisors and administrators.

Types of materials:
• Availability of up-to-date, quality materials.
• Range of material types.
• Compatibility of material content with teacher approach.
• Compatibility of material content with learner needs.
• Availability of effective materials previously developed by colleagues.
• Availability of technology and other resources, in addition to textbooks.

Teachers' instructional approaches:
• Personal knowledge of nature and features of spoken English.
• Use of both pedagogical and real-life materials to support learning.
• Evaluation of the fit of learners' speaking needs with materials.
• Extent of flexibility in using and adapting materials.
• Previous experience in developing teacher-made material.
• Previous experience in adapting and extending material.
• Knowledge of other resources available for learning.

Think about it

To what extent do the factors outlined above affect your selection of materials? Are there other factors influencing your situation that are not included in the list? In your teaching context, how do you go about selecting or adapting materials? If possible, discuss your ideas with a colleague.

Inevitably for all teachers, questions about the suitability and flexibility of the materials their students use in the course will arise. One way in which teachers may respond to these dilemmas is to personalize materials and resources to better match the types of speaking contexts, participants, and topics that are familiar to learners (see Lewis 2007; Lindstromberg 2004). When considering the materials for the course and how they promote effective learning, it is useful to ask: Do the materials promote the speaking skills that are most needed by the students? Do they facilitate the cognitive aspects of learning? Do they extend students' knowledge of metalinguistic strategies? Do they highlight the cultural and social purposes of different kinds of tasks and texts? Do learners encounter genuine reasons to communicate and to speak and act as themselves?

Considering outcomes

Both during and also at the end of the speaking course, attention needs to be placed on considering the course outcomes. Outcomes are concerned with what has been achieved by the learners as a result of participating in the course, and the extent to which the course has met its goals and objectives. There are two components that need to be considered: assessment of learning and learner progress, and evaluation of the effectiveness and success of the course as a whole.

Role of assessment in program outcomes

Assessment of student progress plays a vital part in planning any speaking program. As already suggested, assessment occurs not just at the end of the program, but should be integrated into classroom tasks throughout the course so that teachers can check on learner progress and modify the content where necessary. This kind of intermittent assessment is called *formative* assessment, as it allows for the continued formation of learning. Assessment that takes place at the end of the course is known as *summative* assessment, since it sums up what overall progress learners have achieved as a result of completing the course.

Formative assessment is most likely to be informal, and many tasks and texts included in the course content will inevitably lend themselves to teacher and student observations on progress being made in relation to the speaking skills and strategies included. Examples of activities that might be used for student assessment are informal tests, role plays, or interviews (see Chapter 12 for further discussion). Teachers can use formative assessment to give individual feedback to students or to discuss individual learning plans, as well as to diagnose overall difficulties the whole class might be experiencing. As a result, adjustments can be made during the course to topics, tasks, and texts, and to the kinds of activities used.

Summative assessment is likely to be more formal with students being assessed according to rating scales, tests, or descriptors of speaking competency required within the program, such as the oral-production descriptors below from the Common European Framework.

If formal descriptors or texts are not used, teachers may be involved in conducting other types of summative assessment, using procedures such as assessing student portfolios, recorded presentations, or role-play performances. We will discuss the assessment of speaking in greater detail in Chapter 12.

	OVERALL ORAL DEVELOPMENT
C2	Can produce clear, smoothly flowing well-structured speech with an effective logical structure which helps the recipient to notice and remember significant points.
C1	Can give clear, detailed descriptions and presentations on complex subjects, integrating sub-themes, developing particular points, and rounding off with an appropriate conclusion.
B2	Can give clear, systematically developed descriptions and presentations, with appropriate highlighting of significant points and relevant supporting detail. Can give clear, detailed descriptions and presentations on a wide range of subjects in his / her field of interest, expanding and supporting the ideas with subsidiary points and relevant examples.
B1	Can reasonably fluently sustain a straightforward description of one of a variety of subjects within his / her field of interest, presenting it as a linear sequence of points.
A2	Can give a simple description or presentation of people, living or working conditions, daily routines, likes / dislikes, etc. as a short series of simple phrases and sentences linked into a list.
A1	Can produce simple, mainly isolated phrases about people and places.

Figure 8.10: CEFR oral-production descriptors.

Role of evaluation in program outcomes

Evaluation differs from assessment in that it takes a much broader account of the various factors contributing to the success of the program. Brown (1989: 223) defines evaluation as follows:

> The systematic collection and analysis of all relevant information necessary to promote the improvement of a curriculum and assess its effectiveness and efficiency, as well as the participants' attitudes within the context of the particular institution involved.

Given the broad scope of evaluation, a course could be evaluated on a number of different aspects, including:

- The students' achievement on tests and other forms of assessment.
- The needs analysis and assessment processes for determining the content of the syllabus.
- The placement of the students.
- The coverage of the content of the syllabus.
- The topics, tasks, and texts selected.
- The materials and resources selected.
- The appropriacy of the formative and summative assessment processes.

Like assessment, evaluation can also be formative or summative. Formative evaluation will focus on evaluating aspects of the course as it is being developed and implemented, in order to refine and improve it. Formative assessment is likely to be particularly important where a speaking course is being trialed for the first time. Formative assessment can be considered a "forward-looking" process, aimed at enhancing the eventual outcomes of the course and maximizing the learning experience for the learners and the teacher.

Summative evaluation occurs at the end of a course. It evaluates the course as a whole from the point of view of its strengths and weaknesses, and whether it has met the stated goals and objectives. On the basis of this summative evaluation, recommendations are then made for how a course should be changed, or, in some cases, whether it should continue at all in its present form. Summative evaluation often includes getting input from various "stakeholders." Apart from the teachers and learners in the program, stakeholders could involve external input from administrators, parents, employers, academics, consultants, or even bureaucrats concerned with program policy development. Views and opinions on the effectiveness of the course are typically sought through interviews, questionnaires, or other forms of feedback, such as materials evaluations. In contrast to formative evaluation, summative evaluation primarily looks backward over the course as a whole, although with the ultimate purpose of making recommendations for the future.

Think about it

In your teaching context, are formal processes in place for evaluating speaking courses? If not, how is evaluation conducted? Who is involved in the evaluation process? What input do learners have in the evaluation of the course?

Summary

This chapter has responded to the questions posed by the teacher in Graves' example at the beginning of this chapter. These are key questions likely to be asked by English teachers around the world who are involved in creating an effective speaking course. We have considered in broad detail the essential steps, components, and processes involved in planning, including:

- Consideration of the learner group and learner characteristics: the age, language level, linguistic and cultural background of the learners, and their previous experience learning English. An effective speaking course should place the learners at the heart of the planning process.
- Assessing and analyzing learners' needs as a basis for understanding what will need to be included in the course.
- The role in the planning process of setting clear goals and objectives, in order to steer the course in the right direction.
- Deriving syllabus content, and developing and selecting materials and resources based on learner needs and course goals and objectives.
- Processes for considering course outcomes through formative and summative assessment of learner achievement.
- The role of evaluation in determining the effectiveness of the course and in identifying further course modification and development.

Group-learning tasks

1. With colleagues, share your strategies and instruments for conducting a needs assessment. If you do not usually conduct a needs assessment, prepare one that would help you find out more about your learners' perceptions of their needs. If necessary, use or adapt the ideas in this

chapter. To what extent could you involve your learners in preparing a needs assessment?

2. Keeping in mind the characteristics of the learner groups you teach and their needs, develop a set of goals and objectives for a specified speaking course (your current course or one you will soon teach). Do this task first as an individual activity, and then share your proposals with your colleagues. Compare your ideas, and ask for feedback on each other's proposals. Would you modify, omit, or add to what you have already written as a result of this discussion?

3. Share the topics, tasks, or texts that you use in your course with your colleagues. Explain the types of activities you use for teaching. Provide feedback on each other's ideas, and discuss how you could use or adapt the activities for your learner group.

4. With your group, collect samples of the speaking materials used in your courses. Evaluate them individually, using the points below. Then compare your responses across the group. Consider ways that materials considered by the group to be less effective could be modified or extended.

	Strongly agree	Neutral	Strongly disagree
The materials are motivating.			
The materials appeal to students' interests.			
The materials meet students' learning needs.			
The materials allow for success in practicing speaking.			
The materials are at the appropriate level of difficulty.			
The materials contain sequences of activities that scaffold learning appropriately.			
The materials allow for a focus on accuracy as well as fluency.			

Further reading

Feez, S. (1999) *Text-based Syllabus Design*, Sydney: NSW Adult Migrant English Service and National Centre for English Language Teaching and Research.

Burns, A. and Richards, J. C. (eds.) (2012) *The Cambridge Guide to Pedagogy and Practice in Second Language Teaching*, New York: Cambridge University Press.

Richards, J. C. (2000) *Curriculum Development in Language Teaching*, New York: Cambridge University Press.

Thornbury, S. (2005) *How to Teach Speaking*, Harlow: Pearson Education / Longman.

PART IV
CLASSROOM PRACTICES AND PROCESSES

9 *Speaking tasks*

The teaching-speaking cycle presented in Chapter 7 consists of a number of stages that work together to develop learners' speaking competence in a holistic manner. It focuses on the skills and knowledge that learners need to develop their speaking, as well as addressing metacognitive and affective aspects of their learning. Each stage of the cycle requires appropriate kinds of learning tasks and materials. Examples of tasks were introduced in Chapter 8 when we discussed how teachers can plan units of work in a speaking program. This chapter continues the discussion by focusing on details of types of speaking tasks that can be used to develop fluency, accuracy, and complexity in learners' speech production. The chapter will address the following questions:

1. What kinds of speaking tasks can be used to promote communication and fluency during speaking practice?
2. How can teachers organize students into pairs and groups for speaking practice?
3. What must teachers consider when planning speaking tasks or adapting activities for speaking?

The following topics are discussed:

* Three types of speaking tasks:
  a. Communication-gap task (information and context gaps).
  b. Discussion tasks.
  c. Monologic tasks.
* Organization of pair and group work.
* Considerations when planning speaking tasks.

Introduction

In Chapter 5, we discussed two types of spoken interactions, namely, conversations and encounters in which language is used for interactional (interpersonal) purposes, and those where it is used for transactional (pragmatic) purposes. While second language learners may be familiar with interacting in both of these ways in their first language, they invariably face different kinds of challenges when they have to speak in a language they are still trying to acquire. Their performance is affected by a number of cognitive and affective factors, and they need a great deal of help and support from teachers to develop their speaking competence. The methodological framework in Chapter 6 and the teaching-speaking cycle in Chapter 7 offer a principled approach to planning and organizing learning activities that can help learners develop their speaking in a holistic manner. In this chapter, we show how teachers can plan and design their own tasks for learners to practice their speaking. We describe three types of speaking tasks that can help to promote speaking proficiency. These tasks can be used in Stages 3 and 5 of the teaching-speaking cycle, the stages where tasks are introduced for the first time to practice fluency and subsequently repeated to promote greater fluency, as well as accuracy and complexity. We also discuss how to organize learners during pair and group work, and suggest some techniques for doing so. Finally, we highlight some key considerations that teachers need to bear in mind when planning speaking tasks or adapting existing activities for speaking practice.

Types of speaking tasks

The main purpose of using speaking tasks is to provide learners with opportunities to practice their speaking so that they can achieve greater fluency. Not all speaking tasks are the same, however. Some may require learners to work on simple activities while other tasks are complex, as are the outcomes of the tasks. In this section, we present three types of speaking tasks that make different demands on learners' skills and linguistic knowledge. These are *communication-gap* tasks, *discussion* tasks, and *monologic* tasks.

To participate in communication-gap and discussion tasks, learners typically work in pairs or small groups to achieve the specified outcomes. The tasks involve a combination of transactional and interpersonal interaction. Learners focus on getting the information and views they need while, at the same time, maintaining some interpersonal interaction. Interpersonal interaction results as they seek cooperation to complete the task, or explore with others their opinions and ideas. Through this kind of collaboration, learners practice different core speaking skills, draw on their knowledge about language and discourse, and use strategies to enhance their communication. In contrast, monologic tasks are those that require the learner to produce pieces of extended discourse individually. The form of interaction is mainly transactional, as the purpose is typically to convey information to the listeners, for example, in a presentation or a talk. The context may be formal or informal, and feedback from listeners is typically received after the information has been communicated. In the next section, we will describe each type of task in greater detail and offer some examples for each one.

Communication-gap tasks

Gaps are common in real-life communication. Participants in an interaction do not share the same information or background knowledge. That is the whole purpose of communication – to close some of the gaps that exist between us and the people we are interacting with. In a casual conversation, we share information (jokes, gossip) that others may not know. When we listen to someone give a speech, we look out for things that we do not know about, for example, facts or views that we hope the speaker will provide us with. For most people, the gaps create an incentive to continue with the interaction. In the language classroom, teachers can make use of speaking tasks that have two kinds of communication gaps: information and context.

In *information-gap* tasks, learners are given different sets of information for a task. They need to work together in pairs or small groups to share the information, in order to achieve a pre-defined goal, and typically follow these steps:

1. Understand the information that they have.
2. Explain to one another the type of information they need.
3. Orally communicate with their partners or members in the group the information they have processed.
4. Ask questions to clarify or confirm when meaning is not clear.
5. Ask for repetition as often as necessary.
6. Complete the gap in the information in whatever form is required.

The information given to each learner may be presented in a number of ways, including printed handouts, recorded audio or video texts, short reading texts, pictures or diagrams, and printed texts with illustrations. We can compare an information-gap task to a jigsaw puzzle. In the speaking task, learners have different pieces of the puzzle that they have to present through the spoken language. Using the information that they have, learners have to speak to one another to complete the task collaboratively. Their focus should primarily be on conveying meaning through whatever linguistic resources they have or whatever preparation they have done beforehand. Information-gap tasks are very versatile, and we can use them to get learners to practice many important speech function skills, such as describing, comparing, contrasting, listing, summarizing, explaining, and clarifying meaning.

For *context-gap* tasks, learners in both pairs or groups are given the same set of information, such as a set of pictures and a list of words. They have to use the information to construct new content for their listeners. These tasks are called context-gap tasks because they allow individual learners to create a context for the information that they are sharing, encouraging them to express their meaning by drawing on their knowledge of the language. Compared with information-gap tasks, context-gap tasks give learners greater flexibility in the way they use and communicate the information that they have. Typically, information is given as small, unrelated chunks to the learner who will be doing the speaking. The learner's task is to use the various pieces of information to construct a piece of coherent text. An example of a context-gap task, as mentioned above, is asking learners to tell a story using a series of randomized pictures or words. Although the other learners can see the pictures or the words, they have to listen closely to the story as it unfolds.

Context-gap tasks are in general more cognitively challenging for the learners, compared with information-gap tasks. Learners have to put together pieces of text that involve dynamic relationships, such as the way characters in a story interact, the way an event unfolds, or the steps that are involved in a procedure. The challenge is not only for the speakers. The listeners will have to make sense of what is being said, without first knowing what the context is. The context is built up slowly as they listen to and interpret the input. Participants in a context-gap task will have to do more than just listen for details. They need to listen globally, as well as predict what they are going to hear.

Figure 9.1 presents examples of communication-gap tasks and the outcomes that the tasks generate, and includes a description of the procedure for carrying out the different kinds of tasks.

Task	Communicative outcomes	Type of gap
a. Read / listen and compare.	Lists of similarities and differences.	Information.
b. Sequence and complete.	Descriptions of pictures and completed text.	Information.
c. Construct and compare.	Descriptions of procedures / process.	Information / context.
d. Ask and answer.	Completed questionnaires.	Information / context.
e. Select and narrate.	Short narrative texts.	Context.

Figure 9.1: A sample of communication-gap tasks.

(continued)

a. Read / listen and compare.

Outcomes:	Lists of similarities and differences.
Resources:	Short narratives: two versions of a story printed as handouts or recorded for playback.
Procedure 1:	Students work in pairs as A and B.
	They are given one version of the story.
	Each student reads the text and tries to remember as many details as possible.
	Pairs tell each other what they have read.
	They identify three similarities and three differences in the two versions of the story.
Procedure 2:	Students work in pairs as A and B.
	They are given one version of the story.
	Both students read their version of the story individually to understand it first.
	Student A reads aloud his / her story while Student B listens without reading his / her text.
	Student B then identifies three similarities and three differences in the two versions of the story.
Option(s):	For Procedure 1, the students could be given different recorded versions to listen to. They take notes as they listen, and use the notes to retell the story to each other.

b. Sequence and complete.

Outcomes:	Sequenced pictures / diagrams and completed text.
Resources:	Pictures or diagrams printed on handouts.
Procedure:	Student A has a complete cartoon sequence (at least four frames) with dialogue in speech balloons.
	Student B gets a handout with the frames jumbled up. The words in the speech balloons are blanked out.
	Student A describes the frames in the cartoon strip sequentially, and Student B sequences the jumbled frames.
	Next, Student A dictates the words from the speech bubble. Student B fills in the words in the speech bubbles.
Option(s):	Use a diagram depicting a process or procedure (e.g., a flow chart).

c. Construct and compare.

Outcomes:	Descriptions of procedures / process.
Resources:	Handouts with a list of food ingredients. (Pictures can be used instead of words.)
Procedure 1:	Students work in pairs as A and B.
	They are given one set of ingredients each.
	Each one must look at the ingredients and suggest a dish that can be prepared using all the ingredients.
	Each student then describes how he / she would prepare the dish with the ingredients.

Figure 9.1: A sample of communication-gap tasks.

(continued)

Procedure 2:   Students work in pairs as A and B.

Each student is given a different set of ingredients.

Pairs decide what dish they can prepare with the ingredients given.

Student A tells Student B how he / she intends to prepare the dish, without telling him / her what the dish is.

Student B can ask questions to clarify, while listening to the description.

Option(s):   Weak students can be given jumbled sentences referring to various stages in the process. They can work on the task collaboratively by sequencing the stages in a process.

d. Ask and answer.

Outcomes: Completed questionnaires.

Resources: A list of printed questions with space for answers.

Procedure: Each student approaches another one with a set of questions.

Students take turns asking the questions and completing their questionnaire with the answers they get.

When everyone has completed the activity after a predetermined number of minutes, students go back to their places.

The teacher calls on some students to tell others about the students they have spoken to.

Option(s):   Instead of using the questions given by the teacher, students draw up a list of questions that they would like to ask their classmates.

e. Select and narrate.

Outcomes: Short narrative texts.

Resources: A set of ten pictures of objects, events, and faces.

Procedure: Students work in pairs as A and B.

Each student has the same set of pictures. Individually, students select eight of the pictures and use them to develop a short story based on the pictures.

Students listen to each other tell the story.

After both students have told the story, they discuss why they have chosen these particular pictures and how they have used them to tell their story.

Option(s):   Students work together, as a pair, to select the pictures and jointly construct the story.

They join up with another pair to narrate their story.

Figure 9.1: A sample of communication-gap tasks.

Try it

Take a look at some speaking tasks in a coursebook. Are there any communication-gap tasks? Can you change an information-gap task into a context-gap task, and vice versa? State at least one way in which this modification will change the type of language and speaking skills that students will need to use compared to the original version?

Discussion tasks

Discussion tasks contain a genuine communicative purpose that may be absent in some communication-gap tasks. Learners have to share their personal ideas with one another by drawing on their own background knowledge and experience. They also often have to negotiate with one another as they attempt to arrive at a solution that is acceptable to all. Group-discussion tasks can take place through simulations. Simulations are "classroom activities which reproduce or simulate real situations and which often involve dramatization and group discussion" (Richards & Schmidt 2002: 487). In simulations, learners take on a role, such as a politician, a parent, or a judge, and they are given scenarios to work with where a solution is needed. Unlike strict role plays where each learner is told how to behave (e.g., lodge a complaint) and, in some cases, what to say (e.g., using role or cue cards), simulations allow learners to rely on their own knowledge and experience to deal with the simulated problem, as they would if they were actually the people whose roles they adopt.

Learners may also simply participate in a discussion as themselves. They are given a real-life issue or problem, and work together to make recommendations or proposals and offer solutions. The topics for discussion need not always be from the teacher. Learners could also identify an issue or problem themselves that they want to discuss. In addition to dealing with real or hypothetical issues and problems, small-group discussions are also excellent opportunities for learners to solve language-related tasks that involve the four skills of speaking, listening, reading, and writing in an integrated manner. For example, learners can work together to discuss the plot of a story, and jointly write it to be read aloud to the class. Alternatively, they may be asked to prepare the beginning or the ending of a story.

To get learners to engage in a discussion, teachers have to provide them with relevant prompts, which can be in the form of written or spoken language. For example, learners could be given the details of a scenario or problem in a printed handout, or they could be asked to listen to a recording of a situation and use that as the basis for their discussion. In some discussions, learners may have to discuss the content of what they read or hear. For example, in a simulation activity where the learners take on the role of judges in a singing competition, they can be asked to listen to audio recordings, or to watch video recordings of several "competitors" and base their decision on the actual performance of the individuals.

A benefit of group discussion tasks is that they can potentially develop high-level thinking and reasoning skills. The fact that the prompts or scenarios are taken from real-life situations will offer motivating contexts for learners to use language to communicate. Discussions are abstract tasks and are useful in helping learners develop the type of decontextualized skills that we referred to in Chapter 1. Learners have to find ways of communicating the ideas in their head to other people as clearly as they can. Their listeners do not know what the learners may want to say and, therefore, will rely on them to make their views explicit. Discussion tasks can be quite challenging for learners if they are to do them well.

Teachers can set goals that are achievable by varying the degree of difficulty or challenge of a discussion task, which can be done by changing the communicative outcomes of the task. Some outcomes can be relatively straightforward, but the process of arriving at these outcomes may be very demanding. Take, for example, an outcome such as a group having to discuss and arrive at a consensus on how some information should be reorganized. This can take the form of ranking (*first, second, third*, etc.) or matching (linking text with the relevant pictures). The level of difficulty can vary depending on whether learners have to work with abstract concepts, such as views and ideas, or more concrete prompts, such as pictures.

Figure 9.2 presents examples of discussion tasks and the outcomes that the discussions lead to. They can be carried out as simulation activities or as straightforward group discussion. A description of the procedure for carrying out the tasks follow. These tasks and their procedures serve as examples of what teachers can do, and teachers are encouraged to use these tasks, as well as adapt them freely to meet the needs of their students.

It is useful to note that not all discussions must lead to a communicative outcome, as Figure 9.2 shows. Teachers can also organize philosophical discussions that allow learners to express themselves creatively and critically. The purpose is not to achieve an outcome, but purely to give learners a chance to practice their speaking skills by tackling an abstract topic.

Task	Communicative outcomes
a. Discuss and propose.	Recommendations.
b. Discuss and organize.	Organized information.
c. Discuss and judge.	Evaluation.
d. Discuss and solve.	Solution.
e. Discuss and plan.	An action plan.

a. Discuss and propose.

Outcomes:	Recommendations
Resources:	—
Procedure 1:	In a simulation, students assume the roles of teachers in a high school.
	The school intends to select three students to represent it as its young ambassadors in an international event.
	The students draw up a list of criteria used for short-listing and finally selecting the chosen three.
	They present their list to the rest of the class.
Procedure 2:	Students are asked to design a gadget that would enhance the quality of life of a group of senior citizens.
	The students discuss a challenge that senior citizens face and the function of their proposed gadget.
	They discuss the components of the gadget and details of its design.
	When they reach an agreement, the design is drawn up on a flip chart and displayed for others to see.
Option(s):	After completing the discussion tasks, the groups can be asked to share their outcomes with another group, instead of with the whole class. This would provide more opportunities for the learners to interact with one another, thereby increasing talking time.

b. Discuss and organize.

Outcomes:	Organized information.
Resources:	Statements printed on pieces of paper.
Procedure 1:	Students are given ten statements on an issue, such as students taking on part-time work.
	They discuss and identify the statements, which either support or oppose the issue.
	They organize the statements into two groups: "Support" and "Oppose."

Figure 9.2: A sample of discussion tasks.

(continued)

Procedure 2: Students brainstorm a list of items commonly found in a woman's handbag or a student's schoolbag.

They select ten items considered to be useful and rank them in order of importance.

They compare their lists and ranked items with other groups.

Option(s): After they have done the task, students can be asked to make up similar tasks. This will generate another round of discussion.

c. Discuss and judge.

Outcomes: Evaluation.

Resources: Recordings or printed materials.

Procedure 1: Students assume the role of judges in an art competition.

They are given a number of pictures of paintings by famous artists.

Pretending that the pictures are pieces entered in the competition, the students discuss and select the top three winners.

The student judges must be prepared to defend their results with other groups who have the same task.

Procedure 2: Students watch three TV commercials that promote a similar type of product (e.g., perfume, airlines, breakfast cereals, etc.).

They discuss and reach a consensus on the one that they find most effective.

The groups present their choices to the rest of the class.

Option(s): The students can be asked to watch a recording of prime-time news and decide which item was the most newsworthy.

d. Discuss and solve.

Outcomes: Solution.

Resources: Information that is needed to arrive at a possible solution.

Procedure 1: Students brainstorm a list of problems in the world.

Working in groups, the students select one problem.

They propose possible solutions to the problem.

Procedure 2: Students assume the role of detectives who have to solve a crime.

They are given a number of clues that they must use.

Through a sequence of logical deduction, the group arrives at a solution.

Option(s): Students can be asked to suggest a problem that another group has to solve.

Figure 9.2: A sample of discussion tasks.

(continued)

e. Discuss and plan.

Outcomes:	An action plan.
Resources:	A scenario that requires some planning to take place.
Procedure 1:	Students take on the role of different members in a family: father, mother, or children.
	They have to find ways to increase their household income and reduce their utilities bill.
	The "family" works out a plan of action that involves the entire family, as well as individuals.
	The plan should include specific targets and steps for achieving the targets.
Procedure 2:	The students are given a day off from classes in their school or college.
	They discuss how they intend to use the day so that they can practice their English and have fun at the same time.
	The plan should include specific targets and steps for achieving the targets.
Option(s):	Students can be asked to select somebody they have read about, or heard of, who needs help. They discuss and draw up a plan for how to offer help to the person, and follow up by actually putting their plan into action.

Figure 9.2: A sample of discussion tasks.

Discuss it

In small groups, suggest a list of hypothetical problems that you can use for tasks with a group of learners of your choice. Identify the speaking and listening skills that learners can practice through these tasks.

Monologic tasks

A monologue in the context of language learning can be defined as an extended piece of discourse that an individual produces for an audience in formal or informal situations. Monologic tasks are undertaken by learners individually, but are best conducted within small groups. Small group work not only reduces the language anxiety that many learners face, but also maximizes the use of class time and gives more learners a chance to talk. There can also be occasional opportunities for students to speak in front of their class. In monologic tasks, learners get a chance to speak extensively on a topic without any initial interruptions. Questions may follow from what has been said when other learners are asked to respond to what they hear, but the speakers should be given a specified period of time to speak before this happens. In monologic tasks, learners may be asked to share their views on issues, personal experiences, stories or jokes, or even simple topics that they may have little knowledge or experience of, requiring them to make up the content as they go along. Monologic tasks can fall along a continuum from planned, edited, and rehearsed speech to speech that is spontaneous, unedited, and creative.

Tasks that require learners to produce extended discourse give them opportunities to use what has been referred to as "decontextualized oral language skills." Decontextualized language use is the ability to talk about topics that are beyond the immediate context, and it requires linguistic skills to make the meaning of these topics clear to listeners who do not have the same background knowledge. In monologic tasks, learners typically have to learn to introduce, maintain, and close a topic; use cohesive devices to organize extended discourse; and anticipate and share listeners' perspectives. Effective decontextualized language use is dependent upon good grammatical and pragmatic competence, as well as knowledge of appropriate vocabulary for particular topics. Equally important is knowledge of how the discourse can be organized appropriately, according to the type of genre it falls under. Many language learners may not have a high level of command over these aspects of the language, but these competencies and knowledge of discourse can be developed and enhanced in the language classroom.

Figure 9.3 presents examples of monologic tasks. They may look more challenging than the previous two types of speaking tasks, but teachers can, in fact, use them with learners of different age groups. The level of challenge can be modified by changing the topic, adjusting the scope of the monologue, and varying planning time. For example, a task can be made simple by allowing the learners to select a topic of their choice, determine the scope of the topic, and plan the speech before it is delivered. On the other hand, learners could also be asked to pick a topic randomly and speak about it without any preparation. In the case of young learners, the task can be limited to genres that they are familiar with, such as narratives and information reports.

In addition to the types of monologic tasks mentioned in Figure 9.3, we can also allow learners to work on tasks where they need to adjust their delivery according to what their listeners already know. For example, after learners have watched a film together, they could be asked to give their individual views on it. This type of speech will assume a certain degree of shared knowledge, and so the speaker can dispense with certain details, such as the plot or the characters. To make the task slightly more challenging, learners could be asked to share their views about a film that the others have not seen. Now that the listeners are "at a distance" and share only limited amounts of background information, the speakers will have to adjust what they need to say accordingly.

Task	Communicative outcomes
a. Tell a story.	Narrative texts.
b. Respond and share.	Personal reflections or reactions.
c. Share personal anecdotes.	Recounts of an incident or event.
d. Give a talk.	A range of texts that includes one or more of the following: explanation, process and procedure, description, or exposition (persuasive text).

a. Tell a story.
Outcomes: A narrative text.
Resources: Pieces of paper with titles of famous fables and fairy tales.
Procedure 1:   Students sit in small groups of three to four.
    The first person to speak picks a title from a box.
    He / she tells the story.
    The next person in the group continues in the same way.
Procedure 2:   Students sit in small groups of three to four.
    They take turns retelling a story that they have read recently.
Option(s):   Students could be given a time limit for each story. For Procedure 2, they can also retell a movie that they have watched or a story that they have heard.

b. Respond and share.
Outcomes: A personal reflection or reaction.
Resources: Objects; recordings (e.g., songs, stories, parts of a movie, interview, or documentary).
Procedure 1:   Students sit in pairs or in a group of three.
    They draw an object from a bag without looking inside.
    They have to think about the first thing they associate the object with.
    They have one minute to think about what they want to say before sharing their personal response with the group.
Procedure 2:   Students sit in pairs or in a group of three.
    They listen together to a recording such as a song.

Figure 9.3: A sample of monologic tasks.

(continued)

	They have one minute to think about what they want to say about the song.
	They share their response with the others.
Option(s):	Instead of objects, use pictures of places, people, and animals. To replace recordings, use a piece of short written text, such as an interesting dialogue.

c. Share a personal anecdote.

Outcomes:	A recount of an incident or event.
Resources:	—
Procedure 1:	Students sit in pairs or in a group of three.
	They take turns talking about an interesting thing that happened to them or someone they know.
	After everyone has spoken, they decide which account is the most interesting.
	The person with the most interesting anecdote goes to another group to retell it while the rest of the group listens to a student from another group.
Procedure 2:	Students sit in pairs or in a group of three.
	Each student shows a photograph he or she has brought to class.
	Students take turns telling the group something interesting that happened that is associated with the photograph.
	The person with the most interesting anecdote goes to another group to retell it while the rest of the group listens to a student from another group.
Option(s)	More advanced learners can be asked to tell their favorite joke to their group.

Figure 9.3: A sample of monologic tasks.

Discuss it

Monologic tasks can be carried out by learners individually, and then recorded and shared with their teachers and classmates, using the technology and electronic platforms that are widely available these days. With two other colleagues, discuss some ways such sharing can be done.

Organization of pair and group work

An important part of any speaking practice activity is the formation of pairs and groups. This section introduces ways in which teachers can organize students in novel ways for participation in the speaking tasks presented

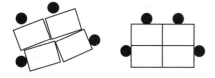

Front of the class

Figure 9.4: Suggested seating arrangement for students working in groups in a big class.

earlier, particularly discussion and monologic tasks. Teachers should bear in mind the following points when organizing students into groups: group size, arranging groups, selecting group members, and building good relations (Jacobs & Goh 2007). It is best to keep the group size relatively small. Here we recommend a size of three or four. Due to the unpredictability of the number of students in each class, there are bound to be groups where the sizes are different, so some groups in a class may have three students while others have four. Although five students is still possible, groups this large should be avoided because groups larger than four will give learners few opportunities to speak in the limited time available in class. Groups of four are generally considered to be ideal by many experts of group work, although groups of three may, in some situations, be preferable for the monologic tasks we have just described.

When arranging groups, it is useful to ensure that there is room for students and the teacher to move around. This will allow the teacher to monitor the progress of each group, as well as assist students when needed. In some situations, the noise generated from group work may be a concern. Teachers can tell their students to sit close together and use their normal conversation voice (although this can prove to be a challenge when students become very excited about what they are doing!). In classrooms where the desks have been prearranged in permanent positions that are not ideal for group interaction, students can be asked to carry their chairs to different corners of the class and sit together. When working with a big class, as in many school situations, it may be useful to ensure that students sit in a way where their backs are not entirely to the teacher and the front of the class, if the teacher needs to monitor what is happening at a glance.

How should students be selected to form groups? To ensure that students get the most out of their interaction in terms of practice and development of skills, it is best to have a balance of self-selected groups, as well as groups that the teacher forms. In the latter, students will have to work with people they are not as familiar with. Experts recommend forming heterogeneous or mixed groups, taking in consideration the students' first language, gender, ethnic group, and even levels of diligence and motivation. While these are general recommendations, teachers in some countries must also consider religious and cultural sensitivities when putting students into groups. Some techniques that have been suggested for selecting students include random selection by asking students to count around the class and sit with those having the same number, or allowing students to select their own groups, but following a set of criteria that the teacher gives. For example, a teacher may decide that the group must not have students with the same L1.

Discuss it

What criteria would you use when organizing learners into groups? Compare your criteria with your colleagues' criteria.

Techniques for organizing pairs and groups

Teachers can experiment with different ways of forming groups and putting students together at different stages of the discussion and monologic tasks. Figure 9.5 below presents a number of techniques that encourage cooperative learning, techniques that are relevant to the speaking class.

Considerations when planning speaking tasks

Teachers know that language learners need opportunities to speak in the target language in the classroom if they are to improve their speaking performance. These opportunities are typically in the form of pair or group communicative activities, where learners are put in situations where they are encouraged or "forced" to speak in the language. What should teachers do to plan activities that are relevant to learners' needs and sufficiently engaging so that learners want to participate in them? The following are six important considerations when developing materials and tasks for speaking practice:

- Provide contexts for communication to take place.
- Create gaps and other cognitive challenges.
- Specify communicative outcomes.
- Encourage focus on meaning.
- Identify features for pre-task planning and post-task focus.
- Select strategies for task repetition.

a. Circle of speakers.

Each member in the group has a number (1, 2, 3, or 4). Members take turns speaking, and when the group has finished the task, the teacher may call a number, and the person with that number repeats what he / she has said.

b. Cooperative controversy.

Each member in the group has a number (1, 2, 3, or 4). Numbers 1 and 3 adopt a position in support of a point of view, while 2 and 4 adopt the opposing position.

c. Everyone can explain.

Each member in the group has a number (1, 2, 3, or 4). Members take turns talking about their ideas, and then reach a consensus on the best response. The teacher calls a number, and the student with that number explains the group's response to the rest of the class.

d. Gallery tour.

After a group has completed its task, members post their responses on the classroom wall. Two of the group members stay behind to explain what their group has done, while the rest of the group joins other students as visitors to the "gallery."

e. One visitor – many hosts.

Students form a group to complete a task. Once it is completed, one of the group members leaves the group and joins another group to share what his / her group's responses were.

f. Presentation alternation.

After the groups have completed their task, they join another group and take turns presenting the outcomes of their speaking task.

g. Talk–pair–switch.

Students form pairs to work on a task. Once they have achieved the outcome, they switch partners with another group, and each student tells the new partner what they have talked about with the old partner.

h. Talking tokens.

Students in a group are given five tokens each. They give up one token every time they speak. Students who use all five tokens can only ask questions. When all the tokens are used up, they get back their tokens, and the process starts again.

i. Think–pair–square.

Students form a group of four. They think about how they would respond to the question(s) in the task. They share their answers with a partner. The four students come together and discuss how to develop a better answer.

j. Walk–stop–pair.

Students stand up and walk around the room, When the teacher signals for them to stop, they form a pair with whoever is standing nearest to them. Pairs complete the task, and the process repeats.

Figure 9.5: Techniques for organizing pair and group work (based on Jacobs & Goh 2007).

Provide contexts for communication to take place

It seems an obvious point that to encourage learners to learn to communicate in the target language, we need to provide them with opportunities to speak. It is not uncommon, however, to find speaking activities in some language classrooms that provide nothing more than exercises and drills, where learners repeat sentences with specific language forms and read aloud dialogues based on selected scenarios. While some might argue that these activities can benefit learners, the activities, in themselves, do not sufficiently prepare learners for real-life communication and, therefore, offer them very little in the way of learning how to communicate orally in the target language.

To prepare learners for real-world communication, teachers need to plan speaking tasks that are built as far as possible on authentic communicative contexts. By "contexts," we mean situations where learners know what topic they have to talk about, what their respective roles are, and what discourse procedures they should engage in to complete the task. The situation should reflect the kinds of real-world needs that our learners face, whether for communication in their new country, using English for specific academic purposes, or other kinds of needs such as travel, work, and socializing. (See Chapter 8 on conducting needs analysis.)

By focusing on establishing a communicative context for a learning activity, teachers can avoid the type of isolated-form practice activities mentioned earlier. This does not mean, however, that teachers should not focus on form in speaking lessons. The methodological framework proposed in this book argues that language accuracy is also a desired outcome of learning to speak a second language, and the teaching speaking cycle (Chapter 7) has specified stages in a unit of work where a focus on language and discourse can help learners in their speaking development.

Create gaps and other cognitive challenges

In real-life communication, we speak because we have a purpose in mind. To encourage learners to interact in the target language, tasks should create a purpose that motivates learners to speak. In other words, learners should feel there is a genuine need to communicate with one another. Teachers can create this feeling by ensuring that there are gaps in the learners' knowledge that can only be filled by talking with their partners or other members in a group. Such activities have been referred to as "information-gap activities," as described at the beginning of this chapter. For example, each learner has a version of a picture and needs to describe details of the picture to help his or her partner identify the differences or complete the picture.

Gaps, however, are not limited to factual knowledge. They can also exist in opinions; that is to say, participants in a group do not know what others in the group think about a particular topic, issue, or problem. The purpose of such a task is for learners to express their views to one another. An example of such a task is when we present learners with a specific problem for which a solution is required. In pairs or groups, learners discuss what that solution might be. Other similar kinds of discussion tasks may require learners to reach a consensus about the issues they are discussing, or draw up a list of pros and cons to assist decision making. These are referred to here as opinion-gap tasks.

Clearly, opinion-gap tasks are more challenging and may require advanced oral communication skills, such as negotiating agreement, and listening skills, such as making inferences and predictions. To help learners in their discussion, teachers often select problems that are relevant to the learners' interest or background. These types of speaking tasks are, therefore, motivating for learners of all ages, as many are eager to share what they know. As the tasks allow learners to draw on their own store of knowledge, they can facilitate the conceptualization of messages and the formulation of meaning learners want to convey.

Specify communicative outcomes

Communicative outcomes refer to the end product of a communication task. For example, in one task where learners talk about places they have each visited, they not only have to exchange information about places, but they have to produce a list of interesting facts about each of these places. This list is the communicative outcome for the task. In another task, learners may have to explain a solution to a problem presented by the teacher. Yet in another task, the outcome may be a story that individual learners have to narrate to entertain their listeners. Because they have to identify the outcomes for a speaking task, teachers are "forced" to think about the specific speaking skills and linguistic knowledge that learners need in order to complete the task well. Starting from the end point will, therefore, help teachers identify the skills and knowledge that their students will need to use in a speaking task.

While clear and specific outcomes are important for teachers when planning and evaluating their lessons, they are no less important for learners. When teachers explain the outcomes clearly, learners will know what they need to accomplish in pairs or as a group. Knowing what is required in each situation will lead learners to anticipate the language and other resources they might need to complete the task and achieve their goal. This can encourage them to use appropriate pre-task planning and monitoring strategies to improve their performance, or use communication strategies to compensate for gaps in their language and enhance their message. With a clear communicative outcome as the target, learners can also be encouraged to evaluate their individual performances systematically.

Encourage focus on meaning

One of the important goals of speaking lessons is to encourage learners to communicate their ideas and intentions by drawing on their linguistic resources and knowledge available for dealing with a task. The primary focus of such tasks should be an exchange of meaning and the promotion of fluency. Fluency is defined here as the ability to communicate ideas effectively with few pauses and hesitations, causing minimal comprehension difficulties for the listener. This can be achieved for each task when learners have some command over relevant aspects of grammar and structure of genres, have sufficient vocabulary to express key ideas, and have pronunciation that is intelligible to the listeners.

Identify features for pre-task planning and post-task focus

The speaking task is the "centerpiece" in the teaching-speaking cycle, as it is concerned directly with speaking practice. There are, however, other important learning activities in the other stages of the cycle that play an important role in supporting the overall development of students' speaking competence. One of these is the pre-task planning stage, where learners are given a "head start" by drawing from language and knowledge support provided, in order to plan what to say during the main speaking task. The stages that follow the speaking task can also contribute to learners' overall speaking development. In the stage that immediately follows the speaking task, learners can be helped to focus on selected features of the task that can help them further develop their language, skills, or strategies relevant to the task. As part of the planning of a speaking task, teachers need to decide which features of the task they want to focus on before and after students do the task.

Select strategies for task repetition

Task repetition can help learners develop greater fluency in the spoken language required for the task. It can also lessen learners' attention on meaning (since the ideas are now repeated) so that they can attend more to form. When learners repeat a task, they may use a wider variety of utterances to communicate their initial ideas, thus improving their language complexity. In the proposed cycle for speaking instruction, the speaking task is repeated at least once for the above reasons. It is useful, therefore, for you to consider how this can be done to keep the appeal of the task. Below are three decisions you will need to make:

a. Task design: repeat an entire task or only selected parts.
b. Time: do immediately after an earlier attempt or following an interval of several days.
c. Participants: keep same learners in the dyad or group, or mix different people from other groups.

(See Chapters 6 and 7 again for a discussion of task repetition.)

Discuss it

Of the six considerations for planning speaking tasks, which one do you think is the easiest to do and which is the most challenging? Explain why.

Summary

In this chapter, we presented three types of speaking tasks that can offer different contexts for learners to develop their speaking skills and strategies. The tasks focus on bridging communication gaps and, through discussions, allowing students to bring their own knowledge and opinions to bear on a range of topics and issues. They also give learners the opportunity to produce extended pieces of discourse in different genres commonly found in social and academic settings. As speaking tasks are typically carried out with a partner or in a group, we have also offered some suggestions on how to organize learners for pair and group work. The tasks can serve as examples of how teachers can plan their own activities for speaking lessons. They can also be a point of reference when teachers plan to adapt activities for speaking that are found in the prescribed materials they work with. Whether teachers intend to design their own tasks or adapt existing ones, there are a few points to consider. These include making sure that the context for communication among learners is clearly defined, that there is a genuine gap in the knowledge they share, and that there is sufficient challenge appropriate for the learners. The purpose of speaking tasks is to encourage learners to communicate meaning and to provide learners with opportunities to develop greater fluency in their speech. At the same time, it is important to consider aspects of the task where learners will need help and support. By identifying these aspects, the teacher can decide whether they should be addressed at the pre-task planning stage or as post-task language activities.

Considering this while planning or using a prescribed speaking task will help the teacher take a more holistic approach to speaking development. Speaking activities are not carried out as one-off practice, but seen within the larger framework of the teaching cycle introduced in Chapter 7. As part of this cycle, the teacher also needs to think about how the speaking task can be repeated so that learners will experience its benefits fully. In the next chapter, we will discuss how teachers can include activities that help learners develop their knowledge of language and discourse to further support their speaking development, and we will offer suggestions on how the speaking tasks offered in this chapter can be repeated for further practice by learners.

Group-learning tasks

1. Below is a simple questionnaire that provides a question-and-answer task learners can use to bridge an information gap. The technique for organizing the pair work is walk–stop–pair, where learners walk around the room and stop to talk to the person nearest to them. Suggest how you would adapt the questionnaire for a group of learners you work with, or will be working with.

	Classmate 1 Name: _____	Classmate 2 Name: _____	Classmate 3 Name: _____
What are your hobbies?			
What type of movies do you like to watch?			
What type of music do you like to listen to?			
Why have you chosen to come to study / work / live here?			
What is one thing about you that few people know?			

2. Work with two other colleagues to suggest a list of discussion topics that can be used with (a) young learners and (b) adult learners. Suggest how you would assist young learners in discussion tasks, and how this is different from the kind of support you would offer adult learners. After you have completed the task, one person visits another group to share what you have discussed, while the rest of the group listens to the proposals from a member of another group.

3. The techniques below, taken from Jacobs and Goh (2007), can be used to organize learners for the speaking tasks presented in this chapter. Refer to the various types of communication-gap, discussion, and monologic tasks presented. Select the tasks that you think can be organized by using each of the techniques. You can include as many tasks as you wish for one technique. Some examples have been included for you.

Techniques for organizing pair and group work	Tasks
a. Circle of speakers.	Respond and share.
b. Cooperative controversy.	
c. Everyone can explain.	
d. Gallery tour.	Discuss and plan.
e. One visitor – many hosts.	
f. Presentation alternation.	
g. Talk–pair–switch.	
h. Talking tokens.	
i. Think–pair–square.	
j. Walk–stop–pair.	Ask and answer.

4. Interview some subject teachers in the school or college that your ESL students study in. Find out the kinds of situations in which the learners have to speak English, and what sort of activities the teachers expect the learners to do in the class. Once you have the needed information, plan a communication-gap, discussion, or monologic

task that you think will help your learners practice their speaking skills and strategies for this academic setting.

(If you are unable to interview any teachers, you can also interview your students about their learning needs in their mainstream classrooms. Alternatively, you can examine the syllabus or course content for the subjects that your learners take and infer some speaking activities that would take place during the lessons.)

Further reading

Ernst, G. (1994) "Talking Circle": Conversation and negotiation in the ESL classroom, *TESOL Quarterly*, 28 (2), 293–322.

Jacobs, G. M. and Goh, C. C. M. (2007) *Cooperative Learning in the Language Classroom*, Singapore: SEAMEO Regional Language Centre.

Ho, Y. (2003) Audiotaped dialogue journals: An alternative form of speaking practice, *ELT Journal*, 57 (3), 269–277.

Hsu, H. Y, Wang, S. K., and Comac. L. (2008) Using audio blogs to assist English-Language Learning: An investigation into student perception, *Computer Assisted Language Learning*, 21 (2): 181–198.

10 Enhancing speaking performance

> Conducting speaking tasks alone is not sufficient to help learners improve their speaking proficiency. While learners have a chance to practice speaking during these tasks, they do not have the chance to get feedback on how they have performed, or to receive input on how they can improve. Stages 4 and 5 of the teaching-speaking cycle (see Chapter 7) will give learners the opportunities to receive such feedback and examine the language, discourse, skills, and strategies needed for improvement. The chapter will address the following questions:
>
> 1. What kinds of activities can help learners notice the features of language and discourse, and develop skills and strategies, that can enhance their speaking performance during a particular task?
> 2. How can teachers provide opportunities for learners to repeat speaking tasks so learners can have a chance to apply what they have learned about language and discourse?
>
> The following topics are discussed:
>
> * Going beyond fluency practice.
> * Focusing on language, discourse, skills, and strategies.
> * Repeating tasks.

Introduction

When learners engage in speaking tasks such as those we presented in the previous chapter, they can practice their speaking in a contextualized manner. Although they may try to produce speech that is fluent and accurate, attending to meaning and form at the same time can exert rather heavy demands on them cognitively and affectively. As a result, many learners may find they have to focus mainly on getting their ideas across, rather than simultaneously trying to formulate utterances that are grammatically or phonologically accurate. The purpose of Stage 4 in the teaching-speaking cycle is to address the need to develop greater accuracy in language use and pronunciation. This stage gives learners further opportunities to focus on aspects of the speaking task that they may have overlooked, or not had time to perform adequately when initially doing the task in Stage 3. It also allows learners to develop skills and strategies that can enhance their performance.

225

After learners have had a chance to examine different aspects of the task, Stage 5, which repeats the speaking task, allows them to do the same task again so that they can improve their performance and acquire the language, skills, and strategies that will enhance their overall speaking proficiency. Stages 4 and 5 then are key to successful teaching of speaking because learners focus on areas of language and performance that can help them become better speakers and, at the same time, they get a chance to repeat the language and strategies that they have been taught.

Going beyond fluency practice

After learners have had a chance to practice their fluency in a speaking task, teachers need to draw their attention to selected "parts" of the fluency task they have completed. The focus may be on linguistic aspects, such as pronunciation, vocabulary, and grammar, or on structures of genre or text type. Learners examine selected language forms and vocabulary items, and understand how they are related to the speech functions performed during the task. The focus on linguistic aspects and genres can be done separately or in an integrated manner. For example, learners could be asked to focus on a transcript of a description of a procedure in order to identify the phrases or words used to signal the different "moves" in a specific type of discourse, such as describing processes. By focusing on selected aspects of a task, learners will be able to see how this type of discourse is organized and the way lexico-grammatical features can help to achieve coherence. There are many items of language and types of skills and strategies that learners could focus on at this stage, so teachers must decide which ones are most important. It is certainly not advisable to focus on too many items at one time. A good rule of thumb is to select a maximum of three related items. For example, if it is important to show learners how to use interaction management strategies in a discussion task, the teacher may want to focus on strategies for beginning and wrapping up a discussion, as well as how to offer turns to group members.

Willis (1996) suggests that teachers' "natural" observations of the learners' performance will guide teachers in selecting appropriate areas of a task, and language items that need further attention and analysis. Teachers' observations are useful, as the items that have been identified will be based on actual learning needs. While this further analysis may be easily carried out with small classes, it can be a challenge in some ESL and EFL classes. Many English language classes in Asian schools, for example, have more than 30 students in each class, and the number may go as high as 70 in some

EFL classrooms, in countries like China. In such contexts, it is necessary for teachers to pre-select items for focus based on their assessment of their students' needs, and their teaching objectives.

Pre-selecting items to focus on is also useful for beginning teachers who may lack confidence and skill in dealing with unplanned activities. For example, a teacher may decide to focus on how to manage turn taking or topic change in an interaction. The activity, at this stage, would then involve learners analyzing the language and strategies used for negotiating these moves. We could also involve learners in the selection of the language items or strategies for analysis and practice. For example, teachers could gather valuable information on learners' needs from the reflections and evaluation they do in earlier classes. For example, if many learners have expressed a problem with getting a turn to express their views in group discussions, the teacher can select discourse strategies as learning points to focus on the next time discussion tasks are used in class.

Speaking lessons should go beyond fluency practice to include a language analysis component in which students look critically at language and examine "the relationship between form and meaning" (Willis 1990: 64). Including a grammar focus in a speaking lesson, however, may seem unnecessary because there may be an assumption that good grammar knowledge developed in grammar, or reading and writing, lessons will automatically transfer to speaking and listening. There is little evidence to support this. As part of the acquisition process, learners learn grammar, vocabulary, and even social conventions for structuring texts best from the spoken interaction that they engage in. In other words, they learn form–meaning relationships in context. However, much of this learning may be indirect and is accumulated over long periods of exposure and participation in different kinds of oral interaction. By explicitly focusing on language and discourse, skills, and strategies, teachers can facilitate the acquisition of the selected items and help learners improve their speaking performance directly. As discussed in Chapter 5, spoken discourse also contains features that differ from written discourse, and second language speakers will benefit from knowing about them and how to use them in their speech. In addition, learners will benefit greatly from learning how intonation can help speakers manage their speech by seeing how intonation signals new and shared knowledge with their listeners.

The teaching-speaking cycle extends fluency tasks to include language-focused activities that can expand learners' attention beyond communicating meaning to an understanding of the relationship between meaning and language forms. For learners to improve, they cannot rely solely on their own linguistic resources, or even the type of support that may be provided at the pre-task planning stage. It is necessary for teachers to provide input in the form of models and examples of good oral performance. This sort of teacher modeling, in video / audio recordings and transcripts of spoken texts produced by competent speakers, can help raise learners' metalinguistic awareness, as well as providing them with a mental model of what good spoken performance looks like. In addition to noticing features of a task, learners should also have a chance to repeat the fluency task, but with an added emphasis on accuracy and appropriate use of skills and strategies. Focusing on greater accuracy after the speaking task has been carried out at least once can enhance learning and has the added advantage of increasing learner motivation. This is because learners become aware of the gaps in their linguistic abilities, skills, and strategic competence when they reflect on their performance during the task.

Think about it

Review the discussion on fluency, accuracy, and complexity in Chapter 2. Jot down some ideas on how going beyond fluency tasks can help a specific group of learners you have in mind.

Focusing on language, discourse, skills, and strategies

In this section, we describe how teachers can plan activities that focus on language and discourse, areas that have been previously described in other parts of the book. The activities will involve three stages: noticing / sensitizing, analysis, and part practice. We will discuss grammar, genre, and vocabulary together, while intonation, skills, and strategies are handled separately.

Grammar, genre, and vocabulary

NOTICING

Noticing is an awareness-raising activity and does not require learners to manipulate or produce in speech the items they have noticed. It helps learners become aware of the presence of forms (Batstone 1994). In the teaching-speaking cycle, noticing activities draw students' attention to selected grammatical features of syntax, or the way words are strung together in an utterance. Noticing activities also help learners see how certain grammatical forms may be closely associated with specific kinds of speech genres. These activities can also be used to help learners notice vocabulary, such as formulaic expressions. To help learners notice features of grammar, genre, and vocabulary, the teacher can have them listen to spoken texts and identify the features. Learners can also work with transcripts, while they listen, and underline, circle, box, or highlight relevant aspects of language.

ANALYSIS

After learners have noticed the various forms, the teacher can explain their function to the students. A better way would be for the teachers to first engage the learners in their own discovery of form-function relationships. Learners can be asked to discuss with a partner the functions that the identified features serve in the communication of meaning. For example, if they are working with a transcript of a conversation, they can identify micro-discourse markers (e.g., *right, well)*, and then discuss the role these markers play in interactions. In other words, learners are asked to form their own hypothesis about the functions first, before hearing the teachers' confirmation or explanation.

PART PRACTICE

After the learners have analyzed and discussed the selected language features, they can practice using those features. For example, if formulaic expressions have been focused on in a specific genre for signaling the speaker's intention, the learners can be asked to use these expressions by reviewing what they said during the speaking task. To do this, the teacher should ideally have asked the learners to record themselves when carrying out the task. The learners could then listen to themselves and see those areas where they have performed well, and those that need improvement. If no recordings are used, students could focus on parts of the task where they can incorporate the formulaic expressions, and then practice those parts.

Intonation in discourse

SENSITIZING

Pronunciation-focused activities aim to raise learners' awareness of the communicative role that intonation plays, and to improve their perception and production of these features. Teachers can help learners develop sensitivity to intonation features by first introducing some perception activities where learners have to recognize stress and pitch movements (tones) in context. Stress and pitch may prove to be a challenge for some students who have difficulty perceiving pitch changes in sounds in general, but most learners will eventually become more adept at recognizing pitch, as their ears become more sensitized to the sounds. Sensitizing activities are useful for pronunciation-skill development because the ability to perceive phonological changes will help learners produce the different sounds. Learners can also work with transcripts and underline, highlight, or draw symbols, such as arrows, to indicate the sound movement that they have perceived.

ANALYSIS

As with grammar, analysis activities for intonation can also ask learners to consider the way various intonation features work in the context of the spoken utterances they hear. Instead of prescribing "rules" for pronunciation, the teacher encourages the learners to try to work out the communicative value of intonation choices (e.g., prominence or fall and rise tones) for themselves. For example, learners can examine why prominence is assigned in an utterance, and how it is linked mostly to the stressed syllables in words (e.g., //*HOTter*//). They may also see that in some instances, the normally unstressed syllable is stressed because the speaker wants to emphasize a contrast (e.g., // not just *HOT*// but *hotTER*). Intonation may be more challenging for some learners than learning grammar and vocabulary, and it may take more time for them to learn the features. It is advisable that some instruction on intonation be carried out separately in the language curriculum.

PART PRACTICE

After the learners have analyzed and discussed the intonation features highlighted by the teacher, they can learn to practice them in their speech. For example, if they have focused on prominence as a way of signaling important information in an utterance, they can practice reading aloud parts of a transcript they have highlighted, giving special attention to how prominence is assigned to stressed syllables. Rather than asking learners to read the whole transcript, teachers may find it more useful to focus on some utterances. The idea is not for learners to try and reproduce the entire text in the future, as this would be neither necessary nor possible, but to focus their practice on some manageable portions of the text in order to develop greater phonological awareness. When working with a recording of their own speech, learners can identify parts of their text where they could assign prominence more appropriately. They can first transcribe a part of their speech and identify those parts where prominence is needed to highlight new information to the listeners, and then follow up by saying the utterances aloud.

Speaking skills and strategies

NOTICING

Learners can develop a repertoire of speaking skills and strategies, such as those discussed in Chapter 3 and Chapter 5, by first noticing how other speakers use them. In this stage of the teaching speaking cycle, learners can be asked to share with one another the skills and strategies they had used in a task. This will give learners a chance to become familiar with a range of skills and strategies that they can use. Sometimes, as is the case with many beginning or intermediate-level learners, they actually know what to do because of their experience in their first language. The problem, however, is that they do not have the language to use the skills and strategies appropriately when speaking English.

ANALYSIS

In this part of the activity, learners could listen to competent speakers interacting in similar situations. They could also be asked to watch a video recording, which can also show paralinguistic features that are appropriate for participating in an interaction, such as culturally appropriate gestures. It is important that learners understand the different ways in which a strategy can be used, according to the degree of formality of an interaction. For example, learners may need to pay attention to useful phrases that can help them ask for clarification in casual conversations, as well as during a formal interview.

PART PRACTICE

Having been exposed to specific skills and strategies, and the language needed to use them, learners should spend some time practicing them. For example, they can practice asking for clarification and repetition, and checking comprehension. See Chapter 12 for further discussion of strategy use.

Materials

Teachers will need to have some additional materials for the above activities. Fortunately, many of these can be obtained from textbooks, CDs for listening comprehension, and free podcasts and other widely available resources on the Internet. Teaching materials designed as listening comprehension activities are particularly useful because they tend to include examples of different genres that are appropriate to the needs of general English or ESP learners. The teacher's manuals come with transcripts of the recorded texts, and teachers can use both the recordings and the transcripts for the language-focused activities.

Noticing–analysis–part practice activities are suitable for both adults and young learners, and tailored according to the speaking tasks done. In monologic tasks, older or more proficient learners can be asked to analyze talks that they and others produce. Learners can focus on formulaic expressions for initiating and maintaining the message, or for establishing cohesion. Young learners, on the other hand, often have to tell or retell stories. Listening to or reading the transcript of a story aloud can help younger learners focus on simple grammatical resources, such as the way tense and aspect work to convey meaning explicitly and precisely. They can also identify important formulaic expressions or phrases used to signpost different stages of a narrative, as well as learn how to use intonation to make their stories more interesting.

Repeating tasks

After going through the noticing / sensitizing and analysis activities, learners need to reinforce their new knowledge through further practice. This opportunity is provided in Stage 5 of the teaching-speaking cycle, where learners repeat the task they have done in Stage 3. The rationale for repeating a task done at Stage 3 is based on a cognitive approach to language learning. As discussed in earlier parts of this book, speaking is a cognitively demanding task, particularly for language learners who have to speak in a language they have not quite mastered. As a result, they often experience anxiety and other debilitating emotions, even when engaged in routine classroom tasks. We explained the importance of task repetition in Chapters 6 and 7 and outlined the ways that task repetition has been shown to help learners in their spoken performance in the areas of fluency, accuracy, and complexity. Task repetition also helps learners better frame narratives and develop enhanced knowledge of the narrative genre. In the teaching-speaking cycle, task repetition is purposely done after activities that focus on language, discourse, skills, and strategies so that learners can now have further language resources for improving their first performance.

When repeating a task, teachers need to consider what type of task it is, how much to repeat, when to repeat, and who the learners should repeat the task with (Bygate 2005). Teachers may also consider using a parallel task that is not identical.

Type of task

Many of the tasks presented in the previous chapter lend themselves well to repetition. Nevertheless, for practical reasons, it would be useful to consider whether it is practical to repeat all of them. For example, it may be difficult to repeat an entire discussion task.

Task design

A task can be repeated in its entirety. However, it is just as possible to repeat only a part of the task. For example, learners can be asked to repeat the "question and answer" (communication-gap) task with several other classmates, but for monologic tasks carried out in small groups, such as "respond and share," learners might repeat only their part, without having to meet as a group again.

Timing

A task can be repeated immediately on the same day, or after an interval of a day or several days. If the activities focusing on language, discourse, skills, and strategies are extensive, it is unlikely that the task can be repeated the same day. Sometimes, time constraints will also mean that the task has to be repeated on another day.

Participants

Learners can repeat a task with the same people as the original task; that is, their partners or members of the same group. Alternatively, they can repeat the task with different people. The techniques presented in Chapter 9 for organizing pair and group work are useful strategies for getting learners to repeat the same task with different people.

Parallel tasks

A parallel task is similar to the original task in its nature and demands, but some details have been changed. For example, if students do a "construct and compare" task (communication-gap task) in Stage 3 where they prepare a dish of food, they can repeat the task with some modifications to the list of ingredients they have been given, but the task still requires them to describe the process of preparing a dish, and to use the skills of asking questions, giving answers, and seeking clarification.

Try it

Select a speaking task from Chapter 9 that you think will be appropriate for task repetition. Explain how the task will be repeated. What challenges, if any, might there be when you carry out this form of repetition? How can you avoid or minimize the problems you've identified?

Summary

This chapter presented ideas for helping learners focus on language, discourse, skills, and strategies through three-part activities consisting of noticing / sensitizing, analysis, and part practice. These activities can offer learners the time and space to develop the linguistic and strategic competence needed to cope with future speaking tasks of a similar nature. They go through this process without the anxiety created by real-time, face-to-face interaction. By deliberately including post-speaking activities, this approach also helps to address, at least in part, the need for teachers to give immediate feedback to learners on their individual performance, something they may have had difficulty doing in large classes. The next stage in the teaching-speaking cycle, where the speaking task is repeated, will give learners the opportunity to use the knowledge they have gained from the feedback, thus improving their performance over the first time they did the task.

The tasks presented in the previous chapter are suitable for repetition, but teachers should also find different ways to retain the novelty of the tasks if they do subsequent repetitions. If the entire task is to be repeated, learners could do it with different participants. Alternatively, only a part of the task might be repeated.

Speaking lessons should not be limited to simply asking learners to complete a speaking task. There is more that teachers can do to help them gradually improve their speaking. The attention given to language and discourse, as well as skills and strategies, and the opportunities to do a task again will contribute towards the development of greater automaticity in learners' spoken English. Figure 10.1 shows a sequence of lessons in which language-focused activities and task repetition can be added to the core task, referred to as "Discuss and Plan," after it has been carried out once. Pre-task planning is also illustrated.

Task: Discuss and Plan – an action plan.[1]
Theme / Topic: Family coping with changes.
Speaking skills: Express views and explain reasons.
Language focus: Modality: Modal adverbs (e.g., *possibly, probably*), verbs (e.g. *could, might*), and lexical phrases (e.g. *a possibility, a certainty*).

Stage	Procedure
2 (Pre-task planning.)	Organize students in groups of threes, and set the first scenario for the task: "Sam is ten years old. Recently, he has been reluctant to go to school. Assign yourselves the roles of Sam's father, mother, and teacher. Discuss reasons for Sam's behavior, and work out a plan of action for each of you to help him."
	Give each group a short article[2] on children who are afraid to go to school. Instruct students to scan the article for reasons for anxiety and fear, and suggestions on how to help children with this problem. After the students have read the article, highlight important content words that will be relevant to the fluency activities. Explain those that students do not understand. Ask the students to underline words or make a list of words that they think they will need for their discussion.
3 (Speaking task.) *Discuss and Plan.*	Instruct students to simulate a parent-teacher discussion to: • Identify possible factors that contribute to Sam's reluctance to go to school. • Suggest strategies to help Sam overcome the problem so that he will enjoy school again. • Decide specific tasks that each person will be responsible for. • Set out a time frame for implementing the plan. • List some criteria for monitoring and evaluating progress.
4 (Language-focused activity.)	Have students listen to an audio recording, or view a video recording, of a discussion by a group of competent speakers doing a similar discussion and planning task. Instruct students to listen for the way in which the speakers frame their views and suggestions. Provide them with a checklist of language items that express modality found in the recording (e.g., *I think, I suppose, probably, hopefully, perhaps, ought to*). Students can check off the items when they hear them. Alternatively, use a transcript of the interaction for the noticing activity. Follow up with analysis and discussion of the functions of the language items, and a short practice.
5 Task repetition. *Discuss and Plan.*	Have students change their assigned roles and repeat the task. If they have been referring to the article when doing the task the first time, they should not do so during this phase. Ask students to monitor the forcefulness of their views and use appropriate language items to indicate modality.
6 Reflection on learning.	Have students evaluate their own performance.

Figure 10.1: A sequence of lessons in the teaching-speaking cycle, Stages 2–6 (adapted from Goh 2007).

Notes: This example of a sequence of lessons can be carried out with a class of adolescent or adult learners. Depending on your class length, the activities can spread over several lessons in a week. The suggested activities can be modified for younger learners by changing the roles in the problem-solving task to ones they can readily identify with (for example to Sam's classmates, who have been asked to help Sam). Instead of an article, it may be better to use a series of pictures with supporting words. You will also have to adjust time allocation, overall task demands, and learner involvement during the noticing and analysis phase.

[1] See Chapter 9.

[2] The article should be short to ensure that this does not turn into a reading comprehension lesson. You can also do some research on the topic and provide a short summary of key points.

Group-learning tasks

1. Describe a favorite speaking activity that you use or have experienced as a student. Explain why it is your favorite. What speaking skills do your students practice through this activity? What language items are needed to help speakers convey their meaning clearly and precisely? How is learners' performance affected if they do not use these skills and the words or grammar that you have identified?
2. Select a piece of short, spoken text. If it doesn't have a ready transcript, transcribe it. If the text is a long one, transcribe an important excerpt. Identify key grammatical items in that piece of text that are used for expressing meaning at a) the sentence level and b) the discourse level. Explain how you can help your students notice the grammatical forms present in this text.
3. Go back to the first group-learning task at the end of Chapter 5, and review the activities that you identified as suitable for drawing learners' attention to the various generic stages of a recount. Do you think those activities will be effective? Would you like to change any of the ideas?
4. Select an excerpt from a radio podcast or recording. Identify three to five continuous utterances that you would do some analysis on. Work with a partner to identify prominence, rise or fall-rise tone, and fall tone. Explain to each other the communicative value of these features in the utterances that you have examined.
5. Using the sequence of lessons in Figure 10.1 as a model, plan a similar sequence (Stages 2–6 of the teaching-speaking cycle) with a speaking task selected from Chapter 9.

Further reading

Burns, A. and Joyce, H. (1997) *Focus on Speaking*, Sydney: National Centre for English Language Teaching and Research.

Hewings, M. (1993) *Pronunciation Tasks, Course for Pre-intermediate Learners*, Cambridge: Cambridge University Press.

Riggenbach, H. (1999) Discourse analysis in the language classroom, Vol. 1: *The Spoken Language*, Ann Arbor: The University of Michigan Press.

11 *Raising metacognitive awareness*

> The teacher has an important role in helping learners bring the processes of learning to speak to a conscious level so that the learners can have greater control over their speaking development. This chapter will answer two questions:
>
> 1. What is metacognition, and why is it important for L2 speaking development?
> 2. How can teachers raise learners' metacognitive awareness about speaking?
>
> To answer these questions, we will be addressing the following topics:
>
> * The concept of metacognition.
> * The importance of metacognition.
> * Activities for raising metacognitive awareness.

Introduction

The discussion of the teaching-speaking cycle thus far has been mainly about speaking tasks that teachers can use to provide opportunities for speaking practice. These tasks encourage learners to communicate meaning, as fluently as they can. We have also explained the need to include post-speaking activities to help learners develop their knowledge of language and discourse, and use appropriate discourse and communication strategies to enhance their interaction. In addition, we recommended that teachers repeat the speaking tasks so that learners can recycle the language they used when they did the task the first time, while incorporating some of the language and skills that they learned from the language-focused activities. These stages in the teaching cycle are crucial to helping learners improve their speaking directly. The teaching of speaking, however, will not be complete without attention being given to developing the learners' metacognitive awareness about speaking. By incorporating an explicit metacognitive dimension into a sequence of speaking activities that focus on task, language, and discourse, teachers will adopt an approach that develops speaking holistically. Such a holistic approach will benefit learners, as it recognizes that they are active agents who set learning goals and expectations according to what they perceive to be significant and relevant (Lantolf & Thorne 2006).

237

In this chapter, we will elaborate on the remaining stages of the teaching-speaking cycle, where learners develop their metacognitive awareness of second language speaking and of themselves as second or foreign language speakers. We will explain how teachers can direct learners' attention to the speaking skill at the beginning of each unit of work, as well as the nature and demands of the task they are about to carry out. In addition, we will present practical ways by which learners can reflect on their learning and receive feedback. Our discussion begins with an explanation of what meta-cognition means, what it does for learning in general, and why it is important for overall speaking development.

The concept of metacognition

Several decades after psychologist John Flavell (1976, 1979) proposed it as a way of understanding how people think about their own thinking, the concept of metacognition has become increasingly relevant to the discussion of second language learning. Metacognition, as a construct, refers to people's consciousness of their thinking and behavior: what they are thinking, how they are thinking in relation to a situation or a learning task, and why they are thinking in a particular manner. Metacognition also includes the ability to bring mental processes under conscious scrutiny, thereby allowing the person to regulate or manage these thinking processes.

Flavell's explanation of the construct is as follows:

> "Metacognition" refers to one's knowledge concerning one's own cognitive processes and products or anything related to them, e.g., the learning-relevant properties of information or data. For example, I am engaging in metacognition (metamemory, metalearning, metacognitive-attention, metalanguage, or whatever) if I notice that I am having more trouble learning A than B; if it strikes me that I should double-check C before accepting it as a fact. . . . Metacognition refers, among other things, to active monitoring and consequent regulation and orchestration of these processes in relation to the cognitive objects or data on which they bear, usually in the service of some concrete goal or objective (Flavell 1976: 232).

This capacity to be aware of our mental processes, and to have control over our learning, has been called the "seventh sense," something that learners, even young ones, can develop (Nisbet & Shucksmith 1986). It has been argued that metacognition is not only a part of learners' cognitive development, but that it also promotes further cognitive development, is amenable to classroom instruction, and enables learners to participate actively in regulating and managing their own learning (Marzano et al. 1988). When learners bring their learning processes to a conscious level, they develop a sense of agency over their own learning efforts that can drive them to aspire for greater success (Hacker, Dunlosky & Graesser 2009). Metacognition also allows learners to examine their own feelings about learning and acknowledge those feelings that need to be managed closely. In other words, metacognition enables learners to exercise control over the nature and quality of their learning. This ability to influence, by their own actions, the way things happen, in turn, encourages learners to work harder at achieving their learning goals, and encourages them to develop greater confidence in themselves.

The benefits to language learning of metacognition were first reported by Wenden (1987, 1991, 1998), and then discussed by a number of other second language scholars who further highlighted the benefits of examining learners' metacognition (see Chamot & O'Malley 1991; Cohen 1998; Cohen & Macaro 2007; Matsumoto 1996; Oxford 1991; Victori & Lockhart 1995). An understanding of learners' metacognition will enable teachers to appreciate their students' approach to learning, and offers teachers insights into individual students' learning styles and abilities (Rubin 2001). A recognition of the role of metacognition in teaching and learning speaking can, therefore, help teachers address learners' needs in a focused manner. Learner metacognition is an aspect of learning that previously has not been addressed systematically in other approaches to teaching speaking. By including a metacognitive dimension in our discussion of speaking instruction, we are proposing an approach that not only puts a premium on learners' own contribution to their speaking development, but also strengthens the teaching of linguistic knowledge and skills that are necessary for effective speaking.

The term "metacognitive awareness" is frequently seen in literature discussing learner strategy use and learner autonomy. Its definition, however, is sometimes unclear. In our discussion of metacognitive awareness here, we use the term to refer to manifestations of an individual's metacognition in the following ways: experience, knowledge, and strategy use (see also Vandergrift & Goh 2012). These three dimensions, through which metacognition is demonstrated, are distilled from common perspectives in the field of education and second language learning (see Borkowski 1996; Flavell 1979; Wenden 1991, 2001; Hacker, Dunlosky & Graesser 2009; Pintrich, Wolters & Baxter 2000). (See Figure 11.1.)

First, metacognition can take the form of a cognitive or affective *experience* (Flavell 1979); that is to say, one feels a distinct sense about a thought or a learning demand at the moment it occurs. For example, when

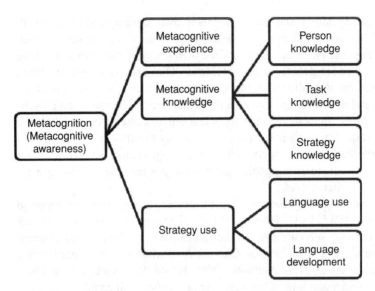

Figure 11.1: Metacognitive awareness in second language learning.

given the chance to respond to something that someone else has said, a second language speaker senses an impending problem in expressing an idea. The person may think, "I know what to say but I don't have the words in English." Metacognitive experiences tend to be short-lived and may be forgotten unless something is done as a result of them. In the example above, the speaker may decide to use a communication strategy such as circumlocution to express an idea that he or she does not have an English word for, or the speaker might ask the listener to repeat what has been said to buy some thinking time. On the other hand, if the speaker senses a difficulty, but does nothing about it, he or she will miss an opportunity to speak and continue in the interaction.

Second, a person's metacognition is demonstrated by the *knowledge* that one has about a particular type of experience or learning. Second language speakers, for example, may know how to structure a talk where information is presented and explained. Additionally, a learner may understand what it takes to become a competent speaker of the language and the obstacles that need to be overcome. Metacognitive knowledge is explained further in the section that follows.

Third, metacognition is also demonstrated through a person's use of *strategies* to solve a problem or enhance learning. Strategy use demonstrates a person's control of his or her own cognition, and the action the person then takes in order to achieve a goal. In the case of second language speaking, these strategies may involve finding ways of enhancing communication and coping with difficulties, as well as structuring and managing discourse. (See Chapters 3 and 5.) Strategies are also crucial to a learner's overall speaking development, in that they help learners plan, monitor, and evaluate their overall learning efforts. Strategies for overall speaking development will be discussed in the section below.

Think about it

Refer to the three dimensions of metacognition discussed above, and give examples from your experience for each of them. You can select examples from any areas of formal or informal learning.

Metacognitive knowledge

Metacognitive knowledge is the self-knowledge a person has about learning, and it is similar in structure and function to other kinds of knowledge that is stored in long-term memory (Borkowski 1998). It has three recognized dimensions – person, task, and strategy – all of which are relevant to learning in general, as well as to second language learning (Flavell, 1979; Wenden 1991). Person knowledge refers to knowledge about how one's learning takes place and the way different factors may influence it. It includes what learners think of themselves as learners, and what personal factors could lead to their success or failure in learning something. It consists of a learner's concept of him- or herself as a learner, the sense of self-efficacy in relation to a task and the problems that one faces, and possible causes as well as solutions. Task knowledge refers to knowledge about the purpose and the nature of a learning task, demands exacted by the task, and what kind of deliberate effort is needed and when it is needed. It includes knowing about the cognitive, social, and affective processes involved in a task, the internal and external factors that affect the success of the task, and ways of improving performance. Finally, strategy knowledge refers to knowledge about strategies that can facilitate learning in general, and those that are likely to be effective in achieving defined learning and communication goals in specific situations. Figure 11.2 highlights examples of metacognitive knowledge from the learners' perspective. The figure is adapted from an original framework applied to second language listening by Vandergrift and Goh (2012).

Person knowledge
Knowledge of the cognitive and affective factors that facilitate one's speaking performance and overall speaking development.

    a. Self-concepts and self-efficacy about speaking:
- I must try not to feel so stressed each time I have to speak on the phone in English.
- I think I'll be able to speak like a native speaker one day.
- I need to think a lot before I say something.

    b. Problems related to L2 speaking, reasons, and possible solutions:
- My problem is not having the words to express some meanings in English.
- I should learn to speak more appropriately in formal situations like interviews.
- If I ask the speaker for clarification, I will have more time to think about my reply.

Task knowledge
Knowledge about the nature and demands of a speaking task, how to approach the task, and when deliberate effort is required.

    a. Mental, affective, and social processes involved in speaking:
- You need to think about what to say and how to say it at the same time.
- It's important to be relaxed when you speak.
- I need to work with my listener during a conversation so we can understand what we are both trying to say.

    b. Differences between spoken and written discourse:
- If I speak the way I write, I might sound "bookish" and unnatural.
- Speech isn't like writing, which can have many neat and complete sentences.
- Telling a story is a bit different from writing one.

    c. Skills for second language speaking:
- It is important to know how to organize a story when you have to retell it.
- Having the right intonation when speaking is useful.
- When I'm in a group discussion, I need to know how to disagree politely.

    d. Cultural and social differences of speakers:
- I must be careful when speaking English to people from other cultures so that I will not sound rude to them.
- I was told that in the U.K., it is OK to start a conversation about the weather.
- In my country, you mustn't call people older than you by their first names.

    e. Factors that influence speaking:
- I need to know enough about the content to talk about it.
- We speak the way our friends and other people in our society speak.
- I should speak English to everyone I meet and not be embarrassed.

    f. Ways of improving overall speaking development:
- I need to get some local friends so I can practice my speaking with them.
- I should learn how different types of speech are organized.
- I need to learn to speak naturally and not repeat sentences that I write down.

Figure 11.2: Metacognitive knowledge about second language speaking.

(continued)

Strategic knowledge
Knowledge about effective strategies for different types of spoken interaction, strategies for specific speaking tasks, and strategies that may not be useful.

a. Strategies for managing communication and discourse:
   - If you don't have the English word, you should use other words to explain yourself and express the same meaning.
   - I learned many useful phrases that I can use in my conversations.
   - If I don't understand, I can always ask someone.
b. Strategies for specific types of speaking tasks:
   - If I have to do pair work, I need to remember how to ask my partner to give better explanations.
   - For talks, I always prepare an outline with a proper introduction and conclusion.
   - In group discussions, it is always useful to know how to disagree politely.
c. Ineffective strategies:
   - When I don't know some key words, I will keep quiet, but I know this isn't good.
   - Memorizing the entire speech is not useful because I may get stuck on one part and won't be able to go on.

Figure 11.2: Metacognitive knowledge about second language speaking (adapted from Vandergrift & Goh 2012).

Think about it

Give examples of metacognitive knowledge about speaking, based on students you work with, or yourself if you have spent some time learning another language.

Strategy use

Strategies in language learning are special techniques learners use to help them enhance their learning and cope with challenges. Following Cohen's (1998) distinction between strategies for language use and strategies for language learning, strategies for speaking consist of those used during spoken interactions (language use), and those used for general speaking development and specific speaking tasks (language learning). (See Figure 11.3 below). Speaking strategies that can facilitate speaking performance during spoken interactions comprise communication and discourse strategies (see Chapters 3 and 5 again). Strategies for language learning comprise self-management strategies that assist learners in their speaking development. This latter group consists of strategies for regulating overall speaking development, and for approaching and managing speaking tasks in the language classroom.

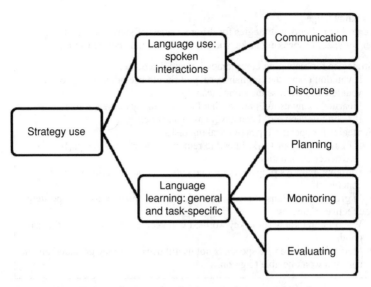

Figure 11.3: Types of strategies for interactions and learning.

Figure 11.4 below presents strategies for language learning according to the three functions of planning, monitoring, and evaluating, as developed by Brown (1978) and applied successfully to language learning (O'Malley & Chamot 1990; Oxford 1990). Commonly referred to as metacognitive strategies, this group of strategies can potentially help language learners develop greater self-regulation when managing their overall speaking development, as well as when approaching specific speaking tasks in the classroom, individually or with their peers. Self-regulation is a process by which individuals adjust their actions and goals in light of environmental conditions, so as to achieve the desired results for their learning (Boekarts, Pintrich & Zeidner 2000). Planning strategies enable learners to set learning objectives and consider the means by which these objectives can be achieved. Monitoring strategies enable learners to check on their progress with the goal of speaking development in mind, and also to ascertain whether they are addressing the demands of a speaking task adequately when the task is being carried out. Finally, evaluating strategies enable learners to determine the outcomes of their plan for speaking development, as well as assess the success of their efforts in accomplishing a speaking task in class. Figure 11.4 shows examples of metacognitive strategies that are relevant to second language speaking development, in general and task-specific situations.

	General development	Task specific
Planning	• Set personal goals, and develop an appropriate action plan for my speaking development. • Identify areas of speaking competence that require deliberate effort on my part. • Seek opportunities to practice my speaking skills and improve my pronunciation.	• Preview requirements of the task and task outcomes. • Review or prepare language and content I will need for the speaking task. • Identify communication and discourse strategies that can facilitate my interaction or speech.
Monitoring	• Reflect on my speaking development at appropriate junctures in the plan. • Determine whether my short-term goals have been achieved and how far away I am from long-term goals. • Check and see if I am still making the same mistakes, or have the same affective problems, after a period of study.	• Check my overall performance during a speaking task. • Check the appropriateness and accuracy of what I say during a speaking task. • Correct my use of language when speaking. • Recognize any negative emotions during speaking.
Evaluating	• Assess my progress over a period of time against some external measures, e.g., test performance. • Assess the effectiveness of my learning and practice methods. • Assess the appropriateness of my learning goals and plans. • Identify problem areas that I still need to work on.	• Check the appropriateness and accuracy of what I have said when the task is over. • Decide whether the strategies I selected and use for completing a task have been useful. • Assess my overall success at a task.

Figure 11.4: Metacognitive strategies and learning objectives in L2 speaking development.

Think about it

Consider the kinds of guidance and support that learners would need in order to apply the three metacognitive strategies given above.

The importance of metacognition

Educational research shows that successful learners are individuals who think about their learning and can develop ways to manage and direct this endeavor (Alexander 2008). They are keenly aware of their own learning processes and perceptive of the demands of their learning tasks. Furthermore, they have a wide repertoire of strategies that they can apply and adapt to meet the needs of specific contexts. Learners who are less effective, on the other hand, are known to be less reflective of the way they learn, and are usually less conscious of task demands and appropriate ways of approaching learning tasks. These effects of metacognition have been postulated by Flavell (1979: 908):

> I believe that metacognitive knowledge can have a number of concrete and important effects on the cognitive enterprises of children and adults. It can lead you to select, evaluate, revise, and abandon cognitive tasks, goals, and strategies in light of their relationships with one another and with your own abilities and interests with respect to that enterprise. Similarly, it can lead to any of a wide variety of metacognitive experiences concerning self, tasks, goals, and strategies, and can also help you interpret the meaning and behavioral implications of these metacognitive experiences.

Learners' metacognition can directly influence the process, and even the outcome, of their learning (Borkowski 1996; Palmer and Goetz 1988). If they know the demands of a task and have a rich knowledge of strategies, learners can choose the appropriate strategies when addressing a particular communication or learning need. Learners with rich strategic knowledge are also more successful at transferring strategies appropriately to a new learning task (Gagnè, Yekovich & Yekovich (1993). In second language speaking, language learners' perception of what speaking requires can influence the strategies they select or abandon (Zhang & Goh 2006). It can also influence their learning path because learners will be in a better position to modify their plans, adjust their goals, and review their needs. Second language research has provided evidence of learners' metacognitive knowledge (Wenden 1999; Cotterall & Murray 2009), and the contribution metacognitive knowledge has made to improved listening skills (Cross, 2009; Vandergrift & Tafaghodtari 2010); reading (Carrell 1989; Zhang 2010); pronunciation (He 2011); and writing (Victori 1999). Metacognitive awareness is also linked to learner motivation (Vandergrift 2005), and it has been reported to enhance self-confidence (Goh & Taib 2006).

Raising metacognitive awareness

The teaching-speaking cycle has three stages (1, 2, and 6) where teachers can help learners bring their metacognitive knowledge to the surface. In the last stage (7) teachers provide feedback to learners on their learning and performance, so this stage adds to metacognitive knowledge, as well. The aim of the activities done during all four stages is to increase learners' awareness of what is involved in learning to speak another language, and to encourage them to consider how they can further improve their own performance by setting goals for future tasks. The activities will deepen learners' understanding of themselves as L2 speakers, the nature and demands of speaking and learning to speak, and the strategies needed for spoken interaction and speaking development. The activities are also a means by which learners can tap into their task knowledge, as they prepare for the task they are about to engage in. By integrating speaking activities and metacognitive ones, the teaching-speaking cycle provides the necessary support, challenge, and motivation to engage language learners in developing the skill of speaking.

The importance of the various stages in the cycle was first highlighted in Chapter 7. Although the stages each have an explicit focus, they are not completely independent of each other in the learning process. For example, activities that highlight language, discourse, skills, and strategies in Stage 4 have a metacognitive element because they raise learners' awareness of the features of speech and effective ways of speaking, and this awareness is part of the learners' task knowledge and strategy knowledge, respectively.

In the following section, we will relate the activities in the four stages (1, 2, 6, and 7) more closely to the metacognitive framework explained earlier in this chapter. We will also provide more examples of prompts that teachers can use at the reflection stage to direct learners' attention to different aspects of their learning.

Focusing on speaking

Stage 1 of the teaching-speaking cycle gives learners the opportunity to think about the skill of speaking in general, as well as attend to the speaking task at hand. It serves one or both of the purposes below:

- It encourages learners to plan for overall speaking development.
- It prepares learners to approach the speaking task for the day.

In this stage, learners work with prompts based on planning strategies to guide them in setting personal goals. For example, teachers can encourage learners to consider the feedback received on their performance in previous lessons or similar tasks done in the past. They can also ask learners to identify one or two areas of their speaking competence that they should pay attention to when participating in the task in Stage 3. Stage 1 is also a time for learners to focus on person knowledge, as mentioned earlier in this chapter. It is what they know about themselves as second language speakers, their strengths and problems, and why these problems occur (see Figure 7.2 in Chapter 7).

Clearly, learners cannot focus their attention on all the above at the same time. The teacher may vary the focus according to the timing of the unit of work on speaking. For example, at the start of a program or a new semester, learners can reflect on their past achievements and work on an action plan for speaking development. In the same way, if the cycle is at the end of a course of study, asking learners to evaluate their development would be appropriate. You may wish to give the following handout (Figure 11.5) to your students.

Planning for a new term and managing your progress

You are about to begin a new term, and it will be useful for you to take stock of what you have learned and make new plans. Research tells us that it is important for students to take time to think about their own learning, and find ways of managing it. The questions below are meant to help you in your reflection and planning.

Part 1: Thinking back

    a. What did you find most enjoyable in your last English course?
    b. What speaking skills did you learn?
    c. What kind of speaking activities did you find most useful for your speaking development?
    d. Are you satisfied with the progress you have made?
    e. Do you think the methods you adopted for practicing speaking were useful?
    f. What are some areas of speaking that you still need to work on?

Part 2: Thinking forward

    a. What goals for speaking do you have for this new term? Why are they important?
    b. How do you plan to achieve your goals?
    c. Whose help do you need to carry out your plan? How would you involve them?
    d. What are two dates during this term when you will be spending time checking on your own progress? Write them down.
    e. How will you know that you have made any progress?

Figure 11.5: Thinking about speaking at the beginning of a new term.

Preparing for speaking

Stage 2 of the teaching-speaking cycle is where teachers provide input on the language (e.g., vocabulary) or the content needed for the task, and guide learners in their pre-task planning. A consideration of the various aspects of task knowledge is most relevant here. Teachers can select from the items of task knowledge in Figure 11.2 that are most appropriate. For example, learners can be asked to consider the cultural and social differences between spoken interactions in their country and the country in which they are learning English. If learners are preparing a monologic task, they can be asked to consider the differences between spoken and written discourse, when they are preparing for their speech.

Learners can also be asked to preview the requirements of the speaking tasks and the outcomes they are expected to produce. Figure 11.6 gives an example of a set of guiding questions that learners could use individually or with a partner to prepare for a monologic task (see Chapter 9) that requires them to do a poster presentation in a gallery tour setting, an activity common in academic learning contexts.

Sometimes, the focus of a task may not be on the product or communicative outcome, but on the process. If this is the case, learners must be reminded of the aim of the task. For example, in a discussion task, the teacher may want learners to develop their skill at interaction management and exploring ideas. If this is the case, then learners need to understand that they should spend as much time as possible on the discussion task and not be in a hurry to arrive at an outcome. At the same time, learners may also

---

Preparing for a poster presentation

Part 1: Defining the goal

   a. What is the aim of this presentation?
   b. What am I expected to explain?
   c. What objectives do I want to achieve?

Part 2: Action plan

   a. What are some things I know about poster presentation that I can apply to the new task?
   b. To achieve the objectives for this task, what do I need to do?
   c. What questions would I likely be asked? Do I have answers for these questions? If not, what can I do to prepare for them?
   d. What difficulties would I likely face? What strategies can I use to manage these difficulties?

Figure 11.6: Raising awareness of task knowledge in pre-task planning.

need to review useful phrases and formulaic expressions needed for applying communication and discourse strategies. Emphasizing the importance of the process itself will prevent learners from focusing only on the results of the discussion and will encourage them to practice the process skills that the teacher thinks are important.

Reflecting on speaking

In Stage 6 of the teaching-speaking cycle, learners get to step back from the activities and reflect on their performance, after they have completed the various activities related to the speaking task. Reflections have two characteristics: descriptive, where learners recall in writing or speech what they did; and evaluative, where learners critically assess their own performance in a speaking task or on other activities related to it. Figure 11.7 suggests the use of a speaking diary, based on a similar idea developed for listening (Goh 2002). The template shown in Figure 11.7 can be made more structured by including some questions that focus on specific areas of learning. Although the templates suggest that the reflections will be in writing, it is perfectly possible for learners to record their reflections in speech and upload the file for teachers to access. This will also give learners further opportunities to practice their speaking.

Speaking diary Write down your thoughts about your learning experience this week. Here are some questions to help you get started. a. What did you learn to do this week in your speaking class? b. Were the activities useful for helping you improve your speaking? c. Did you have any problems? If you did, what did you do to help you cope? d. What did you learn about speaking? e. What useful expressions / skills / strategies did you learn? f. Do you feel confident that you can do the same thing again another time?	Teacher's response:

Figure 11.7: A suggested template for a speaking diary.

For reflection that is directed at a task, teachers can give learners a checklist to assess their own performance. For example, in the monologic task involving the poster presentation referred to earlier, learners can be asked to assess their own performance of the presentation. Figure 11.8

Self-assessment of a monologic task

Part 1: My performance

Put a check ✓ in the box that best shows what you think. Write any thoughts you have.

	Agree.	Not sure.	Disagree.	My thoughts.
1. I prepared well for the task.				
2. I am happy with my performance today.				
3. My classmates showed that they enjoyed listening to me.				
4. I felt nervous.				
5. I made few grammatical mistakes.				
6. I used the right formulaic expressions.				
7. My pronunciation was clear.				
8. I used suitable words and phrases to help my audience notice what I wanted to say.				
9. I feel my pace was just right.				
10. I spoke too fast throughout.				
11. I had too many pauses and hesitations.				
12. I spoke confidently.				

Part 2: My plan

List two to three things you would like to improve on before you do another similar task. Write your thoughts in the box.

Things I would like to improve on:

Figure 11.8: Self-assessment checklist for a monologic task.

gives a self-assessment checklist, where the reflection can be done quite quickly, as in the speaking diary, without too much writing. This checklist can also be used for peer-assessment, where learners assess each other's performance.

Improving speaking

The last stage of the teaching-speaking cycle is where the teacher gives feedback on speaking performance and responds to learners' written or spoken reflections. Learners can also be asked to give feedback to one another. The important point about feedback is that the teacher should decide on a few important areas to focus on. Based on the prompts used, the teacher's feedback can be on learners' reflections on person, task, or strategy knowledge, as well as commenting on learners' use of strategies. The feedback can also be based on the learners' actual speaking performance that the teacher has observed during the speaking tasks, or post-speaking activities where language use is discussed. All of this feedback will be useful for the learners as they begin the next cycle of speaking lessons. Thus, the goal of feedback is to help learners increase their knowledge about themselves as second language speakers, and their knowledge of how they can improve their speaking further.

Summary

The teaching of speaking will not be complete without including ways of helping learners develop their metacognitive awareness. This chapter completes the exemplification of activities in the teaching-speaking cycle by elaborating upon the aims and nature of metacognitive activities in Stages 1, 2, 6, and 7. The aim of these activities is to raise learners' metacognitive awareness about learning to speak another language. This chapter is based on the principle that language learners who have a high degree of metacognitive awareness about second language speaking will be more capable of regulating their own learning. With heightened metacognitive awareness, learners can draw on their person, task, and strategy knowledge and, at the same time, actively plan and monitor their performance. By developing their metacognitive awareness, learners can acquire a greater feeling of control as they develop new ways of managing their own speaking development.

Group-learning tasks

1. Review what you understand by "metacognition." Plan an activity where you can tell your learners about metacognitive awareness and what it can do to help them in their language learning, particularly in speaking development.
2. Interview some learners about their experiences in learning to speak a second / foreign language. Organize the learners' comments according to the framework for metacognitive knowledge and strategies presented in Figures 11.2 and 11.4. Compare your observations with other colleagues.
3. This task has two parts. The first part is an integrative task, where you consolidate all that you have learned about planning with the teaching-speaking cycle. The second part gives you a chance to experience part of the teaching cycle.
    a. Plan a unit of work on speaking, using the teaching-speaking cycle as the framework. Ensure that the right kinds of tasks and activities are used at every stage. When you have finished, present your plan in a poster to your colleagues or others in your class. If you are in a course, your course instructor will organize a "gallery tour," and you will get a chance to explain your work and answer questions based on it.
    b. When you have finished your presentation, play the role of students, and do the activity. Then assess your own performance, using the checklist in Figure 11.7. Did you find the checklist useful? How would you improve it?
4. Review the tasks at the end of all the chapters in this book. Select a few that you think have been helpful in raising your metacognitive awareness about teaching speaking. Which aspects of metacognitive awareness did each of these tasks raise? Which aspects of strategy use, if any, did the tasks focus on?

Further reading

Evans, R. and Jones, D. (2008) *Metacognitive approaches to developing oracy: Developing speaking and listening with young children*, London: Routledge.
Hughes, R. (2010) Materials to develop the speaking skill, In Harwood, N. (ed.) *English Language Teaching Materials: Theory and Practice*, Cambridge: Cambridge University Press, 207–224.

Tan, Y. H. and Tan, S. C. (2010) A metacognitive approach to enhancing Chinese language speaking skills with audioblogs, *Australasian Journal of Educational Technology*, 26 (7), 1075–1089.

Wenden, A. (2001) A metacognitive knowledge in SLA: The neglected variable, In M. P. Breen (ed.) *Learner Contributions to Language Learning: New Directions in Research*, Harlow: Pearson Education / Longman, 44–64.

12 *Assessing speaking*

In this final chapter, we discuss the topic of assessing speaking. Assessment of speaking is both an important and a challenging area of a speaking program. The way in which judgements about students' speaking abilities can be made will vary according to the purposes for assessing and the point at which assessments are made. Assessment can also have a profound effect on what speaking skills the teacher chooses to teach, as the fact that the students will ultimately be assessed at the end of a course means that teachers may "teach to the test." Not all instruction, however, is directed at test taking and, in some courses, the teachers may have considerable flexibility in selecting what will be assessed and how assessment will be conducted.

In this chapter, we address three main questions:

1. What is the role of assessment in speaking programs?
2. What issues must be considered to ensure sound and reliable forms of assessment?
3. What types of speaking assessment tasks are available to teachers?

To answer the questions, we will discuss the following topics:

- When and how assessment in speaking should occur.
- Principles for sound assessment practices.
- Tasks and activities for assessing speaking.
- Procedures for rating and scoring assessments.

In Chapter 8, we touched briefly on assessment, when outlining the main steps and procedures in planning and designing a speaking course. There, we made the point that assessment is a component of course planning and design that should occur throughout the course. Not only is assessment a vital aspect of diagnosing learner needs on an ongoing basis, but it also enables teachers and learners to analyze what progress has been made in learning, as a result of the course. In short, assessment is an integral part of a learner-centered speaking program.

Apart from its importance as a part of course design, and in enabling learners to evaluate what progress they have made, around the world, assessment has become increasingly important in recent years. Ministries of education require evidence of what achievement learners are making as a result of the financial investment that is being made in the teaching of English.

255

Policymakers want accountability from educators, regarding the effectiveness of English-language tuition. They also want to see how programs create logical and sequenced educational "pathways," as students progress from early tuition to more advanced stages. Administrators, in schools and colleges, require mechanisms for passing on information about what has already been achieved to other teachers so that the transition from one level of learning to the next can be transparent. Students and parents also express the need to know how learners are progressing, especially in a globalized world, where the learning of English is seen as increasingly important for future study and employment opportunities. Assessment and testing lie at the center of all of these concerns, as they provide concrete records of progression and achievement.

Think about it

Consider the various factors related to testing that are outlined above. In your view, what impact do they have on your teaching of speaking?

In our discussion of assessment, we will make a distinction between *summative* assessment; that is, the assessment of students at the culmination of a course or other specified period of learning; and *formative* assessment, which is related to the ongoing development of knowledge and skills. We discussed both these concepts previously in Chapter 8. We will first look briefly at some of the major tests used to assess speaking, but the main focus of this chapter will be on what teachers themselves can do to carry out classroom-based assessment.

Tests of speaking

In this section, we discuss some of the international tests available for testing speaking. However, as our main focus is on classroom-based assessment, we touch only very briefly on major tests of speaking.

The testing of speaking skills has become increasingly important, not only because progress and achievement need to be recorded within educational institutions, but also because certain levels of language skills may be required for progression into further study and / or employment. In many countries, students must achieve certain levels of skills in tests – such as the International English Language Testing Service (IELTS), the Test of English as a Foreign Language (TOEFL), or the Test of English for International Communication (TOEIC) – before they gain admission to universities or to other forms of post-secondary education and training. "Gate-keeping" tests of this type that determine whether students proceed to future educational pathways are considered "high-stakes" tests (Brindley 1989).

In Chapter 8, in the section on assessment as part of course planning, we referred to the Common European Framework of Reference (Council of Europe 2010), which is now widely used as a set of criteria for measuring assessment of the various language skills, including speaking. The CEFR assesses both spoken *macrofunctions* and *microfunctions*. Macrofunctions are chunks of language serving the same functional purpose (e.g., narratives, descriptions, explanations), similar to the notion of genre or types of talk we discussed in Chapter 5. Microfunctions are more individual functions such as apologizing, inviting, complimenting, and so on, which relate to turns in talk (see also Chapter 5). Six spoken microfunctions are included in the CEFR:

- Giving and asking for factual information (e.g., describing, reporting, asking).
- Expressing and asking about attitudes (e.g., agreement / disagreement, knowledge / ignorance, permission).
- Suasion (e.g., suggesting, requesting, warning).
- Socializing (e.g., attracting attention, addressing, greeting, introducing).
- Structuring discourse (e.g., opening, summarizing, changing the theme, closing).
- Communication repair (e.g., signaling non-understanding, appealing for assistance, paraphrasing).

The Cambridge Certificate in English Language Speaking (CELS) is a test linked with the CEFR. CELS can be taken at three levels corresponding to B1, B2, and C1. (See Chapter 8 and Task 3 in the Group-learning tasks at the end of this chapter for the oral-production descriptors for each level of the Common European Framework of Reference.) Four categories of assessment scales are included in the CELS: a) grammar and vocabulary; b) discourse management; c) pronunciation; and d) interactive communication.

The grammar and vocabulary category involves testing accurate and appropriate use of lexico-grammar in tasks provided at each level.

Discourse management tests the ability of the candidate to produce connected and coherent speech over several utterances to convey information or put forward opinions.

Pronunciation assesses the ability to produce speech comprehensibly, using appropriate production of individual sounds, linking strategies, stress, and intonation. First-language accents should not impede the ability to be comprehensive.

Finally, interactive communication measures the candidate's ability to initiate and respond appropriately to fulfill the task. Candidates should show they have the ability not only to use language functionally and maintain or repair communication, but also to move the interaction towards an appropriate conclusion.

If teachers are teaching a speaking course where students will eventually be taking a formal international test, such as CELS or the other tests mentioned in this section, they will, of course, need to familiarize themselves thoroughly with the requirements of the test. They also need to make the test requirements explicit to their students, and assist them in preparing for it, by ensuring substantial amounts of practice with tasks such as the ones they will go on to complete during the test.

Discuss it

Are your students preparing for a formal test? With your colleagues, examine the descriptors or criteria for speaking at the level(s) you are teaching. Share your ideas on how you prepare your students for the test. Also, discuss strategies that the learners in your class use to help themselves prepare. If your learners are not good at self-directing their preparation, brainstorm ways they can be encouraged to be more autonomous.

Outcomes-based assessment

Many educational systems have moved in the last decade or so toward assessing students based on outcomes or using standards, frameworks, and benchmarks to assess performance. Outcomes-based assessment (see Brindley 1998) means that the learner's performance is assessed against a series of external criteria that describe the ability to perform a certain task or job. In some contexts, outcomes-based assessment is also referred to as competency-based assessment, a form of assessment that comes primarily from industry and business, where the competencies needed to perform a job are used to evaluate people's performance. In an outcomes-based system, it is possible for students to partially achieve the outcome, since they may be strong on some performance criteria and less strong on others.

Figure 12.1 below is an example of learning outcomes for students studying in an Australian national program for adult immigrants. The curriculum framework used in this program consists of four certificates: the Certificates in Spoken and Written English (CSWE) I-IV, each level of which equates roughly with the levels A1-B2 of the CEFR. At the most advanced level, students have an option to undertake modules of English study that aim to assist them in seeking employment, CSWE IV (E). One of the modules is Skill C: Language skills for telephoning in job-seeking contexts.

The example in Figure 12.1 shows the two sets of learning outcomes students are expected to achieve for Skill C: C1 (Prepare for a job-seeking telephone call) and C2 (Negotiate a complex transactional telephone conversation).

Outcomes-based assessment, which refers to assessment of learners' performance against specified criteria, contrasts with norm-referenced assessment, where students' performances are compared with each other. Norm-referencing, a more traditional form of assessment, is illustrated in the way students' scores at school are listed from the highest to the lowest. Luoma (2004) points out that these two forms of assessment tend to form a continuum with the grading that is used, showing an inclination for one form or another. In this chapter, we focus on criterion-referenced or outcomes-based assessment.

Principles of assessment

It has not always been the case, in situations assessing speaking, that students are aware of what is being assessed. A common tendency has been to assess students without making the criteria for assessment clear to them. Research on assessment over the last two decades has highlighted various principles that should be applied in assessment settings, in order to make assessments fairer, more equitable, and transparent to students. Here, we outline briefly the factors teachers should take into account, as far as possible, when assessing speaking.

- Students should be informed when they are being assessed.
- Students should be informed how they will be assessed.
- Teachers should make the criteria for assessment explicit to the students.
- The ratings, scores, marks, or grades attached to the criteria should be explained to students.

All of these factors have to do with the conditions under which students are assessed. One important issue is how the teacher will communicate

Module name: Language skills for telephoning in job-seeking contexts

Module code: CSWE IV (E) C

Nominal hours: 75

Module purpose: This module covers the language skills required when using the telephone to inquire about advertised jobs, employment opportunities, or work-experience placement. The module also prepares learners to respond appropriately to employers who are using informal interviews.

Summary of learning outcomes:
C1   Prepare for a job-seeking telephone call.
C2   Negotiate a complex transactional telephone conversation.

Assessment strategy:
Learning outcomes for this module may be assessed together using the same task.

Evidence may be gathered, for example, through:

- Teacher observation of satisfactory performance.
- Observed role plays.
- Audio / video recordings to assess performance.

Delivery mode:
The module may be delivered by telephone or face-to-face.
To deliver this module, the teacher will need to research an organization relevant to the learner's job-seeking context.

Module: CSWE IV (E) C

Language skills for telephoning in job-seeking contexts

Learning outcome: CSWE IV (E) C1
Prepare for a job-seeking telephone call.

Assessment criteria	Conditions and method of assessment
1.1 Research target organization. 1.2 Identify contact person within organization, e.g., name, position. 1.3 Outline range of questions to elicit information sought. 1.4 Prepare responses to questions likely to be asked by organization.	**Sample tasks** Learners prepare, for example: • File incorporating research notes. • Research worksheet.

Figure 12.1: Example of assessment criteria in an outcomes-based curriculum (Certificate in Spoken and Written English Module IV (E) C 2008; reproduced with permission).

(continued)

Module: CSWE IV (E) C

Language skills for telephoning in job-seeking contexts

Learning outcome: CSWE IV (E) C2

Negotiate a complex transactional telephone conversation.

Assessment criteria	Conditions and method of assessment
2.1 Participate effectively in a complex transactional telephone conversation. 2.2 Initiate a call, identify self, and state business clearly and appropriately. 2.3 Use appropriate staging for telephone exchanges, e.g., greeting, body of the call, pre-closing and closing. 2.4 Ask for information / offer a service. 2.5 Demonstrate understanding of intent of interlocutor, e.g., intent may include initiating an informal interview or providing information. 2.6 Make statements, ask and answer questions, and give feedback. 2.7 Sustain conversation, e.g., take turns, confirm, clarify, repair, identify topic shifts. 2.8 Link ideas cohesively by using appropriate reference and conjunctions, e.g., addition, time, cause, consequence, condition, and comparison. 2.9 Use accurate vocabulary and grammatical structures appropriate to setting and register. 2.10 Pronounce utterances intelligibly, i.e., so that delivery does not impede comprehension, or use strategies such as reformulation or repetition to clarify meaning. 2.11 Use pausing, stress, and intonation to communicate meaning.	Call can be simulated or authentic. Interlocutor must be a fluent English speaker. **Sample tasks** Learners undertake role play, inquiring, for example, about: • An employment / work-experience opportunity. • A position, [and then they] participate in a short informal interview. • A position [alone]. Learners participate in a short informal interview. Learners may role play a telephone call to [an] organization [they have previously] researched for C1.

Figure 12.1: Example of assessment criteria in an outcomes-based curriculum (Certificate in Spoken and Written English Module IV (E) C 2008; reproduced with permission).

information about assessment methods, criteria, and rating systems to the students. Teachers may need to ask questions, such as: Does the students' language level allow for explanations in English, or should I use their L1? If students are from mixed first-language backgrounds, what strategies can I employ to make sure they all understand the information? Are students at an age where they will understand what assessment is? If not, what strategies can I use to explain the concept of assessment? Are students aware of how the assessment criteria fit into the overall requirements of the course they are taking, and are they aware of the assessment demands of the educational system? In preparing their students for assessment, it is important that teachers take these issues into account and develop ways to provide clear explanations to them.

Discuss it

With your colleagues, discuss the conditions under which you currently organize student assessment. Use some of the questions above as a trigger for parts of your discussion. Consider ways in which changes or improvements might be made to current practices.

In addition to these conditions, there are characteristics of good assessment that need to be established:

- Assessment methods and criteria should relate back to the goals and objectives for the course. In other words, the students should not be assessed on speaking skills and knowledge that the course has not covered. Therefore, in their planning of course objectives, teachers should be thinking ahead to the outcomes that can be expected from each objective.
- Assessment must be reliable. Reliability in assessment has to do with consistency, and both *intra-rater* and *inter-rater* reliability need to be achieved. Intra-rater reliability means that the same assessor is able to rate students' task performances consistently over several days, using the same criteria. Inter-rater reliability means that different assessors are able to reach agreement about a student's task performance.
- Assessment must be valid. In other words, assessment should assess what it claims to assess; it should have face-validity. For example, a speaking assessment that requires students to provide written responses would not be considered a valid test of students' spoken competence. Content validity (assessing what has been taught) is another important type of validity.

- Assessment should be based on clear criteria and shared descriptors. In other words, if assessment is to work effectively and fairly, and have meaning for other teachers in the educational system or school, a "common language of assessment" is needed. The way in which achievement is described should be comprehensible and meaningful to other teachers.

Thornbury (2006) comments, justifiably, that assessment of speaking is by no means straightforward. In comparison with assessment of grammar or writing, where responses can easily be recorded in written form, speaking must be assessed *through* speaking. The teacher must arrange for the time and opportunity for students to demonstrate their spoken skills, and also must devise tasks enabling students to do so. Therefore, it is particularly important that the criteria for speaking assessment be realistic and clear. Fortunately, one solution to the problem of finding the time for classroom assessment is that many of the activities used in class to practice speaking can be the same as those used to assess speaking. Formative assessment processes, in particular, benefit in this respect. In addition, as Thornbury points out, the "washback effect" of a speaking test is likely to encourage students (and even teachers) to produce more oral language in class. Washback has to do with the effect or influence the test and its criteria have on the way course content and skills practice are planned. If a teacher and students know that students need to pass a certain type of test in the future, they are likely to prepare for that test as part of the course.

Classroom-based assessment

Luoma (2004:121) provides a useful example of an end-of-course speaking test, devised by a teacher. The teacher's purpose in administering the test is described as follows:

> The aim of this test is to assess the examinee's ability to express [his or her] ideas in English, take the interlocutor's contributions into account and make use of them in discussion, and collaborate in the creation of interaction. Social appropriateness is not assessed explicitly.
>
> Ability to express [one's] own ideas is reflected in:
> - Intelligible pronunciation.
> - Knowledge of relevant vocabulary.
> - Ability to react in reasonable time and in relevant, meaningful chunks.
> - Sufficiently accurate knowledge of grammar.

Ability to take into account and make use of the interlocutor's turns, and ability to collaborate in the creation of interaction are reflected in:

- Signaling of known and new themes through phrasing, grammar, and stress.
- Repetition and reformulation of words and phrases from previous turns.
- Relevance of turn content, in light of previous turn and discourse history.
- Willingness to talk, [and] willingness and ability to elaborate.

The background to the test described above is that the teacher developed it for her own particular learning context, bearing in mind the course she had taught, and what she wanted her students to achieve. As she developed the course herself, she did not have to refer to other testers or external criteria. Over time, she had gained experience in improving the way she carried out tests with her students, and in formulating criteria for assessing the skills she wanted them to demonstrate. The test she used is a summative one, carried out at the end of the course, which complemented the continuous assessment she did to diagnose learner progress and identify the skills that still needed development. This test and the procedures the teacher used are examples of classroom-based assessment.

Classroom-based assessment, sometimes referred to as school-based, teacher-based, or alternative assessment, can be formative or summative. In some language-teaching situations, the teacher is responsible for both types of assessment, and formative assessment will be aimed at enabling students to achieve the outcomes stated for a particular course. Classroom-based assessment typically involves the assessment that a teacher carries out to gain information on the progress that is being made, as a result of teaching the course. In the next section, we discuss some of the ways teachers can carry out speaking assessments in class.

Assessment specifications

Before designing the tasks, it is useful to consider the specifics of the assessment process and how it will be structured overall. Assessment specifications involve considering questions such as the following:

- What is the purpose of the assessment?
- Who are the students to be assessed?
- What is the level of the assessment?
- What skills or knowledge are being assessed?
- How many tasks do the students need to undertake to complete the assessment?

- How long will they have to complete the task(s)?
- Are all of the tasks weighted equally?
- What communicative situation does the assessment target?
- What type and length of texts are involved in the assessment?
- What language skills and knowledge are being assessed?
- What language features are being assessed?
- What tasks do students have to perform?
- What instructions will be given to the students about completing the tasks?
- What criteria will be used to assess the performance?
- How will the performance be rated and scored?

Not all of these specifications will be required for every assessment process, and formal specifications are less necessary in classroom situations than in large testing systems. Nevertheless, the specifications are valuable for teachers to consider, as they make the development of the assessment process more systematic, and they also link assessment to the teaching and learning process, as well as the goals and objectives for the course.

Tasks and activities for conducting classroom-based assessment

Before discussing the types of tasks that can be used for speaking assessment, we comment here on how speaking performances can be collected and planned. Some tasks are assessed, as students perform them, by the person who does the assessing. However, one disadvantage of this approach is that the assessor must administer the task, control its administration (keeping time, supplying information and materials), and assess the student's performance, using the assessment criteria, all at the same time. Recording the task performance on audio or video is a more reliable way of conducting the assessment. It has the advantage of allowing the teacher to revisit the performance at a later time and also to involve other assessors in the assessment, thereby increasing inter-rater reliability. It also means that performances can be reviewed more than once if necessary.

Depending on whether the aim of assessment is summative or formative, tasks for assessing speaking can be of two types, either designed to pinpoint specific features or skills of speaking, or designed to replicate naturalistic interactions learners need to engage in. "Pedagogic" or "language and skills-focused" tasks aim to assess the communicative skills that enable speaking, while "real-life" or "target" tasks reflect interactions that might be found beyond the classroom (Nunan 1989).

A pedagogic task might ask learners to discuss a picture where different items are missing. The learners would then interact to ask questions to identify the items, and where they are located in the picture. This is unlikely to be a task performed in the "real world," but it can usefully test skills like being able to describe positions, use prepositions appropriately, and provide descriptions of items. It also promotes collaboration and exchange of meaning in two-way interaction. A real-life task assesses what speakers might say in a particular social context, which could involve an interactional purpose (chatting to colleagues at a party, making polite conversation with a stranger), or a transactional situation (visiting a travel agency, making inquiries about a course). Real-life assessments usually involve simulations, or role plays, that attempt to get close to the kind of interactions that occur in real-life contexts. These kinds of assessments are often central in English for Specific Purposes (ESP) courses where students might be training for various professions, for example, in medical, legal, financial, business, or hospitality contexts. Having looked at these two different ways to consider types of tasks, pedagogic and real life, we now make suggestions for different assessment task types.

Interviews

An interview between an assessor and a test candidate is a common way of testing speaking. The interview can require the student to undertake a variety of task types. Generally the focus is on "pedagogical" assessment, but interviews can also be used to simulate real-life contexts, such as a job interview or an enrollment interview.

INDIVIDUAL INTERVIEWS

Individual interviews involve the students and teacher in completing some kind of interaction. One of the challenges for the teacher is occupying other students in the class while the interview takes place, so plans will have to be made for them to complete other tasks. Individual interviews can present problems because the students may be anxious and unable to perform to their best ability, or unable to engage in what might be expected to be a relaxed and informal conversation. There may also be what are termed "interviewer effects," where the interactional style of the interviewer (e.g., the way he / she asks the questions or controls what the speaker says) can impede the student's best performance. Thornbury (2007) suggests that having a casual chat at the beginning of the interview, and giving students time to prepare what they will say, can help. Also, objectivity can be increased if the same questions are asked of each student, and a colleague is available to jointly assess the candidate.

PAIRED INTERVIEWS

These interviews involve pairs of students rather than individuals. (Swain 2001) sees three advantages in administering speaking tasks to pairs of students. First, they are an alternative to the traditional single interview and provide more extensive evidence for what speakers can do in performing the task. Second, they strengthen the relationship between teaching and assessing, as they encourage the use of greater pair work in class. Third, they are more economical in terms of time than individual interviews. Paired interviews also mean that the interaction may be more natural, as the assessor is not the one who controls the flow of the talk.

GROUP INTERVIEWS

Group-interaction tasks can also be a practical way of assessing speaking. They enable more interaction among students and can demonstrate, in particular, how speakers negotiate for turns. They also cut down on the time needed for individual assessment. Fulcher (1996) describes how he used a group task involving a discussion of education in participants' home countries. Each student was given a task card, with ideas about what could be discussed at the beginning of the task. They were then given ten minutes to prepare individually, after which they were asked to discuss the topic together for 15 minutes, but they were not given explicit instructions on how to structure the discussion.

Different kinds of specific tasks can form part of the interview. Below, we discuss a variety of interview task types, with examples of how they could be administered individually or in pairs / groups.

Description tasks
Students are asked to describe an object, location, or picture. Assessors need to decide the level of the learner, the length of an acceptable description, and what specific aspects of the description (e.g., spatial, people, location) are the most important for successful achievement. Here is an example of an individual and a paired description assessment task:

INDIVIDUAL: Describe a member of your family.
PAIRED / GROUP: I will give each of you a picture to describe. Describe your picture to each other for about two minutes. Then ask each other questions about the picture.

Narrative tasks

As we described in Chapter 5 when referring to genres of speaking, these tasks allow students to demonstrate how well they can recount a sequence of time, people, and events *(who, what, when, where)*. For these tasks, students are often given a set of pictures and asked to retell the events. Individual narrative tasks have the disadvantage of involving the speaker in a monologue, where there is no possibility for interaction. Paired tasks, where two speakers construct the story together, allow for demonstration of more natural interactional features of spoken narrative. Examples of individual and paired narrative tasks are:

INDIVIDUAL: I am going to give you a set of pictures that tell a story. Each picture is numbered in the order of the story. You have three minutes to study the pictures and to prepare to tell the story.

PAIRED: This test is about a story that is told in six pictures, which are numbered in the order of the events. Partner A has Pictures 1, 3, and 5. Partner B has pictures 2, 4, and 6. Take three minutes to study your pictures and to prepare to talk about them. You will take turns talking about your pictures so that you can tell the story together.

Instruction tasks

Instruction tasks involve talking about procedures for doing something. Students must be successful in describing directions or instructions clearly so that their interlocutors understand what to do. In individual tasks, instructions do not include interaction on the part of the listener. In paired tasks, the interaction between speaker and listener is an important part of what is assessed. Instruction tasks can be particularly useful when students are enrolled in an ESP course where they have to perform specific kinds of professional tasks.

INDIVIDUAL: I'm going to ask you to give me directions for how to get to a particular place. Tell me how to get from school to your house.

PAIRED: I'm going to describe a task that will involve giving instructions.

To Partner A
Your partner has left an important book at home, and he or she needs it for homework. Your partner does not have time to go and get it. You know where he or she lives and you

agree to help. Listen to your partner's instructions, and ask questions if there is anything you don't understand. Check the instructions with your partner by explaining a) what you will do when you get to his or her house; b) where you will look to find the book.

To Partner B
You must give your partner instructions on how to find the book. Tell your partner exactly what to do. Then check that your partner understands by asking him or her to summarize a) what to do when he or she gets to your house; b) where to find the book.

Decision-making tasks
These tasks involve discussing an issue from more than one point of view. The test-takers then come to a decision about the best alternatives they have discussed. Usually, the arguments for and against decisions are not clear-cut, so the speakers must justify their point of view and put forward their arguments. This type of task is usually interactive and involves negotiation among speakers. However, it can be used individually to get the speaker to articulate various points of view and then explain why one of them is chosen as the final decision. These kinds of tasks are commonly used in communicative classrooms and provide good practice for learners in interactive negotiation skills.

INDIVIDUAL: You and your classmates have just discovered that you can choose among five different options where to go for a class trip in the local area. Here are some pictures of the places that you could visit. Study the pictures for two minutes, and then describe the attraction of each place for the school visit. Finally, give your opinion on which one you would prefer, and explain why.

PAIRED / GROUP: You have been asked to design a poster that outlines the best ways to practice and improve speaking skills. It will be displayed at a student language learning conference in your school. Discuss your ideas and rank them in the order of importance in which they will appear on the poster.

Explanation and prediction tasks
These tasks are very suitable for students studying in academic programs or in ESP programs. They require the student to explain information often

found in graph or table form and extrapolate from the information to explain or predict the meaning. To complete the task, students need to explain the background, identify the components of the information or processes they are explaining, and organize them in a coherent order so that listeners understand the information. Explaining and predicting tasks lend themselves best to individual assessment, as they tend to be monologic (see Chapter 4). However, they can include an interactive component by moving from explanation and prediction to a discussion of the implications of the information.

INDIVIDUAL: The graph used for this task shows the population figures in our country over the last five years. Please study the table for two minutes, and then tell me about the following:

1. The information provided in the graph.
2. The reasons for the changes you see in the graph.

PAIRED / GROUP: The graph used for this task shows the population figures in our country over the last five years. Please study the table for two minutes. Then discuss the following issues:

1. What problems could arise from the trends in population numbers?
2. What advantages could there be in these population trends?

All of the assessment tasks we have discussed so far are appropriate to interview situations. However, not all tasks have to be completed in this way. We now turn to other kinds of assessment tasks that can be used in speaking classrooms.

Role plays and simulations
Role plays are often used as activities in communicative classrooms and, therefore, lend themselves well to assessment situations. Role plays are also appropriate for pair / group assessment because, otherwise, one part of the role play has to be taken by the assessor or another student, which can make what the individual says rather artificial. The situation selected for the role play should be as familiar to the students as possible and close to their real-life experiences. For example, there is no point in making a young student who may be unfamiliar with medical consultations play the part of a doctor. Nevertheless, role plays can be a versatile way of assessing

spoken communication skills, as they allow students to take on a role, rather than talking to an assessor, and they, therefore, provide scope for enabling students to demonstrate speaking abilities appropriate to the role.

In some cases, material is provided to stimulate the interaction, such as course information for students who must role play requesting information about enrolling in a course. However, in such cases, it is important that the skills required in reading the information do not outweigh the interaction that the speakers must engage in. Role plays can also align more closely with real-life tasks that students need to carry out. In that respect, they may contrast with the pedagogic tasks that are usually used in interviews.

Simulations are similar to role plays, allowing students to act out imagined communicative situations. Usually, students are provided with a situation within a specific context, some guidelines about what they should discuss, and possibly a stimulus, such as a recording they should listen to in order to get an idea of the kind of interaction that is required.

Below is an example of a role-play task that students might be asked to undertake for the purpose of assessment.

Your class has been informed that a student from another country has been awarded a scholarship to spend six months at your school, and will be joining your class.

Partner A
You have been selected to tell the student about the school on the first day that he or she arrives. Decide what important information about the school you will tell the student, and, in your conversation, answer any questions he or she might have. You have five minutes to prepare the information and five minutes to talk to your partner.

Partner B
You are the visiting student who will soon arrive at the school. Decide what you would like to know about the school. In your conversation with your partner, ask questions to find out the information you need. You have five minutes to prepare the questions and five minutes to talk to your partner.

Class-presentation tasks
Students are often asked to prepare short classroom presentations, and tasks of this type can also be used for assessment purposes. They involve preparing a short talk on a subject relevant to the course, and to the student's level and interests. Presentations are sometimes followed by question and answer sessions, which provide even more opportunity for the assessor to evaluate how students respond interactively. One of the advantages of a

classroom presentation is that it removes the "assessor effect" that is present in interviews. It also allows students to demonstrate their ability to present spoken information logically in an extended turn.

One of the disadvantages of this task is that students may not have the need to give presentations (apart from undergoing assessments), and so the teacher should decide whether this kind of assessment is really an appropriate way to assess the student's skills. Presentations are probably most relevant in academic or specific-purpose courses, where students are likely to be required to make individual presentations outside of the language class. One other disadvantage of presentations is the nervousness and anxiety many people experience in presenting publicly. In a classroom, students may be particularly anxious about addressing their peers; in which case, they are unlikely to give their most effective performances. One way a teacher can offset this potential problem is to ask students to record presentations, which can be evaluated after the time of the performance. Teachers then have the opportunity to involve other assessors and to ensure as much agreement as possible on the criteria used to judge the performance, and on the final grade.

Self- and peer assessment

In many language programs, students are increasingly being encouraged to take more responsibility for their learning and to develop autonomous learning strategies. Teacher assessment can be complemented well by self- and peer assessment. In situations where students are not used to taking responsibility for their learning, let alone assessing themselves, teachers may need to introduce them gradually to these concepts, and help them see the benefits for their learning of assessing themselves or each other. Students can be sensitized to the benefits through class-discussions, reflection sessions, and buddy systems, where they support each other in developing their speaking skills.

Self-assessment, as the term suggests, involves students in assessing their own performances. The most efficient way for students to do this in speaking classes is to have them record performances either inside the classroom, or preferably in a lab or self-access center, or elsewhere, such as at home, and then evaluate their performance according to a simple set of criteria. Figure 12.2 is one example of the kind of template that could be used. The students insert, in the box, the smiley face that best represents their response to the question, and can also add a comment.

Depending on the age of the learners and the speaking skills being taught, teachers can modify the assessment template to highlight different features of speaking. In addition, with or without the teacher's assistance, students

How did I do on this task?

Name_____   Date_____

	☺	☺	☹
Did I speak fluently without too many pauses and hesitations?	Comment	Comment	Comment
Did I structure what I said accurately?	Comment	Comment	Comment
Did I use grammar appropriately?	Comment	Comment	Comment
Did I use vocabulary appropriately?	Comment	Comment	Comment
Was I able to use good strategies to keep the interaction going?	Comment	Comment	Comment

Figure 12.2: Example of self-assessment rating scale.

can be encouraged to develop their own self-assessment templates and to identify different spoken discourse features where they wish to improve. For example, they may want to improve their use of turn taking, giving feedback, or using communicative repair strategies. In this way, students can compare their own evaluations of their performances with their teacher's evaluations.

Peer assessment makes use of students as assessors of each other's performances and is increasingly being used, in speaking classrooms, as a supplement to teacher assessment, enabling students to get a more rounded picture of their achievements. Peer assessment allows students who are not involved in the speaking task to become more experienced in listening to spoken English, to engage more deeply with the learning goals and expected outcomes of the speaking course, and to learn from each other. Teachers also benefit from peer assessment, as they can share the task of assessment with their students and raise their own awareness of how assessment is carried out.

There are several challenges to introducing peer assessment in a speaking class. First, students may not be familiar with the concept of peer assessment and may have doubts about its worth. Teachers may then need to spend time discussing with their students how peer assessment works, and its benefits for speaking development, and they may need to agree on some ground rules with the class for the role they will play during peer assessment. Second, students may not be used to working with explicit assessment criteria and will need to be given some initial training on what the criteria mean, how they apply to the speaking skills students are learning in class, and how to use the criteria during peer assessment. Luoma (2004) suggests that teachers avoid linguistic terms in the criteria and concentrate instead on criteria related to the task. She also suggests that developing the criteria jointly with the students will help them understand and use the criteria more effectively.

Rating and scoring assessment tasks

The final aspects of assessment we discuss in this chapter are the issues of rating and scoring. Rating has to do with assessing the student's performance against specified criteria, while scoring involves determining what mark or grade the student should get, based on the assessment against the criteria. Thus, rating and scoring are concerned with providing an evaluation of the student's speaking performance in the form of a grade or score.

Rating and scoring are the final stages in the ongoing cycle of assessment – from test need to test development and administration, and from the performance to the assessment of the performance. Although the focus in assessment often seems to be on the tasks themselves, as Luoma (2004: 171) argues, "The validity of the scores depends equally as much on the rating criteria and the relationship between the criteria and the tasks." In other words, task criteria need to relate closely to the tasks themselves. Likewise, assessment tasks should be closely related to the goals and objectives of the course.

In order to put the criteria into practice, the process of rating needs to be carefully considered. How tasks are rated will depend on the structure of the assessment. Teachers will need to consider questions, such as: Does the assessment need to be scored task by task? Are short responses involved? Is there equal weighting between tasks? Points given to each task or task component can be in the form of scores (14 / 20, 80 / 100, and so on), which can then be categorized into achievement bands or grades. In longer performances, rating scales rather than scores are often used. Scales may be designed for different kinds of tasks, so that a narrative task might be rated for fluency, genre organization, use of past tense, and appropriate time sequencing, and a discussion task might be rated according to comprehensibility, turn-taking ability, feedback strategies, and variety of vocabulary.

Figure 12.3 is an example of a numerical rating scale for a discussion task. This scale assesses students on categories of language, production, participation, expression, and coherence. In each of these categories, scores can be given for different features.

	1	2	3	4	5
Language: • Structure and organization. • Grammar and vocabulary. • Accuracy.					
Production • Fluency. • Syllable / word pronunciation. • Intonation, stress, and rhythm.					
Participation • Turn taking. • Maintenance of interaction. • Feedback.					
Expression • Clarity of ideas. • Quality of ideas.					
Coherence • Linking of ideas. • Justification of point of view.					

Figure 12.3: Discussion task numerical-rating scale.

Very often rating scales are formulated in terms of "can-do" statements; for example, "Can organize the structure of the text appropriately," or "Can produce fluent utterances." It is useful for both teachers and students to use a rating form for assessment, where the criteria are listed, and numbers or letter grades can be indicated for each criterion. Forms can also include space for comments on the performance or for noting the reasons a particular rating was allocated. Comments are a valuable way of providing feedback to students, because they provide more information about the quality of the performance and where improvements might be made.

Discuss it

With your colleagues, discuss the criteria you use to rate your students' speaking performance. Are you required to use generic ratings (a one-size-fits-all approach to assessing their performance), or do you use different ratings for different kinds of tasks?

The scores that result from the rating of a performance against the task criteria are usually provided in the form of a number or grade. Two types of scoring are generally used in assessment: *holistic* scoring and *analytic* scoring. Holistic scoring involves providing an overall score based on the performance as a whole, thus giving a holistic impression of the quality of the performance. The advantages of holistic scoring are that it does not take up as much time as analytical scoring, it provides an adequate account of the quality of the performance and the standards reached, and it gives students a single perspective on their achievement level. However, unlike analytic scoring, it doesn't pinpoint specific areas for development. Analytic scoring involves giving separate scores for different components of the task. The benefit of analytical scoring is that it breaks down areas of strength and weakness so that students have a better idea of what aspects of speaking skills they need to work on. Clearly, however, analytic scoring takes more time, something that for teachers is often in short supply. Thornbury (2006) warns also that although analytic scoring may be fairer and more reliable because several factors are taken into account, assessors may become distracted if there are too many criteria to consider and may lose sight of the overall performance picture. He recommends using approximately four or five categories for analytic assessment.

Try it

If possible, discuss with your students what kind of scores they prefer to get (you can do this in L1 if that makes the discussion more effective). Ask them to consider the advantages and disadvantages of receiving holistic or analytic scores. With your students, develop criteria for both types of scoring, and ask them to use these criteria for self-assessment.

Before we leave this section, we look at just one more aspect of speaking that is not always considered in speaking programs: assessing pronunciation. Here, we offer a final example of a checklist that can be used by the teacher to rate pronunciation. The rating scale could also be used by students to self-assess, with adaptation to the wording of the ratings, according to the students' level of speaking.

Name _____	Date _____		
Suprasegmentals			
Speech rate: _____			
	Very slow	Appropriate	Very fast
Volume: _____			
	Very low	Appropriate	Very loud
Intonation: _____			
	Too flat	Appropriate	Too marked
Word linking / flow: _____			
	Inadequate	Sometimes adequate	Adequate
Utterance-level word stress: _____			
	Inadequate	Sometimes adequate	Adequate
Segmentals			
Vowel sounds: _____			
	Inadequate	Sometimes adequate	Adequate
Consonant sounds: _____			
	Inadequate	Sometimes adequate	Adequate
Syllable stress: _____			
	Inadequate	Sometimes adequate	Adequate
Word endings: _____			
	Inadequate	Sometimes adequate	Adequate

Figure 12.4: Rating scale for pronunciation.

Summary

This chapter has considered a number of issues in assessing speaking. While referring briefly to existing formal tests for speaking, the main focus of the chapter has been on what teachers can do in the classroom to assess speaking skills and abilities. The main points to note from this chapter are:

- Key principles of assessment that teachers should be aware of in preparing classroom-based assessments. In order to have reliable, valid, and fair assessment, teachers need to keep these principles, at the beginning of this chapter, in mind when preparing assessment tasks.
- The close relationship of assessment to students' needs, course goals, objectives, and outcomes. Assessment, whether formative or summative, informs each component of the planning of a speaking course.
- The range of tasks that can be used to assess speaking. Many of these tasks are similar to tasks used to teach speaking. Ongoing assessment of students' performance on these tasks enables the teacher to fine-tune the teaching of speaking, according to ongoing learning needs and the rate of student development.
- The benefits to students of raising their awareness about self- and peer assessment, in addition to teacher assessment. By sensitizing students to ways they can assess their own performance, teachers can assist them in taking more responsibility for their speaking progress.
- Features of rating and scoring that need to be considered to ensure valid, reliable, and fair classroom assessment of speaking.

Postscript

This discussion of assessment brings us to the end of this volume on teaching speaking through a holistic approach. As with other skills, development in students' ability to speak English can only take place through the extensive use of that skill in the classroom. If teachers are to enhance students' ability to communicate orally, the teacher must provide ample opportunity for speaking practice. As we have argued in this book, however, it is not enough simply to let learners talk. Speaking development requires the teacher's intervention and expertise in raising learner awareness of how spoken language operates in a wide variety of natural contexts, what features of grammar, vocabulary, and discourse typify spoken English, what aspects of pronunciation contribute to meaning and comprehensibility, and what cognitive and metacognitve strategies can be employed to enhance knowledge and skills.

Our hope in writing this book is that we have successfully drawn attention to both the theory and practice of teaching speaking, and that the ideas we have presented are of value to our readers. We also hope that the activities and tasks interspersed throughout this volume will provide teachers of speaking with opportunities for reflection, action, and discussion that will enhance their understanding of how best to support their students' oral language learning.

Group-learning tasks

1. In Chapter 8, we presented the following example of a course goal and course objectives. With your group, develop a rating scale that could be used to assess students' performance at the end of this course. Provide examples of what discourse features you would expect to see in a particular casual conversation text type. The discussion in Chapter 5 will also help you with this task.

   Goal: To develop the knowledge and skills for engaging in casual conversations.
   Course objectives: Students will develop the skills to:
   - Initiate a topic in a casual conversation.
   - Select vocabulary appropriate to the topic.
   - Give appropriate feedback responses.
   - Provide relevant evaluative comments.
   - Take turns at appropriate points in the conversation.
   - Ask for clarification and repetition.
   - Use discourse strategies for repairing misunderstanding.
   - Use discourse strategies to close a conversation.
   - Use appropriate intonation and stress patterns to express meaning intelligibly.

2. Select an assessment task type from the ones discussed in this chapter. Develop a task and administer it to your students (or to some of your students if time is limited), using either an individual or paired / group approach. Record the students' performance, and use these samples for the next task.

3. Form groups, preferably with colleagues who teach students at different language levels from your students. In your group, collect the recorded samples of your students' oral performances. Use the six bands from the Common European Framework (CEF) on the next page to evaluate the level of each performance. Discuss the reasons for your evaluation.

	OVERALL ORAL DEVELOPMENT
C2	Can produce clear, smoothly flowing well-structured speech with an effective logical structure [that] helps the recipient notice and remember significant points.
C1	Can give clear, detailed description and presentation on complex subjects, integrating sub-themes, developing particular points, and rounding off with an appropriate conclusion.
B2	Can give clear, systematically developed descriptions and presentations, with appropriate highlighting of significant points and relevant supporting detail. Can give clear, detailed descriptions and presentations on a wide range of subjects to his / her field of interest, expanding and supporting the ideas with subsidiary points and relevant examples.
B1	Can reasonably fluently sustain a straightforward description of one of a variety of subjects within his / her field of interest, presenting it as a linear sequence of points.
A2	Can give a simple description or presentation of people, living or working conditions, daily routines, likes / dislikes, etc., as a short series of simple phrases and sentences linked into a list.
A1	Can produce simple mainly isolated phrases about people and places.

Further reading

Bachman, L. and Palmer, A. (1996) *Language Testing in Practice*, Oxford: Oxford University Press.

Brindley, G. (1989) The role of needs analysis in adult ESL program design, In R.K. Johnson (ed.), *The Second Language Curriculum*, New York: Cambridge University Press, 63–78.

Brindley, G. (1998) Outcomes-based assessment and reporting in language-learning programmes: A review of the issues, *Language Testing*, 15, 45–85.

Council of Europe (2010) *Common European Framework of Reference for Languages*, Cambridge: Cambridge University Press.

Davison, C. and Leung, C. (eds.) (2009) Special issue on classroom-based assessment, *TESOL Quarterly*, 43 (3).

Fulcher, G. (1996) Does thick description lead to smart tests? A data-based approach to rating scale construction, *Language Testing*, 13 (2), 208–238.

Luoma, S. (2004) *Assessing speaking*, Cambridge: Cambridge University Press.

McKay, P. (2006) *Assessing Young Language Learners*, Cambridge: Cambridge University Press.

NSW AMES (2008) Certificates in Spoken and Written English, Levels I–IV, Sydney: NSW Adult Migrant English Service.

Nunan, D. (1989) *Designing Tasks for the Communicative Classroom*, Cambridge: Cambridge University Press.

Swain, M. (2001) Examining dialogue: Another approach to content specification and to validating inferences drawn from test scores, *Language Testing*, 18 (3), 275–302.

References

Aida, Y. (1994) Examination of Horwitz, Horwitz, and Cope's construct of foreign language anxiety: The case of students of Japanese, *The Modern Language Journal*, 78 (2), 155–168.

Alexander, P. A. (2008) Why this and why now? Introduction to the special issue on metacognition, self-regulation, and self-regulated learning, *Educational Psychology Review*, 20 (4), 369–372.

Arnold, J., and Brown, H. D. (1999) A map of the terrain, In J. Arnold (ed.) *Affect in Language Learning*, Cambridge: Cambridge University Press, 1–24.

Austin, J. L. (1962) *How to Do Things with Words*, London: Oxford University Press.

Bachman, L. and Palmer, A. (1996) *Language Testing in Practice*, Oxford: Oxford University Press.

Baker, S. C. and MacIntyre, P. D. (2000) The role of gender and immersion in communication and second language orientations, *Language Learning*, 50 (2), 311–341.

Barnes, D. (1988) The politics of oracy, In M. Maclure, T. Phillips, and A. Wilkinson (eds.) *Oracy matters: The Development of Talking and Listening in Education*, Philadelphia: Open University Press, 45–56.

Bechtel, W. and Abrahamsen, A. (1991) *Connectionism and the Mind: An Introduction to Parallel Processing in Networks*, Oxford: Blackwell Publishing Ltd.

Bernstein, B. B. (1975) Language and socialization, In S. Rogers (ed.) *Children and Language: Readings in Early Language and Socialization*, London: Oxford University Press, (original work published 1971), 329–345.

Biber, D. et al. (1999) *Longman Grammar of Spoken and Written English*, New York: Pearson Education / Longman.

Bock, K. and Levelt, W. (1994) Language production: grammatical encoding, In M. A. Gernsbacher (ed.) *Handbook of psycholinguistics*, San Diego: Academic Press, 945–984.

Borkowski, J. G. (1996) Metacognition: theory or chapter heading? *Learning and Individual Differences*, 8 (4), 391–402.

Brazil, D. (1997) *The Communicative Value of Intonation in English*, Cambridge: Cambridge University Press.

Brice, A. and Montgomery, J. (1996) Adolescent pragmatic skills: A comparison of Latino students in English as a second language and speech and language programs, *Language, Speech, and Hearing Services in Schools*, 27 (1), 68–81.

Brice, A. E. (1992) The adolescent pragmatics screening scale: Rationale and development, *Howard Journal of Communications*, 3 (3), 177–193.

283

Brindley, G. (1989) The role of needs analysis in adult ESL program design, In R. K. Johnson (ed.) *The Second Language Curriculum*, New York: Cambridge University Press, 63–78.

Brindley, G. (1998) Outcomes-based assessment and reporting in language learning programmes: A review of the issues, *Language Testing*, 15 (1), 45–85.

Brown, A. L. (1978) Knowing when, where, and how to remember: A problem of metacognition, In R. Glaser (ed.) *Advances in Instructional Psychology* (Vol. 1), Hillsdale, NJ: Erlbaum, 77–165.

Brown, G. and Yule, G. (1983) *Discourse Analysis*, Cambridge: Cambridge University Press.

Brown, H. D. (1994) *Principles of Language Learning and Teaching*, Englewood Cliffs, NJ: Prentice Hall.

Brown, J. D. (1989) Language program evaluation: A synthesis of existing possibilities, In R. K. Johnson (ed.) *The Second Language Curriculum*, Cambridge: Cambridge University Press, 224–243.

Bruer, J. T. (1998 / 1999) Education, In W. Bechtel and G. Graham (eds.) *A Companion to Cognitive Science*, Oxford: Blackwell Publishing Ltd., 681–690.

Burden, P. (2004) The teacher as facilitator: Reducing anxiety in the EFL university classroom, *JALT Hokkaido Journal*, 8, 3–18.

Burns, A. (1998) Teaching speaking, *Annual Review of Applied Linguistics*, 18, 102–123.

Burns, A. (2001) Analysing spoken discourse: implications for TESOL, In A. Burns and C. Coffin (eds.) *Analysing English in its Social Context*, London: Routledge, 123–148.

Burns, A. and Joyce, H. (1997) *Focus on Speaking*, Sydney: National Centre for English Language Teaching and Research.

Burns, A., Joyce, H., and Gollin, S. (1996) *"I See What You Mean," Using Spoken Discourse in the Classroom: A Handbook for Teachers*, Sydney: National Centre for English Language Teaching and Research.

Burns, A. and Richards, J. C. (eds.) (2012) *The Cambridge Guide to Pedagogy and Practice in Second Language Teaching*, New York: Cambridge University Press.

Burns, A. and Seidlhofer, B. (2010) Speaking and pronunciation, In N. Schmitt (ed.) *An Introduction to Applied Linguistics*, London: Hodder, 197–214.

Bygate, M. (1987) *Speaking*, Oxford: Oxford University Press.

Bygate, M. (1998) Theoretical perspectives on speaking, *Annual Review of Applied Linguistics*, 18, 20–42.

Bygate, M. (2001) Effects of task repetition on the structure and control of oral language, In M. Bygate, P. Skehan, and M. Swain (eds.) *Researching Pedagogic Tasks: Second Language Learning, Teaching, and Testing*, Harlow: Pearson Education / Longman, 23–48.

Bygate, M. (2005) Oral second language abilities as expertise, In K. Johnson (ed.) *Expertise in Second Language Learning and Teaching*, Baisingstoke: Palgrave Macmillan.

Callaghan, M. and Rothery, J. (1988) *Teaching factual writing: Report of the Disadvantaged Schools Program Literacy Project*, Sydney: Metropolitan East Disadvantaged Schools Program.

Canale, M. (1983) On some dimensions of language proficiency, In J. W. Oller Jr. (ed.) *Issues in Language Testing Research*, Rowley, MA: Newbury House, 333–342.

Canale, M. and Swain, M. (1980) Theoretical bases of communicative approaches to second language teaching and testing, *Applied Linguistics*, 1 (1), 1–47.

Candlin, C. N. (1987) Towards task-based language learning, In C. Candlin and D. F. Murphy (eds.) *Language Learning Tasks*, Englewood Cliffs, NJ: Prentice Hall.

Carter, R. (1997) Speaking Englishes, speaking cultures, using CANCODE, *Prospect*, 12 (2), 4–11.

Carter, R. (1998) Orders of reality: CANCODE, communication, and culture, *ELT Journal*, 52 (1), 43–64.

Carter, R. and McCarthy, M. (1997) *Exploring Spoken English*, Cambridge: Cambridge University Press.

Carter, R. and McCarthy, M. (2006) *Cambridge Grammar of English*, Cambridge: Cambridge University Press.

Carter, R. et al. (2008) *Working with Texts: A Core Introduction to Language Analysis*, London: Routledge.

Channell, J. (1994) *Vague Language*, Oxford: Oxford University Press.

Cheng, Y., Horwitz, E. K., and Schallert, D. L. (1999) Language anxiety: Differentiating writing and speaking components, *Language Learning*, 49 (3), 417–446.

Cohen, A. D. (1998) *Strategies in Learning and Using a Second Language*, London: Longman.

Corson, D. (1988) *Oral Language Across the Curriculum*, Clevedon: Multilingual Matters Ltd.

Corson, D. (2001) *Language Diversity and Education*, Mahwah, NJ: Lawrence Erlbaum Associates.

Cotterall, S. and Murray, G. (2009) Enhancing metacognitive knowledge: Structure, affordances and self, *System*, 37 (1), 34–45.

Council of Europe (2010) *Common European Framework of Reference for Languages*, Cambridge: Cambridge University Press.

Coxhead, A. (2000) A new academic word list, *TESOL Quarterly*, 34 (2), 213–238.

Cummins, J. (2000) Language proficiency in academic contexts, In J. Cummins (ed.) *Language, Power, and Pedagogy: Bilingual Children in the Crossfire*, U.K.: Multilingual Matters Ltd., 57–85.

Davison, C. and Leung, C. (eds.) (2009) Special issue on classroom-based assessment, *TESOL Quarterly*, 43 (3).

Dell, G. S. (1986) A spreading-activation theory of retrieval in sentence production, *Psychological Review*, 93 (3), 286–321.

Derwing, T. M., Munro, M. J., and Wiebe, G. (1998) Evidence in favor of a broad framework for pronunciation instruction, *Language Learning*, 48 (3), 393–410.

Dickinson, D. K. and Tabors, P. O. (eds.) (2001) *Beginning Literacy with Language: Young Children Learning at Home and School*, Baltimore, MD: Paul H. Brookes Publishing.

Dörnyei, Z. (1995) On the teachability of communication strategies, *TESOL Quarterly*, 29 (1), 55–85.

Dörnyei, Z. and Scott, M. L. (1997) Communication strategies in a second language: Definitions and taxonomies, *Language Learning*, 47 (1), 173–210.

Dörnyei, Z. and Thurrell, S. (1994) Teaching conversational skills intensively: Course content and rationale, *ELT Journal*, 48 (1), 40–49.

Duranti, A. (1983) Samoan speechmaking across social events: One genre in and out of a "fono," *Language in Society*, 12 (1), 1–22.

Edwards, C., and Willis, J. (eds.) (2005) Teachers Exploring Tasks in English Language Teaching, Hampshire: Palgrave Macmillan.

Eggins, S. (1990) The analysis of spoken discourse, Paper presented at the NCELTR Spoken Discourse Project Workshop, Sydney: Macquarie University.

Eggins, S. (1994) *An Introduction to Systemic Functional Linguistics*, London: Pinter.

Eggins, S. and Slade, D. (1997) *Analysing Casual Conversation*, London: Equinox Publishing Ltd.

Ellis, R. (2005) Planning and task-based performance: Theory and research, In R. Ellis (ed.) *Planning and Task Performance in a Second Language*, Amsterdam: John Benjamins Publishing Company, 3–34.

Ernst, G. (1994) "Talking Circle": Conversation and negotiation in the ESL classroom, *TESOL Quarterly*, 28 (2), 293–322.

Evans, R. and Jones, D. (eds.) (2008) *Metacognitive Approaches to Developing Oracy: Developing Speaking and Listening with Young Children*, London: Routledge.

Faerch, C. and Kasper, G. (1983) *Strategies in Interlanguage Communication*, London: Longman.

Feez, S. (1999) *Text-based Syllabus Design*, Sydney: NSW Adult Migrant English Service and National Centre for English Language Teaching and Research.

Flavell, J. H. (1979) Metacognition and cognitive monitoring: A new area of cognitive–developmental inquiry, *American Psychologist*, 34 (10), 906–911.

Foss, K. and Reitzel, A. (1991) A relational model for managing second language anxiety, In E. K. Horwitz and D. J. Young (eds.) *Language Anxiety: From Theory and Research to Classroom Implications*, Englewood Cliffs, NJ: Prentice Hall.

Foster, P. and Skehan, P. (1996) The influence of planning on performance in task-based learning, *Studies in Second Language Acquisition*, 18 (3), 299–324.

Fulcher, G. (1996) Does thick description lead to smart tests? A data-based approach to rating scale construction, *Language Testing*, 13 (2), 208–238.

Gagne, E. D., Yekovich, C. W., and Yekovich, F. R. (1993) *The Cognitive Psychology of School Learning* (2nd ed.), New York: Harper Collins.

Garman, M. (1990) *Psycholinguistics*, Cambridge: Cambridge University Press.

Gass, S. M. (1997) *Input, Interaction, and the Second Language Learner*, Mahwah, NJ: Lawrence Erlbaum.

Gibbons, P. (2001) Learning a new register in a second language, In C. N. Candlin and N. Mercer (eds.) *English Language Teaching in its Social Context*, London: Routledge, 258–270.

Gibbons, P. (2002) *Scaffolding Language, Scaffolding Learning: Teaching Second Language Learners in the Mainstream Classroom*, Portsmouth, NH: Heinemann.

Gilmore, A. (2004) A comparison of textbook and authentic interactions, *ELT Journal*, 58 (4), 363–374.

Goh, C. (1997) Metacognitive awareness and second language listeners, *ELT Journal*, 51 (4), 361–369.

Goh, C. (2000) A discourse approach to the description of intonation in Singapore English, In A. Brown, D. Deterding and E. L. Low (eds.) *The English Language in Singapore: Research on Pronunciation*, Singapore: Singapore Association for Applied Linguistics, 35–45.

Goh, C. (2008) Metacognitive instruction for second language listening development, *RELC Journal*, 39(2), 188–213.

Goh, C. C. M. (2007) *Teaching Speaking in the Language Classroom*, Singapore: SEAMEO Regional Language Centre.

Goh, C. C. M. and Silver, R. E. (2006) *Language Learning: Home, School and Society*, Singapore: Pearson Education / Longman.

Gor, K. and Chernigovskaya, T. (2005) Formal instruction and the acquisition of verbal morphology, In A. Housen and M. Pierrard (eds.) *Investigations in Instructed Second Language Acquisition*, Berlin: Mouton de Gruyter, 131–164.

Graf, M. (2011) *Including and Supporting Learners of English as an Additional Language*, London: Continuum International Publishing Group.

Grainger, T. (2004) *The Routledge Falmer Reader in Language and Literacy*, London: Routledge Falmer.

Graves, K. (1996) *Teachers as Course Developers*, New York: Cambridge University Press.

Hacker, D. J., Dunlosky, J., and Graesser, A. C. (2009) A growing sense of "agency," In D. J. Hacker, J. Dunlosky, and A. C. Graesser (eds.) *Handbook of Metacognition in Education*, New York: Routledge, 1–4.

Halliday, M. A. K. (1985) *An Introduction to Functional Grammar*, London: Edward Arnold.

Halliday, M. A. K. (1970) *A Course in Spoken English Intonation*, Oxford: Oxford University Press.

Halliday, M. A. K. (1975) *Learning How to Mean: Explorations in the Development of Language*, London: Edward Arnold.

Halliday, M. A. K. (1989) *Spoken and Written Language*, Oxford: Oxford University Press.

Hammond, J. et al. (1992) *English for Social Purposes: A Handbook for Teachers of Adult Literacy*, Sydney: National Centre for English Language Teaching and Research.

Han, L. Y. (2001) *A Study of Secondary Three Students' Language Anxiety*, (unpublished M.A. dissertation), Singapore: Nanyang Technological University.

Hashimoto, Y. (2002) Motivation and willingness to communicate as predictors of reported L2 use: The Japanese ESL context, *Second Language Studies*, 20 (2), 29–70.

Hatch, E. (1978) Acquisition of syntax in a second language, *Understanding second and foreign language learning: Issues and approaches*, Rowley, MA: Newbury House, 34–70.

He, L. (2011) Metacognition in EFL pronunciation learning among Chinese tertiary learners, *Applied Language Learning*, China.

Heath, S. B. (1983) *Ways with Words: Language, Life, and Work in Communities and Classrooms*, Cambridge: Cambridge University Press.

Hewings, M. (1993) *Pronunciation Tasks: A Course for Pre-intermediate Learners*, Cambridge: Cambridge University Press.

Ho, Y. (2003) Audiotaped dialogue journals: An alternative form of speaking practice, *ELT Journal*, 57 (3), 269–277.

Horwitz, E. K. (2001) Language anxiety and achievement, *Annual Review of Applied Linguistics*, 21, 112–126.

Horwitz, E. K., Horwitz, M. B., and Cope, J. (1986) Foreign language classroom anxiety, *The Modern Language Journal*, 70 (2), 125–132.

Hsu, H. Y., Wang, S. K., and Comac, L. (2008) Using audioblogs to assist English-language learning: An investigation into student perception, *Computer Assisted Language Learning*, 21 (2), 181–198.

Huang, X. H., and Van Naerssen, M. (1987) Learning strategies for oral communication, *Applied Linguistics*, 8 (3), 287–307.

Hughes, R. (2002) *Teaching and Researching Speaking*, London: Longman.

Hughes, R. (2010) Materials to develop the speaking skill, In N. Harwood (ed.) *English Language Teaching Materials: Theory and Practice*, Cambridge: Cambridge University Press, 207–224.

Hymes, D. (1971) *On Communicative Competence*, Philadelphia: University of Pennsylvania Press, Excerpts reprinted in J. B. Pride and J. Holmes, J (ed.) *Sociolinguistics: Selected Readings*, Hammondsworth, Middlesex: Penguin, 271–293.

Jacobs, G. M. and Goh, C. C. M. (2007) *Cooperative Learning in the Language Classroom*, Singapore: SEAMEO Regional Language Centre.

Johnson, K. (1996) *Language Teaching and Skill Learning*, Oxford: Blackwell.

Johnson, K. and Morrow, K. (eds.) (1981) *Communication in the Classroom*, London: Longman.

Jourdain, S. (2000) A native-like ability to circumlocute, *The Modern Language Journal*, 84 (2), 185–195.

Kellerman, E. and Bialystok, E. (1997) On psychological plausibility in the study of communication strategies, In G. Kasper and E. Kellerman (eds.) *Communication Strategies*, London: Longman, 31–48.

Konishi, K. and Tarone, E. (2004) English constructions used in compensatory strategies: Baseline data for communicative EFL instruction, In D. Boxer and A. D. Cohen (eds.) *Studying Speaking to Inform Second Language Learning*, Clevedon: Multilingual Matters, 174–198.

Kuo, I. C. V. (2006) Addressing the issue of teaching English as a lingua franca, *ELT Journal*, 60 (3), 213–221.

Larkin, S. (2010) *Metacognition in Young Children*, New York: Routledge.

Levelt, W. J. M. (1989) *Speaking: From Intention to Articulation*, Cambridge, MA: The MIT Press.

Levelt, W. J. M., Roelofs, A. and Meyer, A. S. (1999) A theory of lexical access in speech production, *Behavioral and Brain Sciences*, 22 (1), 1–75.

Lewis, G. (2007) *Teenagers*, Oxford: Oxford University Press.

Lindstromberg, S. (ed.) (2004) *Language Activities for Teenagers*, Cambridge: Cambridge University Press.

Littlemore, J. (2001) An empirical study of the relationship between cognitive style and the use of communication strategy, *Applied Linguistics*, 22 (2), 241–265.

Littlewood, W. (1992) *Teaching Oral Communication: A Methodological Framework*, Oxford: Blackwell Publishing Ltd.

Long, M. H. (1996) The role of the linguistic environment in second language acquisition, In W. C. Ritchie and T. K. Bhatia (eds.) *Handbook of Second Language Acquisition*, New York: Academic Press, 413–468.

Luoma, S. (2004) *Assessing speaking*, Cambridge: Cambridge University Press.

Lun-Tan, Y. S. (2001) *Managing Second Language Speaking Anxiety in NUS Postgraduate Foreign Students: A Classroom Intervention*, (unpublished M.A. dissertation), Singapore: Nanyang Technological University.

Lynch, T. (1997) Nudge, nudge: Teacher interventions in task-based learner talk, *ELT Journal*, 51 (4), 317–325.

Lynch, T., and Maclean, J. (2001) A case of exercising: Effects of immediate task repetition on learners' performance, In M. Bygate, P. Skehan and M. Swain (eds.) *Researching Pedagogic Tasks: Second Language Learning, Teaching and Testing*, Harlow: Pearson Education / Longman, 141–162.

MacIntyre, P. D. and Gardner, R. C. (1991) Methods and results in the study of anxiety and language learning: A review of the literature, *Language Learning*, 41 (1), 85–117.

MacIntyre, P. D. and Gardner, R. C. (1994) The subtle effects of language anxiety on cognitive processing in the second language, *Language Learning*, 44 (2), 283–305.

MacIntyre, P. D., Noels, K. A., and Clement, R. (1997) Biases in self ratings of second language proficiency: The role of language anxiety, *Language Learning*, 47 (2), 265–287.

Mackey, A. (1999) Input, interaction, and second language development: An empirical study of question formation in ESL, *Studies in Second Language Acquisition*, 21 (4), 557–587.

Mackey, A., and Oliver, R. (2002) Interactional feedback and children's L2 development, *System*, 30 (4), 459–477.

Mackey, A., and Silver, R. (2005) Interactional tasks and English L2 learning by immigrant children in Singapore, *System*, 33 (2), 239–260.

Mak, B. S. Y. and White, C. (1996) Communication apprehension of Chinese ESL students, *Hong Kong Journal of Applied Linguistics*, 2 (1), 81–96.

Martin, J. R. (2009) Language, register, and genre, In C. Coffin, T. M. Lillis, and K. O'Halloran (eds.) *Applied Linguistics Methods: A Reader*, London: Routledge, 12–32.

Maybin, J., Mercer, N., and Stierer, B. (1992) "Scaffolding": Learning in the classroom, In K. Norman (ed.) *Thinking Voices: The Work of the National Oracy Project*, London: Hodder and Stoughton, 186–195.

McCarthy, M. (1991) *Discourse Analysis for Language Teachers*, Cambridge: Cambridge University Press.

McCarthy, M. (1998) *Spoken Language and Applied Linguistics*, Cambridge: Cambridge University Press.

McCarthy, M. (2003) Talking back: "Small" interactional response tokens in everyday conversation, *Research on Language and Social Interaction*, 36 (1), 33–63.

McCarthy, M. and Carter, R. (1995) Spoken grammar: What is it and how can we teach it? *ELT Journal*, 49 (3), 207–218.

McCarthy, M., Matthiessen, C., and Slade, D., Discourse analysis, In N. Schmitt (ed.) *An Introduction to Applied Linguistics*, London: Hodder, 53–69.

McCarthy, M. and O'Keeffe, A. (2004) Research in the teaching of speaking, *Annual Review of Applied Linguistics*, 24, 26–43.

McKay, S. L. (2002) *Teaching English as an International Language*, Oxford: Oxford University Press.

McKay, P. (2006) *Assessing Young Language Learners*, Cambridge: Cambridge University Press.

McLaughlin, B. (1987) *Theories of Second-language Learning*, London: Edward Arnold.

McLaughlin, B. and Heredia, R. (1996) Information-processing approaches to research on second language acquisition and use, In W. C. Ritchie and T. K. Bhatia (eds.) *Handbook of Second Language Acquisition*, San Diego: Academic Press, 213–228.

Mercer, N. (2000) *Words and minds: How We Use Language to Think Together*, New York: Routledge.

Mercer, N. (2001) Language for teaching a language, In C. N. Candlin and N. Mercer (eds.) *English Language Teaching in its Social Context: A Reader*, London: Routledge, 243–257.

Mitchell, T. F. (1957) The language of buying and selling in Cyrenaica: A situational statement, *Hesperis*, 44, 31–71.

Nakatani, Y. (2005) The effects of awareness raising training on oral communication strategy use, *The Modern Language Journal*, 89 (1), 76–91.

Nakatani, Y. and Goh, C. (2007) A review of oral communication strategies: Focus on interactionist and psycholinguistic perspectives, In A. D. Cohen and E. Macaro (eds.) *Language Learner Strategies: Thirty Years of Research and Practice*, Oxford: Oxford University Press, 207–227.

NSW AMES (2008) Certificates in Spoken and Written English, Levels I–IV, Sydney: NSW Adult Migrant English Service.

Nunan, D. (1989) *Designing Tasks for the Communicative Classroom*, Cambridge: Cambridge University Press.

O'keeffe, A., McCarthy, M., and Carter, R. (2007) *From Corpus to Classroom: Language Use and Language Teaching*, Cambridge: Cambridge University Press.

Ohata, K. (2005) Potential sources of anxiety for Japanese learners of English: Preliminary case interviews with five Japanese college students in the U.S, *TESL-EJ*, 9 (3), 1–21.

Onwuegbuzie, A. J., Bailey, P., and Daley, C. E. (1999) Factors associated with foreign language anxiety, *Applied Psycholinguistics*, 20 (2), 217–239.

Ortega, L. (1999) Planning and focus on form in L2 oral performance, *Studies in Second Language Acquisition*, 21 (1), 109–148.

Owens, R. E. (2001) *Language Development: An Introduction* (5th ed.), Boston: Allyn and Bacon.

Oyama, S. (1976) A sensitive period for the acquisition of a non-native phonological system, *Journal of Psycholinguistic Research*, 5 (3), 261–285.

Phillips, E. M. (1992) The effects of language anxiety on students' oral test performance and attitudes, *The Modern Language Journal*, 76 (1), 14–26.

Pichler, P. and Eppler, E. M. (2009) *Gender and Spoken Interaction*, London: Palgrave Macmillan.

Pintrich, P. R., Wolters, C., and Baxter, G. (2000) Assessing metacognition and self-regulated learning, In G. Schraw and J. C. Impara (eds.) *Issues in the Measurement of Metacognition*, Lincoln, NE: Buros Institute of Mental Measurement, 43–97.

Poulisse, N., Bongaerts, T., and Kellerman, E. (1990) *The use of Compensatory Strategies by Dutch Learners of English*, Dordrecht: Foris Publications USA.

Reppen, R. (2010) *Using Corpora in the Language Classroom*, Cambridge: Cambridge University Press.

Richards, J. C. (1990) *The Language Teaching Matrix*, Cambridge: Cambridge University Press.

Richards, J. C. (2000) *Curriculum Development in Language Teaching*, New York: Cambridge University Press.

Richards, J. C. (2006) Materials development and research – making the connection, *RELC Journal*, 37 (1), 5–26.

Riggenbach, H. (1999) Discourse analysis in the language classroom, Vol. 1: *The Spoken Language*, Ann Arbor: The University of Michigan Press.

Rossiter, M. J. (2003) "It's like chicken but bigger": Effects of communication strategy in the ESL classroom, *Canadian Modern Language Review*, 60 (2), 105–121.

Rubin, J. (2001) Language learner self-management, *Journal of Asian Pacific Communication*, 11 (1), 25–37.

Rumelhart, D. E. (1980) Schemata: The building blocks of cognition, In R. J. Spiro, B. C. Bruce, and W. F. Brewer (eds.) *Theoretical Issues in Reading Comprehension: Perspectives from Cognitive Psychology, Linguistics, Artificial Intelligence, and Education*, Hillsdale, NJ: Lawrence Erlbaum Associates.

Rumelhart, D. E., McClelland, J. L., and PDP Research Group (1986) Parallel distributed processing: explorations in the microstructure of cognition, Vol. 1: *Foundations*, Cambridge, MA: MIT Press.

Sacks, H. (1974) An analysis of the course of a joke's telling in conversation, In R. Bauman and J. Sherzer (eds.) *Explorations in the Ethnography of Speaking*, Cambridge: Cambridge University Press, 337–353.

Sacks, H., Schegloff, E. A., and Jefferson, G. (1974) A simplest systematics for the organization of turn-taking for conversation, *Language*, 50 (4), 696–735.

Saito, Y. and Samimy, K. K. (1996) Foreign language anxiety and language performance: A study of learner anxiety in beginning, intermediate, and advanced level college students of Japanese, *Foreign Language Annals*, 29 (2), 239–249.

Schmitt, N. (ed.) (2004) *Formulaic sequences: Acquisition, Processing, and Use*, Amsterdam: John Benjamins Publishing Company.

Schriefers, H., Meyer, A. S., and Levelt, W. J. M. (1990) Exploring the time course of lexical access in language production: Picture-word interference studies, *Journal of Memory and Language*, 29 (1), 86–102.

Scott, M. (1999) *Wordsmith Tools*, Oxford: Oxford University Press.

Sheen, R. (2005) Focus on forms as a means of improving accurate oral production, In A. Housen and M. Pierrard (eds.) *Investigations in Instructed Second Language Acquisition*, Berlin: Mouton de Gruyter, 271–310.

Shiffrin, R. M. and Schneider, W. (1977) Controlled and automatic human information processing: II, Perceptual learning, automatic attending and a general theory, *Psychological Review*, 84 (2), 127–190.

Silva Joyce, H. and Hilton, D. (1999) *We are What We Talk: Teaching and Learning Casual Conversation*, Sydney: NSW Adult Migrant English Service.

Skehan, P. (1996) A framework for the implementation of task-based instruction, *Applied Linguistics*, 17 (1), 38–62.

Skehan, P. (1998a) *A Cognitive Approach to Language Learning*, Oxford: Oxford University Press.

Skehan, P. (1998b) Task-based instruction, *Annual Review of Applied Linguistics*, 18, 268–286.

Slade, D. (1997) Stories and gossip in English: The macro-structure of casual talk, *Prospect*, 12 (2), 43–71.

Snow, C. E. et al. (1995) SHELL: Oral language and early literacy skills in kindergarten and first-grade children, *Journal of Research in Childhood Education*, 10 (1), 37–48.

Spada, N., Lightbrown, P. and White, J. L. (2005) The importance of form / meaning mapping in explicit form-focussed instruction, In A. Housen and M. Pierrard (eds.) *Investigations in Instructed Second Language Acquisition*, Berlin: Mouton de Gruyter, 199–234.

Swain, M. (1985) Communicative competence: Some roles of comprehensible input and comprehensible output in its development, In S. M. Gass and C. G. Madden (eds.) *Input in Second Language Acquisition*, Rowley, MA: Newbury House, 235–253.

Swain, M. (1995) Three functions of output in second language learning, In G. Cook and B. Seidlhofer (eds.) *Principle and Practice in Applied Linguistics*, Oxford: Oxford University Press, 125–144.

Swain, M. (2001) Examining dialogue: Another approach to content specification and to validating inferences drawn from test scores, *Language Testing*, 18 (3), 275–302.

Swales, J. M. (1990) *Genre Analysis*, Cambridge: Cambridge University Press.

Swan, M. (2005) *Practical English Usage*, Oxford: Oxford University Press.

Tan, Y. H. and Tan, S. C. (2010) A metacognitive approach to enhancing Chinese language speaking skills with audioblogs, *Australasian Journal of Educational Technology*, 26 (7), 1075–1089.

Thornbury, S. (2005) *How to Teach Speaking*, Harlow: Pearson Education / Longman.

Thornbury, S. and Slade, D. (2006) *Conversation: From Description to Pedagogy*, Cambridge: Cambridge University Press.

Timmis, I. (2002) Native speaker norms and International English: A classroom view, *ELT Journal*, 56 (3), 240–249.

Tomlinson, B. (2003) *Developing Materials for Language Teaching*, London: Continuum International Publishing Group.

Tsui, A. B. M. (1996) Reticence and anxiety in second language learning, In K. M. Bailey and D. Nunan (eds.) *Voices from the Language Classroom*, Cambridge: Cambridge University Press, 145–168.

Ure, J. N. (1971) Lexical density and register differentiation, In G. E. Perren and J. L. Trim (eds.) *Applications of Linguistics: Selected Papers of the Second International Congress of Applied Linguistics*, Cambridge: Cambridge University Press, 443–452.

Van den Brandon, K. (2012) Task-based language education, In A. Burns and J. C. Richards (eds.) *The Cambridge Guide to Pedagogy and Practice in Second Language Teaching*, New York: Cambridge University Press.

Vancil, M. (1994) *NBA Basketball: An Official Fan's Guide*, London: Carlton Books.

Vandergrift, L. (2005) Relationships among motivation orientations, metacognitive awareness and proficiency in L2 listening, *Applied Linguistics*, 26 (1), 70–89.

Vandergrift, L. and Goh, C. (2012) *Teaching and Learning Second Language Listening: Metacognition in Action*, New York: Routledge.

Ventola, E. (1987) *The Structure of Social Interaction: A Systemic Approach to the Semiotics of Service Encounters*, London: Frances Pinter.

Victori, M. and Lockhart, W. (1995) Enhancing metacognition in self-directed language learning, *System*, 23 (2), 223–234.

Vogely, A. J. (1998) Listening comprehension anxiety: Students' reported sources and solutions, *Foreign Language Annals*, 31 (1), 67–80.

Vygotsky, L. S. (1978) *Mind in Society: The Development of Higher Psychological Processes*, Cambridge, MA: Harvard University Press.

Wang, M. C., Haertel, G. D., and Walberg, H. J. (1990) What influences learning? A content analysis of review literature, *The Journal of Educational Research*, 84 (1), 30–43.

Wenden, A. (1987) Metacognition: An expanded view on the cognitive abilities of L2 learners, *Language Learning*, 37 (4), 573–594.

Wenden, A. (1991) *Learner Strategies for Learner Autonomy: Planning and Implementing Learner Training for Language Learners*, New York: Prentice Hall.

Wenden, A. (1998) Metacognitive knowledge and language learning, *Applied Linguistics*, 19 (4), 515–537.

Wenden, A. (2001) Metacognitive knowledge in SLA: The neglected variable, In M. P. Breen (ed.) *Learner Contributions to Language Learning: New Directions in Research*, Harlow: Pearson Education / Longman, 44–64.

Willis, D. (2004) Towards a new methodology, *English Teaching Professional*, 33, 4–6.

Willis, J. (1996) *A Framework for Task-based Learning*, Edinburgh: Longman.

Willis, J. (2005) Introduction: Aims and explorations into tasks and task-based teaching, In C. Edwards and J. Willis (eds.) *Teachers Exploring Tasks in English language Teaching*, Hampshire: Palgrave Macmillan, 1–12.

Winne, P. H. (1996) A metacognitive view of individual differences in self-regulated learning, *Learning and Individual Differences*, 8 (4), 327–353.

Wong, J. and Waring, H. Z. (2010) *Conversational Analysis and Second Language Pedagogy*, New York: Routledge.

Wood, D., Bruner, J. S., and Ross, G. (1976) The role of tutoring in problem solving, *Journal of Child Psychology and Psychiatry*, 17 (2), 89–100.

Yashima, T. (2002) Willingness to communicate in a second language: The Japanese EFL context, *The Modern Language Journal*, 86 (1), 54–66.

Young, D. J. (1991) Creating a low-anxiety classroom environment: What does language anxiety research suggest? *The Modern Language Journal*, 75 (4), 426–439.

Zeidner, M., Boekaerts, M., and Pintrich, P. (2000) Self-regulation: Directions and challenges for future research, In M. Boekaerts, P. Pintrich, and M. Zeidner (eds.) *Handbook of Self-regulation*, New York: Academic Press, 749–768.

Zhang, D. and Goh, C. C. M. (2006) Strategy knowledge and perceived strategy use: Singaporean students' awareness of listening and speaking strategies, *Language Awareness*, 15 (3), 199–219.

Zhang, L. J. and Zhang, D. L. (2008) Metacognition, metalinguistic knowledge, self-regulation and foreign language teaching and learning, *Foreign Language Education in China Quarterly*, 1 (1), 56–65.

Index

NOTES

NOTES

NOTES

NOTES

NOTES

NOTES

NOTES